Deadly Alibi

On the clear, sunny afternoon of April 4, 1953, a man was observed by several people as he tried to break open the door of a plush Chicago apartment. Not only did the witnesses note the exact time of the incident, but they also recognized the perpetrator—thirty-two-year-old William Brooks . . .

But at his trial, Brooks said he couldn't be guilty because he had been dead at the time. His court-appointed attorney checked out his claim and found, bizarre as it sounded, that it was true . . .

Human Combustion Survivor

Although there are many recorded instances of people bursting into flames for no apparent reason, skeptics contend that human spontaneous combustion is impossible. But you won't convince Jack Angel, of Atlanta, Georgia. Some believe Angel to be the only victim of the phenomenon who has lived to tell the tale.

Also by Charles Berlitz
in Sphere Books:

CHARLES BERLITZ'S WORLD OF STRANGE PHENOMENA
VOLUME 1: MYSTERIOUS AND INCREDIBLE FACTS

CHARLES BERLITZ'S
World of
STRANGE PHENOMENA

VOLUME 2:
Strange People and Amazing Stories

No index
No sources
No bibliography

SPHERE BOOKS LIMITED

A *Sphere* Book

First published in the USA by Wynwood™ Press 1990
First published in Great Britain by Sphere Books Ltd 1990

Copyright © Charles Berlitz and the Stonesong Press, Inc. 1990

Printed and bound in Great Britain by
Cox & Wyman Ltd, Reading

ISBN 0 7474 0304 X

Sphere Books Ltd
A Division of
Macdonald & Co (Publishers) Ltd
Orbit House
1 New Fetter Lane
London EC4A 1AR
A member of Maxwell Macmillan Pergamon Publishing Corporation

Contents

Contents

Contents

Contents

Contents

Contents

Contents

Contents

Contents

Foreword

People generally find it hard to accept concepts and things they've never before considered or seen. Many of the objects and machines that today are everyday necessities were once regarded as frauds or dreams.

How could it have been regarded except as wild imagination or magic to speak of flying through the air or speeding across the landscape borne by a machine? Did it not once sound absurd to suggest that one could travel under the sea without getting wet, or speak to friends in distant cities throughout the world from one's home, or see events happening in far places at the very moment of their occurrence? And finally, was it not a simple reversion to ancient mythology to contemplate flying through space to the moon, other planets, and even further?

Not only were they not believed but many of today's scientific miracles were opposed and disdained during their experimental phases. In 1868, newspapers ran editorials claiming that telephones were pure trickery, designed to delude and fleece the public. For five years after the Wright brothers' successful airplane flight, *Scientific American* steadfastly refused to print a report of or comment on it. In fact, Simon Newcomb of the Smithsonian proved mathematically that the flight of a heavier-than-air machine was impossible. The famous eighteenth-century French scientist Antoine-Laurent Lavoisier stated that meteorites did not exist. He said, "It is impossible for stones to fall from the sky because there are no rocks in the sky." Prior to 1914 the French army command staff decided that airplanes might be useful for military observation but for no other military purpose whatsoever. When the phonograph was first tested at the Paris Academy of Science, the permanent secretary suddenly grasped the demonstrator by the throat, shouting that the sound was the demonstrator practicing ventriloquism, but of course the record continued to play.

Even the atomic theory remained only a convenient theory until August 1945, when it proved itself to be indisputable fact.

There are other imaginative suppositions and themes that science has yet to accept but that in recent decades have achieved a measure of respectability and become the objects of experimental study. Some of these are telepathy, teleportation, telekinesis, precognition, transmigration, foresight, and the existence of a *psyche* (Greek for "soul"). The notion of the existence of a psyche, which implies that the brain has a spiritual component separate from its physicality, is still as mysterious as it was in the Middle Ages. Could this separate entity be an intelligence that can survive death and sometimes even separate from the body during life? There are increasing indications that the psyche is not simply a behavioristic pattern within one's intelligence but something more, perhaps possessing motive and mobile force.

With the new methods of research and experimentation currently available, this mystery, along with the other arcane mysteries of the world and the universe, is now the subject of scientific investigation.

The lines separating the paranormal from the accepted sciences are beginning to fade, and the two in some cases are beginning to blend. What we thought was the ultimate in fantasy may be another fact. As J. B. Haldane observed, "We are living at a time when history is holding its breath and the present is detaching itself from the past like an iceberg that has broken away from its moorings."

CHARLES BERLITZ'S
World of
STRANGE PHENOMENA
VOLUME 2:
Strange People and Amazing Stories

The Future of the Face

For prehistoric man, teeth were both powerful weapons and necessary tools for eating unprocessed foods. But as the human race evolved, developing arsenals of armaments and the ability to produce soft, refined foods, the hard appendages of the jaw have become increasingly less important to survival. The eventual result of all this, according to one tooth expert, is the evolution of a sleek, toothless, hairless version of man.

According to orthodontist David Marshall, "Human jaws have already begun to get smaller and the brain cage has begun to grow. Meanwhile, teeth are losing cusps and tooth roots have started to shrink." Marshall, who has studied the human skull for thirty-five years and established an anatomical museum in Syracuse, New York, now says his research points to definitive changes in man. Indeed, Marshall has found, if evolution is left to its own devices, a few million years from now man will have a bald pate, squeezed, prominent features, and a small jaw.

Unlike prehistoric *Homo sapiens*, however, *we* have greater control over our environment, Marshall asserts. And, he adds, "such things as genetic engineering could very well change the projections."

Underwater Living Dead

The sultans of ancient Turkey, like the Roman emperors, possessed the power of life and death over their subjects. Concubines were particularly susceptible to the whims of an affronted ruler. Under Abdul the Damned, for example, unfaithful or petulant mistresses were sealed inside a weighted sack and dropped from the walls of the palace, which perched on a cliff high above the Bosporos. Although they plummeted to their deaths in the deep water, they didn't quite disappear: Years later, exploring the deep strait that cuts through European Turkey and Asian Turkey, divers found the women still packaged in their sacks but standing upright on the seafloor and swaying in the current as if they were alive.

Scuba divers discovered an even more astounding sight at the bottom of Czechoslovakia's Devil's Lake. In 1957, searching for a young man who presumably drowned while boating, they discovered not one body, but an entire German artillery unit—soldiers in full combat uniform, some sitting in trucks or on caissons, as well as horses standing upright, still in their harnesses. During World War II, the army attempted to cross the frozen lake during a winter retreat from the Russian forces. Under the pressure of such heavy weight, the ice cracked, sending humans and horses to their watery deaths. The extremely cold and deep water, however, preserved them until their discovery twelve years later, seemingly positioned and ready for combat.

Deadly Alibi

On the clear, sunny afternoon of April 4, 1953, a man was observed by several people as he tried to break open the door of a plush Chicago apartment. Not only did the witnesses note the exact time of the incident, but they also recognized the perpetrator—thirty-two-year-old William Brooks.

If ever the Chicago police thought they had an open-and-shut case, it was this one. But they would soon learn that all the clues pointed to a man who had a strange, but perfect, alibi.

When they investigated Brooks, Chicago detectives learned he was a penniless parolee. The case seemed cinched when a search of Brooks's automobile revealed a screwdriver hidden in the upholstery. The tip of the instrument fit exactly into the marks left on the apartment door by the would-be intruder.

But at his trial, Brooks said he couldn't be guilty because he had been dead at the time. His court-appointed attorney checked out his claim and found, bizarre as it sounded, that it was true.

Brooks's tale went like this: After he was discharged from a veterans hospital where he'd been treated for ulcers, in March 1953, his records had been switched with those of another man who had the same name. The problem was, the other man had died in the hospital. On the day of the attempted break-in, Brooks had been at the Veterans Administration office attempting to straighten out this mix-up, so he could receive military disability payments.

Records showed he was sitting in the VA office at the time the crime was committed, awaiting a telegram proving his identity. That telegram finally arrived at 1:44 P.M.

The court quickly found Brooks innocent, thanks to what may be the most unique alibi in history. When the burglary was attempted at 1:30 P.M., William Brooks was, legally, a dead man.

Asteroid Aliens

Space aliens may have found the perfect place to set up a colony—the asteroid belt between Jupiter and Mars.

Astronomer Michael Papagiannis of Boston University points out several reasons why this band of rocks might appeal to space travelers. Not only are the asteroids rich in the raw materials a space colony would need, they are also close enough to the sun to harness solar energy. In addition, the asteroids have gaps that would make convenient parking lots for spaceships.

Papagiannis says the asteroids' rocky terrain would also offer another advantage—natural camouflage for the aliens' activities. But why would extraterrestrials want to hide their space colony from Earth's prying telescopes? "We've made tremendous technological progress," Papagiannis answers. "The aliens may be deciding whether to help us or wipe us out."

21

A Rain of Birds

"Raining cats and dogs" is simply a description for a hard, driving rain. But there have been several recorded instances of dead birds literally raining down from the sky.

In the fall of 1846, according to one respected source, for instance, parts of France were covered with dead or dying birds that fell from the sky along with strange red rain. Scientists in Lyons and Grenoble were unable to figure out what had killed the hundreds of larks, ducks, robins, and quails that dropped from the sky—nor could they decipher what the red "rain" was made of.

Fifty years later, in July 1896, hundreds of dead woodpeckers, catbirds, thrushes, blackbirds, wild ducks, and other birds plummeted to the ground around Baton Rouge, Louisiana. Curiously, some of the ill-fated birds were not even native to that part of the country.

In the summer of 1960, the strange phenomenon occurred again, this time in Capitola, California. Police officer Ed Cunningham first noticed the deluge of dead birds around 2:30 A.M. when large dead birds started crashing around his patrol car. "They were falling so fast and hard they could have knocked me senseless," he recalled. "I thought I had better stay in the car and that's just what I did."

Eventually driving from Capitola for about five miles to West Cliff Drive, however, Cunningham found the shore highway and beach also covered with dead birds. At sunrise, the carnage was even more dramatic—bird carcasses covered power lines, fence posts, shrubbery, and TV antennas.

Authorities identified the large birds as a type of petrel known as the sooty shearing. A few of the creatures survived their plunge to earth and eventually flew away.

But what caused the birds to drop to earth in the first place? Was it smog, weather conditions, disease, poison? Experts who examined the dead birds confirmed they were killed by the fall. But why they stopped flying in the first place and fell like rain from the sky remains a mystery to this day.

Ancient Blonde Mummy

Chinese archaeologists have unearthed the oldest, most complete mummy ever found in China—but the well-preserved woman, who died when she was about forty, isn't Chinese. Instead, the mysterious lady is a blonde Caucasian who perished in China almost four thousand years ago.

The newspaper *China Daily* reported that the woman was about five feet tall, had reddish brown skin and long blonde hair. Because the desert where she was buried is so dry, her skin was well preserved and elastic and her internal organs were found to be virtually intact.

Researchers concluded that the woman was most likely a member of a nomadic group called the Uigurs, who were forerunners of modern Turks. According to Boston Museum of Fine Arts curator Wu Tung, the Uigurs were influenced by the Greeks, Indians, and Chinese.

Physicians in Shanghai who studied the preserved corpse came up with some baffling new information about the blonde mummy of China. Whoever she was, she died with high levels of cholesterol in her muscles—and inexplicable traces of the silvery white met-alloid element antimony in her lungs.

Human Combustion Survivor

Although there are many recorded instances of people bursting into flames for no apparent reason, skeptics contend that human spontaneous combustion is impossible. But you won't convince Jack Angel, of Atlanta, Georgia. Some believe Angel to be the only victim of the phenomenon who has lived to tell the tale.

Once a perfectly healthy salesman who earned $70,000 a year, Angel is today disabled and confined to his home—all because of a bizarre incident that happened when he was in Savannah on a business trip. While taking a nap in his mobile trailer, Angel was jolted awake by searing pain as his body erupted in flames. When physician David Fern arrived at the scene to help the badly burned man, he found that Angel had a hole in his chest, fused vertebrae, and an arm so badly charred it could not be saved.

According to Fern, since no objects in the trailer were even singed, the only explanation for Angel's injuries is spontaneous combustion—an unexplained molecular reaction that literally causes people to burn up.

Computerized Evolution

Has man stopped evolving? Not according to scientist Hans Moravec. But his vision of tomorrow's human is a bit different from the large-skulled, slit-mouthed, hairless humanoid so popular in the science fiction literature of today. Instead, Moravec, an artificial intelligence researcher at the Carnegie-Mellon Robotics Institute, predicts that the path of human evolution is heading straight toward a merger with machines.

Within thirty years, Moravec contends, people will be substituting their weak mortal limbs for more durable robotic parts and the relatively slow human brain will be aided by superintelligent computers. He also believes we'll be able to transfer exact copies of our brain patterns to computer programs that will enable us to think thousands of times faster than ever before possible.

Another giant evolutionary step will take place, Moravec explains, when superhuman robots lose their desire to be individuals and begin to share their programs. For example, an architect who knows nothing about cooking will be able to prepare a gourmet dinner by simply borrowing the memory of a talented chef. And scientists will be able to access brilliant minds and spend their time collectively pondering the mysteries of the universe.

Even further down the evolutionary man/machine trail, Moravec sees the concept of "self" blurring. Eventually, he predicts, all human brains will merge with the brains of both earthly and extraterrestrial life forms. "After years of exchange," he notes, "we might wind up with a single conscious entity whose memory is stored in a vast bank spanning the universe."

Moravec's theory, however, has been held by Hindu philosophers for thousands of years. In the very old Sanskritic records mention is made of the eventual return of all life and all things produced by human brain power to Brahma, the original force, or godhead.

The Devil's Sea

The Bermuda Triangle isn't the only place where ships seem to disappear with alarming regularity. An area in the Pacific Ocean off the coast of central Japan has inexplicably swallowed up so many vessels that the Japanese government has officially designated it a danger zone.

The perilous spot has been known as the Devil's Sea, or the Demon Sea, ever since nine ships disappeared there in 1955; a government expedition ship (the *Kaiō Maru #5*) sent to find them vanished after about ten days. Over the next fifteen years, more than a dozen boats were lost in the Devil's Sea.

Japanese researchers suggest that severe winter weather conditions and huge waves could be the cause of some of the disappearances. They also point out that the Demon Sea has a peculiar trait—true north and magnetic north are aligned there, making it impossible to get an accurate compass reading in the area.

In hopes of unraveling the mystery of the treacherous waters, the Japanese Transport Ministry has launched another on-site investigation of the area. But instead of risking a crew of men, the government is installing a robot-buoy in the Devil's Sea, where for several years it will analyze the wind, weather, and wave conditions in the Japanese equivalent of the Bermuda Triangle.

The Hollow Earth

Belief in a hollow earth surfaces in many cultures around the world. In classical Greece, for example, it was believed that some volcanoes served as entrances to Hades deep within the planet. According to Japanese mythology, an underworld dragon moved beneath Japan, causing the earth to quake. And in Central Asia, the Mahayana Buddhist legend of Arghati depicts the world below Mongolia and Tibet where the King of Earth and his retainers reside.

Some Americans, however, have taken such tales literally. Cyrus Read, for example, founded the Hollow Earth Society in 1870 and succeeded in attracting thousands of members. Even earlier, in 1832, navy Captain John Symmes took his hollow-earth theory to the United States Congress. Within our world, he said, was a "rich, warm land stocked with thrifty vegetables and animals, if not men." To find them, Symmes wanted to sail to the North Pole in search of what he called the "Symmes Hole," enter it, and explore the inner planet. With congressional approval, the secretaries of the Navy and Treasury ordered three ships to be outfitted for the venture but President Andrew Jackson intervened to stop the effort.

Believers in a hollow earth continue to publish books on the subject, some even showing aerial photographs of the North Pole's purported "hole." Adherents of the theory point out that many things in nature—bones, pits, fruits, and animals, for example—are structured around an inner cavity. Therefore, it's logical to assume that the earth is as well.

Hitler and the Hollow Earth

Captured by the Allies during World War II and later released, a German air force pilot named Bender intrigued his countrymen with an exceptional theory. The land, water, and everything else we see on earth are really on the planet's inner shell, he asserted. Smaller than we think they are, the sun and moon actually lie between us and an outer dome that we can't see because of vapor.

Attracted to Bender's theory, Adolf Hitler approved a government-sponsored expedition that might help him win the war. Believing that a hollow earth would facilitate tracking of the British fleet, German scientists as well as air force and navy officers assembled on the Baltic island of Rügen. According to G. S. Kniper, later of the Mount Palomar Observatory, they thought "the concave curvature of the earth would facilitate long-distance observation by means of infrared rays, which are less curved than visible rays."

Their belief in the hollow-earth theory, however, worked against them. Conducted in April 1945, at considerable expense, the elaborate Rügen experiment distracted the attention of key scientific and military personnel from the war effort. It also diverted radar equipment needed for the protection of German cities from Allied air attacks.

The Lasting Legend of Loch Ness

Accounts of Scotland's celebrated Loch Ness monster have emphasized the animal's 40- to 60-foot length, its four short legs or flippers, and the carriage of its reptilian head. The description resembles that of the plesiosaur, which has been extinct for fifty million years.

Records of the Loch Ness monster go as far back as the sixth century, when it was described as a "noted demon . . . a source of terror in the neighborhood." St. Colomba is said to have stopped it from eating a swimmer. Another story relates how Nessie, as the beast is called, dragged two children under the water at a section of the lake now known as Children's Pool. A century ago, hundreds of people reportedly watched as it swam on the water's surface.

In the twentieth century, an increasing number of people have seen the monster in the lake. Perhaps encouraged by the Black and White Whiskey Company's offer of $2.5 million for proof of Nessie's existence, survey teams, for example, have scoured the lake. In 1967, a local politician witnessed the monster and was disqualified as the neutral chairman of a debate on the existence of Nessie. A skeptical Loch Ness hotel owner, Johnny Macdonald, was ranting about it being nothing but myth when the monster reared its head out of the water and cruised past the hotel.

Nessie has been photographed by numerous people, and clocked as it traveled through the water at 30 to 40 miles per hour, creating breaking waves on the shore. At least one underwater flash photograph showed what appears to be an unfriendly horned head looking directly at the camera. And electronic detectors have revealed a 25- to 35-foot-long shape swimming 40 feet below the surface of Loch Ness.

Nessie, however, seems only indirectly dangerous. In 1952, for example, John Cobb was racing across the calm water when his speed boat was struck by powerful waves. The sudden disturbance in the water may have been caused by the surprised monster diving to escape the boat.

Indeed, strangers may not be welcome at all. During the filming of a movie, shot on location at the lake, a model was used for the role of Nessie. During one of the scenes, "something" snapped the tow rope and carried the imitation monster to the bottom of the lake. It was never recovered.

Australian Ice-Age Painting

Rock paintings of the Ice-Age creature diprotodon, a rhinoceros-sized animal that became extinct about six thousand years ago, have been discovered in Europe. But researchers were surprised when they found a similar painting in Australia, home of pouch-bearing, or marsupial, mammals such as the kangaroo. Discovered at a rock shelter north of Cairns, in Queensland, the picture shows the diprotodon with a rope around its neck, suggesting not only that it had lived on the Australian continent but that it had been domesticated as well.

Ezekiel's Vision

When Josef Blumrich, the German space and rocket designer who later became chief of NASA's systems layout branch, read Erich von Däniken's *Chariots of the Gods*, he became annoyed. Von Däniken argued that the biblical Book of Ezekiel contains obvious references to space rockets and ancient astronauts. Blumrich, who had developed Skylab and Saturn V, was irked by the author's ridiculous theory and set out to prove von Däniken was wrong.

Just the opposite happened, however. Blumrich discovered that Ezekiel describes possible spacecraft landing gear and gives a detailed account of what a rocket ship would have looked like to an observer who couldn't have recognized it as such. For example, Ezekiel's reference to the "whirlwind . . . out of the north, a great cloud, and a fire infolding itself" could describe a rocket landing. The "sole of their feet . . . like the sole of a calf's foot" would be landing struts.

The likeness of winged creatures on each of the four sides,

according to Ezekiel, interpreted as the faces of a man, a lion, an ox, and an eagle, was probably suggested as the machine turned, offering a different viewing angle. Interestingly, the Gemini capsule of the modern space age, with its port windows, looks like a long ox face.

The sentence "They had the hands of a man under their wings," moreover, seems to indicate the mechanical arms attached to cylinders. The phrases "burning coals" and "out of the fire went forth lightning" are apt descriptions of a landing. Ezekiel also mentioned changing colors that he compared to the color of jewels, and wheels that touched the earth. Chapter 1 closes with his mention of "the likeness of a throne," and upon the likeness of the throne, a man. Ezekiel added, of course, that "this was the appearance of the likeness of the glory of the Lord."

As a result of his study of the von Däniken book, Blumrich was convinced that Ezekiel had seen a vehicle from space. Instead of disproving von Däniken, Blumrich turned around and wrote his own book, *The Spaceship of Ezekiel*.

Beware the Nuclear Winter

Despite predictions that an atomic war would cause millions, even billions, of deaths, many people have been optimistic that survivors would somehow be able to resume their lives and repair the damage. Some scientists, however, have challenged that supposition.

According to the "nuclear winter" theory of astronomer Carl Sagan and others, a large-scale atomic war would spread dust, soot, and smoke into the atmosphere. With the sun's rays blocked out, lakes, rivers, and parts of the oceans would freeze and the earth's temperatures would drop by at least 75°F. Most of the world's food crops would die off, causing starvation and battles over whatever stored food remained. This, combined with continuing fires ravaging the earth's forests and urban centers, would make the victors no better off than the losers.

Out-of-Place Animals

Claims of kangaroos hopping around North Carolina may sound about as plausible to most folks as sightings of pink elephants. But Loren Coleman, a psychiatric social worker who pursues cryptozoology in his spare time, says there's an explanation other than hallucination for reports of out-of-place animals. Coleman, who has studied dozens of these cases, thinks the animals may have somehow mysteriously "teleported" from one location to another.

"There's a random pattern to these things," Coleman notes. "Sometimes these animals literally come out of the blue." For example, in the early 1980s, kangaroos were spotted in North Carolina, Oklahoma, and Utah, and a penguin was found on a New Jersey beach. Several Florida residents were startled when they came across six-foot-long Nile monitor lizards—creatures that are supposedly found only in their native Africa.

Coleman admits that some scientists would argue these animals were brought into the country, perhaps as babies. "But it's not that simple," he asserts. He points out that he has investigated hundreds of sightings of strange animals, talking to game wardens, police, and ordinary citizens. And while a logical explanation is found in more than half of the cases, at least 20 percent of the sightings remain enigmas.

Touching a Lake Monster

Hundreds of people over several centuries have reported seeing dinosaurlike lake monsters, including Loch Ness's famous Nessie. But a British Columbian woman has gained the distinction of being the only human reported to have actually *touched* one of the creatures.

Barbara Clark's adventure began on a sunny bright morning in July 1974, at Okanagan Lake. She was taking a swim toward a diving platform about a quarter mile offshore when, suddenly, she felt something huge and rough pass her in the water, scratching her legs. Quickly, Barbara threw herself upward, reached out for the raft, and climbed aboard. When she turned around, she saw it—a dark gray, serpentine animal about thirty feet long and four feet wide, swimming five yards away. The creature's head was underwater but its fluked tail was clearly visible.

J. Richard Greenwell, secretary of the International Society of Cryptozoology, an organization that researches reports of unexplained or long-thought-extinct life forms, investigated Barbara Clark's claim and found her a highly credible witness. "She did not come forward until recently," he notes. "She was afraid no one would believe her."

Greenwell points out that even before Europeans settled in the area, local Indians related tales of a monster that dwelled in Okanagan Lake. Over two hundred eyewitness reports of the creature, called Ogopogo by local residents, have been collected over the years—most of them, Greenwell says, describe an animal that sounds strikingly similar to the one Barbara Clark encountered.

Whatever it was that slithered through the dark waters of the lake toward Barbara, it did not seem to be interested in attacking her. Greenwell says its tail may explain why. "The creature's fluked tail points to [its being] a mammal," he notes. "Mammals are very curious. It may have come to Barbara just to see what was splashing in the water."

The Mystery of Oliver

Oliver was discovered in the Congo more than a decade ago, and no one is sure whether he's a mutant, a hybrid, or part of a new species of chimp. He looks like a bald chimpanzee, but his ears are at the top of his head rather than at the center. His nose protrudes much like that of humans, and unlike apes, who prefer walking on their knuckles, Oliver seems to naturally walk upright.

Studied extensively by Ralph Helfer, an animal behaviorist who heads Gentle Jungle, a Burbank, California, organization that trains animal actors, Oliver apparently has forty-seven chromosomes, falling between an ape's forty-eight and a human's forty-six, and suggesting a crossbreed or possibly Down's syndrome. His intelligence, however, rules out a simian form of Down's syndrome. He watches television Westerns and action programs for hours, unlike chimps, which become bored after a few minutes.

Everyone, from Sasquatch hunters to anthropologists, is baffled. "No one thinks he's a chimp, and no one has suggested he's an infant bigfoot," Helfer says. Everyone, however, admits that Oliver is an unusual primate.

Teen Wolf

In 1976, a local village chief found a human child frolicking with three wolf cubs in a forest in the Sultanpur district near Lucknow, India. According to later reports by the Press Trust of India domestic news agency, the boy's nails had grown into claws. Estimated to be about eight years old, he had thick body hair with tangled, matted hair on his head.

Because the boy resembled a bear, the chief called him Bhaloo. Although the name was later changed to Bhaskar, many people simply referred to him as the "wolf boy" because they believed he had been reared by a wolf.

The chief had hoped to civilize the wolf boy but his efforts were unsuccessful. Eventually Bhaskar entered Prem Nivas, a home for the destitute and poor operated by the Missionaries for Charity in Lucknow, 270 miles southeast of New Delhi. He remained there until he died in 1985.

Lost River Found

As most of the world cooled and entered the Ice Age about two million years ago, the area near the borders of Egypt, the Sudan, and Libya drastically changed from grassland to desert. Prehistoric man was probably the last to see the great rivers, valleys, channels, and flood plains that once predominated there. The region has since been hostile to almost all living things; rain is believed to fall only every forty years or even less frequently.

Since ancient times, however, explorers have journeyed into this hostile environment seeking the remnants of *Bahr-bela-ma*, a mammoth river system believed to have existed beneath the sands of the Sahara Desert. In fact, the legend of the "great rivers without water" persisted even though no trace of the supposed river systems was ever found—until 1982.

Studying the earth's terrain, scientists on board the space shuttle captured radar images of an extensive river topography beneath the Saharan sands. According to the U.S. Geological Survey's John McCauley, a leader of the team that conducted the shuttle experiments, it is unlikely that the buried river valleys link to the Nile. The rivers veer to the south and west, the opposite of the Nile's present-day movement. It is possible, he conjectured, that the buried rivers and the Nile once joined in the interior in a basin as large as the Caspian Sea.

Baby Mammoth

Huge prehistoric mammoths once roamed what is now Siberia. During one herd's travels across the frozen tundra about forty thousand years ago, a seven-month-old animal became trapped in silt. The frightened infant probably fought to escape but soon exhausted itself and was drowned in the sedimentary material. The carcass was completely covered and protected from carnivorous animals; the site itself was eventually buried under snowslides that never thawed.

The burial site lay untouched until 1977, when a bulldozer operator uncovered the baby mammoth in a layer of ice, broken stone, and silt in the northern Magadan region. The fully preserved corpse was removed to a deep-freeze chamber, where excited Russian scientists weighed, measured, described, and preserved everything. Previous mammoth finds have been considerably damaged, according to Nikolai Vereschagin, chairman of the Committee for Mammoth Studies of the USSR Academy of Sciences.

The baby mammoth, the first completely preserved specimen ever discovered, offers a fuller idea of the mammoth's external appearance as well as the structure of the animal's internal organs. Soviet researchers were able to study its brain, skeleton, and muscles. They removed the heart, lungs, kidney, stomach, and other internal organs. They may also be able to determine the reasons for the extinction of the behemoths, which were seemingly well adapted to severe climate.

Bikini

Nowadays the name Bikini is more noted as a brief bathing attire rather than the Bikini Island atoll in the Pacific Ocean where the hydrogen bomb was tested from 1946 to 1958. The association of names may stem from the obvious fact that there is so little of either of them, Bikini being only two miles square.

Nevertheless, the island of Bikini formerly contained a number of inhabitants who were quite satisfied with their place in the sea. They were all removed by U.S. authorities as were the native dwellers of Eniwetok, a nearby island that was the site of a series of nuclear blasts in the 1950s.

In 1968 the original inhabitants of both islands were permitted to return, but when the Bikini islanders farmed crops, the yield was found to be radioactive and the confused islanders were shipped out again. Eniwetok, a somewhat larger island, was decontaminated and new palm trees were planted since all vegetation had been blown away by the bomb. The authorities, however, forbade the islanders to eat the coconuts that grew on the newly planted trees.

The natives were disappointed and puzzled, but most of them were familiar with the Bible as a result of the untiring efforts of generations of missionaries, and many of them recalled the mention of an earlier and more pleasant garden where the Supreme Authority had forbidden the dwellers in the garden to eat another apparently harmless fruit: "the fruit of the tree which is in the midst of the garden."

Sunken City

Once the Monte Carlo of the Roman Empire, the ancient city of Baiae boasted luxurious villas and pavilions that were built right into the sea. Possibly encompassing an area four miles long and a quarter mile wide, it was larger than its neighbor Pompeii. Even the emperor Augustus Caesar and the orator, statesman, and philosopher Cicero, among others, kept homes at the resort on the west coast of Naples.

During the second century, Romans constructed a seawall to protect the area from the onslaught of storms. The wall, however, proved insufficient against other natural forces. Eventually, earthquakes and volcanic eruptions caused the coastal resort to descend into the sea.

Today, the great villas and their treasures and other artifacts still lay at the bottom of Italy's Bay of Pozzuoli, but only divers can enjoy the thrill of exploring the well-preserved underwater community. German archaeologist Bernard Andreae, however, has proposed the construction of an airtight plastic bubble to be placed at least over the imperial villa. Andreae, who has taken part in excavations of Baiae, would lay a tube from the shoreline to the bubble, drawing the water out and replacing it with air. Visitors would find not only the remains of the elegant structure, but also reconstructions of the statuary that have been recovered placed where it was during Roman times.

The Kiss of Death

Retreating from the festivities of their wedding reception in northeast China, a young Chinese bride and groom secluded themselves in the nearby bridal suite. There, the newly married lovers would consummate their union, as the groom began to kiss his wife passionately on the neck.

Before long, however, their guests heard a scream. Rushing into the bedroom, they found the newly married lovers unconscious. They rushed the couple to the hospital, but the bride was declared dead on arrival.

The intensity of their passion and the length of the groom's kiss, the doctors determined, had caused heart palpitations. The bride had died from cardiac arrest.

A Recent Disappearance In the Bermuda Triangle

After thirty years as a top pilot in the Ford Motor Company's fleet, having flown such officials as Henry Ford and former Ford executive Lee Iacocca, Dick Yerex retired in 1986. He and his wife left their Gibraltar, Michigan, home and moved to North Palm

Beach, Florida, where Yerex took a job with a local commuter service.

On May 27, 1987, Yerex was on a routine commuter flight en route to pick up passengers on Abaco Island in Bermuda. His twin-engine Cessna was in excellent condition, with no history of mechanical problems. The weather was clear except for occasional light rain. And Yerex had an outstanding record as a pilot. All in all, everything was going well.

Just forty minutes after takeoff, however, Yerex radioed another pilot to inform him of the location of a government satellite balloon. It was the last time anyone heard from him. He was last seen heading into the Bermuda Triangle, the infamous area formed by imaginary lines drawn from Melbourne, Florida, to Bermuda to Puerto Rico and back to Florida.

"The only factual thing we know is that the aircraft took off," said Ron Bird, an air safety investigator with the National Traffic Safety Board in Miami. "Beyond that, anything is possible."

After an extensive but fruitless search, Yerex was listed as missing and presumed dead; his twin-engine Cessna, presumed destroyed.

Mystery Manuscript

In 1912 British book dealer Wilfrid Voynich purchased a 204-page manuscript from a Jesuit college in Italy. Illustrated with multicolored drawings, the mysterious volume was handwritten in an unknown alphabet, and Voynich gave copies to anyone interested in trying to translate it.

There were many attempts to decipher the language, but no one was successful until April 1921, when the University of Pennsylvania's William Romaine Newbold claimed to have broken the code. According to Newbold, Voynich's manuscript was the work of Roger Bacon, the thirteenth-century English Franciscan friar and inventor. The translation indicated that Bacon had built and used microscopes and telescopes four hundred years before they were believed to have been invented.

Not long after Newbold's death, however, his diligent translation was disproved, although no one else came up with a more substantial theory. The manuscript eventually was donated to Yale University, where it remains today—still a mystery to researchers and scholars.

Extraterrestrial Bigfoot

The sounds outside her home late one night in February 1974 startled the Pennsylvania woman. Not taking any chances, she went to the front door armed with a gun and cautiously stepped out onto the porch. Suddenly, she was confronted by a flesh-and-blood bigfoot-like creature six feet away. When she shot the gun, aiming for his middle, she was astonished to see it disappear in a burst of light.

Having heard the shot, the woman's son-in-law rushed to her aid. Once outside, he saw other bigfoot creatures at the edge of the nearby woods. Hovering overhead was a bright red flashing light.

There have been a number of cases in which both UFOs and Bigfoot have been sighted at the same time and in the same area. Another case involving the humanoid creatures and UFOs took place on a farm near Gettysburg, Pennsylvania. A twenty-two-year-old farmer's son named Stephen went to investigate a large, bright red luminous ball sighted one night in October 1973. He and the two ten-year-old boys who accompanied him saw the object hovering close to the ground. Nearby, there were two tall, apelike creatures with green glowing eyes and long, dark hair. When they began to approach the threesome, Stephen fired a shot over their heads. When the creatures continued moving forward, Stephen fired three more times, hitting the largest creature. The UFO suddenly disappeared, and the hairy creatures turned around and walked into the woods.

A Future American Triangle?

The Bermuda Triangle is formed by imaginary lines that run from a point near Melbourne, Florida, to Bermuda to Puerto Rico and back to Florida. It's long been infamous because of the dozens of ships and planes that have disappeared within its boundaries. According to Hugh Cochrane, an authority on deadly triangles throughout the world, such zones are created by energy originating at the bottom of the ocean.

Triangle zones can move, however, just as earthquake zones do, says Cochrane, author of *Gateway to Oblivion*. In fact, that is exactly what the Bermuda Triangle is doing, he claims. And it is moving westward—toward the United States. As a result of the shift inland, he adds, passenger vehicles may not disappear, but there will be more train wrecks and airplane crashes.

Bermuda Triangle's Power Source

Tom Gary, author of *Adventures of an Amateur Psychic*, claims that the Bermuda Triangle's destructive force comes from energy emanating from beneath the sea. "There is speculation that a power structure is still underwater in the Bermuda area," Gary says. The structure, he adds, rests atop a large core that extends down through the crust of the earth. "When conditions are right the power structure works intermittently, causing ship and plane captains to lose control of their crafts."

According to Gary, streaming ions form an electric current that produces a magnetic field and this causes instrument failure in craft in the vicinity. Magnetic compasses, fuel gauges, altitude indicators, and all electrically operated instruments are affected. Adds

Gary, pilots who have survived such activity have reported battery drainage as well.

Strange Theft

One day, a would-be shoplifter walked into a store, tried on a sports jacket, and began to walk out of the store. Before he reached the door, however, the coat exploded. It seems a terrorist group had been planting incendiary devices in department stores and placed one of them in the coat's pocket. The unharmed but embarrassed shoplifter had a rough time convincing the Federal Bureau of Investigation that he wasn't a terrorist.

In another FBI case involving theft and terrorists, Croatian hijackers forced a commercial pilot to land in Paris, where they were apprehended. The passengers were flown home to the United States on another plane, while the crew returned with the hijacked plane to Chicago. No one, however, seemed to know what happened to the terrorists' bomb—until the plane's captain and flight attendants finally admitted they had whisked it away, thinking it would be a great souvenir.

The FBI's files are filled with unusual cases. People, it seems, will steal anything—a North Carolina-bound beer truck filled with nothing but empty bottles, a shipment of ox lips, and even horse manure. Then, there was the case of the talking parrot with a vocabulary of 250 words who could even bark like a dog. With such talent, the bird was a strong enticement to the burglar who nabbed it and then found a family to buy it from him. Police soon learned the whereabouts of the valuable parrot as word of its talents spread through its new neighborhood.

Anything of value, of course, is subject to theft, like 3.13 ounces of frozen bull semen from the world's greatest dairy stud. The semen was stolen from a storage tank at a breeders association in Waupun, Wisconsin, and probably steered toward Canada. Worth $90,000 in the United States, its value would be tripled across the border.

Another bird—actually a store mannequin dressed as a chicken—gained the interest of a passerby. Finding the display irresistible, the man broke the window and ran off with the pseudobird, but he was apprehended a few blocks away.

Bursting into Flames

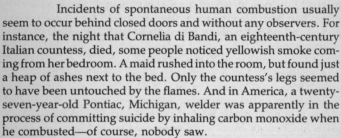

Incidents of spontaneous human combustion usually seem to occur behind closed doors and without any observers. For instance, the night that Cornelia di Bandi, an eighteenth-century Italian countess, died, some people noticed yellowish smoke coming from her bedroom. A maid rushed into the room, but found just a heap of ashes next to the bed. Only the countess's legs seemed to have been untouched by the flames. And in America, a twenty-seven-year-old Pontiac, Michigan, welder was apparently in the process of committing suicide by inhaling carbon monoxide when he combusted—of course, nobody saw.

According to the experts, in fact, the first case with a bona fide witness occurred in 1982, when a Chicago man sitting in his car casually noticed a woman crossing the street. When he turned back for a second glance, she was on fire. Examination by bomb and arson investigators found no foul play involved.

The Dark Star of the Hopi

Hopi tradition, which goes back farther than the tradition of other Indian tribes residing today in the United States of America, preserves accounts of the various world catastrophes that have almost annihilated mankind. Like the Aztecs, the Hopis divided the periods between the catastrophes by "Suns" (the Sun of Water, the Sun of Earth, the Sun of Wind, and the present one, the Sun of Fire).

According to the Hopis, the Sun of Fire is due to end shortly after the year 2000 and will be heralded by the appearance of a dark star, even now approaching Earth. The end of the Sun of Fire will also be indicated by an unusual blue flower that will bloom in the desert. According to tribal reports, a strange blue flower, hitherto unknown, has been found in the desert regions of New Mexico.

Although the Aztecs counted five suns, they agree with the Hopi that the present Sun, the Sun of Fire, will be the last.

Ralph Waldo Emerson and Mrs. Luther

Incidents of spontaneous extrasensory perception occur when people least expect them. Therefore, they're often dismissed as mere coincidence, like the experience of the wife of the nineteenth-century Trinity College mathematician F. S. Luther.

Once a friend asked Mrs. Luther if she had any books about poet Ralph Waldo Emerson. No, she didn't, she replied, and thought no more about it. That night, however, she dreamed she had given such a book to a friend; the friend, in turn, dreamed she had received the text. The next day, the mathematician reported, his wife suddenly and inexplicably turned to the bookshelves. She pulled out a copy of *Century Magazine* and immediately opened to an article entitled "The Homes and Haunts of Emerson."

The Destruction of Mary Reeser

When investigators arrived at Mary Reeser's home in 1951, the front door was too hot to handle. Eventually getting the door opened, they were then confronted by a gust of hot air. They were too late, however, to save Reeser. All they found were her remains in the chair where she had burned to death during the night.

The overstuffed chair was burned down to its springs. The carpet around the chair was charred. Directly above, a patch of ceiling was covered with soot. Unlike other fire deaths in which the skull swells or explodes, Reeser's skull had been shrunken by intense heat. Given the extent of her cremation, according to forensic scientist Wilton Krogman, the entire apartment should have been rightfully consumed. Nothing else in the house had been damaged by the fire, however, not even a pile of papers near the chair.

Numerous theories were proposed to explain Reeser's death, including ignition of methane gas in her body, murder by flamethrower, napalm, even a "ball of fire" that one letter writer claimed to have seen. Krogman himself suggested that Reeser had been burned elsewhere by someone with access to crematorium-type equipment who then returned her remains to the apartment. There, her murderer added such touches as heat-buckled objects and a doorknob that was still hot in the morning.

The coroner, meanwhile, accepted the FBI's theory that Reeser had fallen asleep while smoking and the lit cigarette set her on fire. But the case was never *officially* resolved.

Russian Telepathy

Though paranormal research in the Soviet Union has long been classified as top secret, Russian physiologist Leonid Vasiliev revealed a while back that he and other researchers have been able to give telepathic orders to hypnotized patients. They were, he said, even able to induce hypnosis telepathically.

In one experiment recounted by Vasiliev, for instance, a partially paralyzed woman, whose condition had been diagnosed as psychosomatic, was able to move her left arm and leg with ease while under hypnosis. More important, Vasiliev discovered, when he sent her telepathic directives she would use her limbs—without the use of hypnosis at all.

Demonstrating the ability before an audience of other researchers, Vasiliev blindfolded the woman. Each directive was written down and handed to the group before Vasiliev or his assistant mentally focused on it. Not only was the patient able to pick up the message and obey, but she could even indicate who actually sent the message.

In more recent studies, a committee of Soviet scientists supervised a session using biophysicist Yuri Kamensky in Siberia and actor and journalist Karl Nikolaiev in Moscow. In one test, Nikolaiev correctly described six objects given to Kamensky and identified twelve out of twenty ESP cards.

Interestingly, moreover, the scientists were able to produce independent evidence of the results by connecting Nikolaiev to an electroencephalogram (EEG) machine: As soon as Kamensky began to mentally image the objects, Nikolaiev's brain waves altered.

Based on the EEG results, the scientists devised a technique for sending messages in Morse code. When they instructed Kamensky to imagine he was fighting Nikolaiev, the EEG indicated distinct changes in Nikolaiev's brain waves. Kamensky was able to transmit Morse "dots" and "dashes" by imagining fighting bouts of various lengths: a forty-five-second bout produced a flurry of brain wave activity, interpreted as a dash; a fifteen-second bout was read as a dot. The scientists, two thousand miles away in Moscow, were then able to identify the Russian word *mig* (instant).

The Vultures of Gettysburg

The battle of Gettysburg was one of the bloodiest of the Civil War. After three days of fighting, thousands of slaughtered horses lay among some fifty thousand dead and mortally wounded men strewn across the field. And Plum Run, the stream passing through what is now a national military park, flowed red with blood. It was a smorgasbord for vultures, symbolic sentinels of death.

Today, the carrion-eating birds annually return to Gettysburg, as they have for at least a century, according to park resource specialist Harold J. Greenlee. Virginia Polytechnic Institute and Pennsylvania State University students, working with Greenlee, have been studying the vultures, including their migration patterns. They are also researching Civil War history, looking for mention of the avian scavengers.

"The birds roost on Little Round Top and Big Round Top, hills where some of the heaviest battles took place," Greenlee says. "It's not unreasonable that the vultures could have been attracted to the bodies; they might have scavenged, stayed on for the winter, and then gotten into the habit of coming here." As a result of their investigations, Greenlee and the students hope to explain why nine hundred vultures continue to roost in a national park.

Telepathic Morse Code

Telepathy is an elusive phenomenon, one that tends to occur at unpredictable times and places. Electrochemist and psychic researcher Douglas Dean, however, has found one constant measure of the phenomenon: the volume of blood flowing through the brain changes measurably when people receive messages about a family member or intimate friend. For example, if the communicator concentrated on an image of a person's mother, Dean would be able to tell exactly when the person tuned in to the sender's mind by measuring the movement of his blood.

Using the blood volume measuring instrument called the plethysmograph, Dean went on to develop a Morse Code technique based on his recordings. He interpreted a measurable response to the subject's mental activity as a Morse dot; no response during a specified time was read as a dash. In this manner, Dean has been able to transmit telepathic Morse messages over both short and long distances. In one case, he was able to send such a message from New York to Florida—a distance of twelve hundred miles.

The Mind of an English Clergyman

The nineteenth-century English clergyman Canon Warburton saw his brother catch his foot on the edge of a landing's top stair and fall headfirst to the bottom. Using his hands and elbows, his brother just barely managed to break his fall and prevent serious injury.

Warburton suddenly woke, finding himself in an armchair in his brother's home. The scene he had witnessed had been only a dream. Arriving in London from Oxford to visit his brother, Canon

Warburton had dozed off while awaiting his brother, who had left a note indicating that he had gone to a dance and would return around one o'clock in the morning.

"I have just had as narrow an escape of breaking my neck as I ever had in my life," his brother told him when he returned about half an hour later. "Coming out of the ballroom, I caught my foot and tumbled full length down the stairs."

India's Gravitational Anomaly

Sriharikota, located off the southeast coast of India, is that country's main spacecraft-launching facility. The launch site, however, is notorious for the large number of crashes that occur. Now comes an explanation from Professor Ram S. Srivasta, one of India's most respected space researchers. The disasters occur, Srivasta declares, because the facility is in the middle of "the greatest gravitational anomaly in the world." Srivasta can offer no explanation for the great gravitational swings he has detected at the site. He nonetheless believes that these major variations in gravitational force cause rockets to deviate from course and fall helter-skelter from the Indian sky.

Were the Pyramids Built of Cement Blocks?

Motion pictures like *The Ten Commandments* have left images of thousands of slaves forced to drag huge stones from quarries miles away to the site of pharaohs' tombs, the great pyramids. Barry University chemist Joseph Davidovits, however, presents a different theory: The ancient Egyptians, he says, used concrete, made up of more than two dozen natural ingredients, including limestone and shells. Although the modern Egyptian government denied him permission to verify his theory with on-site sampling, Davidovits believes pouring the stones as the pyramids were built explains their perfect fit.

The Pharos of Alexandria

The highest tower of historical antiquity was most probably the Pharos of Alexandria, an enormous lighthouse guiding ships to and from Alexandria, the Greco-Egyptian metropolis in ancient Egypt. During the night, a great fire burned from its lofty top, and during the day a giant mirror reflected the sun's rays, reputedly visible from thirty miles out over the Mediterranean sea. Its height has been estimated at five hundred to six hundred feet.

To get up and down the towering structure, the lighthouse personnel and garrison had the use of carts, pulled by surefooted asses, which constantly ascended and descended the tower on a series of ramps. The ramps followed a zigzag from level to level, and riders in the carts, soldiers or custodians, could get on or off at the various levels, much like entering or leaving a modern elevator.

This primitive elevator system stopped functioning in the early Middle Ages when Alexandria was captured by the Arabs. Then the Caliph Al-Walid had the Pharos partially dismantled in a search of suspected hidden treasure. Part of the ruined structure was converted into a mosque, but even that was destroyed by an earthquake, and the ruins were carted away for use in other buildings.

About forty years ago divers discovered a large marble column on the sea bottom. It was identified as the *finger* of one of the huge statues that adorned the corners of the great Pharos.

Sucked into the Air by a UFO

In early 1988, forty-eight-year-old Fay Knowles and her three sons were driving near the small village of Mundrabilla on the remote Eyre Highway in the vast desert of southern Australia. Suddenly, their car veered in an unexpected direction—straight up.

The Australian family told police they were pursued by a "huge bright glowing object" that sucked their auto and its shocked passengers into the air. During their bizarre ride, Fay Knowles and her sons noticed that their voices became strangely slurred and abnormally slow. Then the UFO dropped the car back onto the highway, causing a rear tire to blow out. And eerily, three other people in southern Australia saw the unidentified flying object as well.

"The sightings took place hundreds of kilometers apart and these people had no reason to conspire," says police sergeant James Fennell of Ceduna, a town about 370 miles away. Beyond that, he added, an investigation of the Knowles's car showed that it was covered in a thick coating of black ash inside and out. The roof was damaged, too.

"The family members were extremely distraught," Fennell declared. "Something happened out there."

The 1897 Spaceman

On April 19, 1897, something so extraordinary happened in the tiny farming community of Aurora, Texas, that townsfolk talk about it still. According to accounts published in the Dallas and Fort Worth newspapers of the time, on that fateful spring day, a cigar-shaped spaceship roared out of the sky and slammed into Judge J. S. Proctor's home, destroying a window, a water trough, and a flower garden in the process.

S. E. Hayden, a local cotton buyer and newspaper correspondent, reported that the little man who piloted the craft was dismembered by the crash. "However, enough remains were picked up to determine it was not an inhabitant of this world," Hayden wrote in a newspaper article describing the strange event. "The men of the community gathered it up, and it was given a Christian burial in the Aurora cemetery."

The alien's grave marker disappeared several years ago. Residents of Aurora claim they are no longer sure where the grave is and they doubt much could remain in it. But, periodically, areas of the cemetery are dug up—most likely by people hoping to find the remains of the only extraterrestrial said to be buried on planet Earth.

Reward for a UFO: £1,000,000

Kenneth Arnold, an experienced pilot, flying his plane over the Cascade Mountains of Washington in 1947, suddenly saw nine unidentified circular metal objects flying at an estimated speed of 1,300 miles per hour. Since then, many thousands of UFO sightings have been reported over the plains, mountains, deserts, lakes, oceans, and cities of Earth. Although strange objects have been noted in the skies through the centuries, the Arnold sighting seemed to launch an avalanche of reports, which has continued ever since.

Many UFOs have been photographed, but not one has been produced for public inspection. Their landing tracks in the earth have been tested for traces of minerals or chemicals, for geometric signs or mathematical indications, and flight and takeoff patterns have been compared with other international reports.

According to the *People's Almanac* (Bantam, 1981), the Cutty Sark Company of 3 St. James Street, London SW1, has posted a bona fide reward of £1,000,000 to anyone able to capture a "spaceship or other vehicle" that is verified by the Science Museum of London as having "come from outer space." The Cutty Sark Company, makers of Scotch whisky, claims that the reward for a provable UFO is a serious offer, and the company has taken out insurance to cover the possible expense.

Although no one has yet claimed this prize money, a possible candidate is rumored to exist in the form of a crashed flying saucer or spaceship found on July 2, 1947, near Socorro, New Mexico (*The Roswell Incident*: Ace Books, 1988). The saucerlike spaceship was first taken to Roswell Air Force Base and then shipped for further examination, along with its dead humanoid crew, to Muroc Air Force Base in California for inspection by President Eisenhower and others, who maintained regulation military security with the press. After that it was sent to Wright-Patterson Air Force Base, Ohio, where it was held in Building 18A, Area B. Eventually it was sent to Langley Field, Virginia, headquarters of the CIA. Other parts of the wreck are rumored to be at McDill Air Force Base in Florida, and photographs are alleged to be on file or exhibit in the "Blue Room" at Wright-Patterson, where a top-secret exhibit of UFO activity is displayed.

It is unlikely that Cutty Sark will have to make good the reward in the case of the Roswell incident because all corroborative reports concerning it are now classified. Nevertheless, when the incident first occurred, the press gave it wide coverage in interviews with civilians as well as military personnel.

These reports, however, do not qualify for the Cutty Sark award. Cutty Sark will keep its £1,000,000, and its whisky label will continue to feature a sailing ship and not an interplanetary spacecraft. If there is any concrete proof of captured or crashed UFOs held by other nations, it will probably remain secret. During the present world situation, knowledge of the construction and operation of UFOs from space or from Earth itself would represent an extraordinary advantage to the country possessing it.

Giant South Pole Crater

Imagine a hole so huge it would nearly fill the space between Chicago and Indianapolis. An Indiana University–Purdue University scientist John G. Weihaupt says he has proof that such an enormous crater exists, still undiscovered, near the South Pole—the result of the largest meteorite ever to strike the earth.

"We now have evidence that a crater comparable to the largest craters that exist on the moon exists on Earth," Weihaupt contends. He estimates that beneath the ice of northern Antarctica lies a crater a half mile deep and 150 miles wide—four times larger than any other meteorite crater found so far on this planet.

What could have made such an enormous hole? According to Weihaupt, the answer is a mammoth meteorite. Weighing in at around 13 billion tons and measuring 2.5 to 3.75 miles across, the meteorite is believed to have smashed into the earth between 600,000 and 700,000 years ago, at a speed of 44,000 miles per hour.

Although the impact was enormous, when the meteorite hit it spared the earth a greater catastrophe. Weihaupt says his calculations show that the crash lacked enough force to change the planet's axis or rotation.

Ancient Electricity

In 1936, while excavating an ancient Parthian settlement in what is now Iran, Austrian scientist Wilhelm König came across a puzzling object. Although it dated from about 250 B.C., the instrument seemed to have technical workings. In fact, König suspected it was an electricity-producing battery.

Encased in a terra-cotta pot, the tubular object was 2.5 centimeters wide. Made of copper sheeting soldered with a tin-lead alloy, it stood about 12 centimeters high. A tight-fitting copper cap, insulated with pitch, covered one end while the other was sealed with a pitch stopper. Poking out of this was an iron rod insulated with copper. When the contraption was filled with an acid solution (like vinegar, wine, or lemon juice) or with an alkali (for example, lye), König deduced that a working galvanistic element would be produced.

Two experiments—one conducted in the United States in 1957 and another repeated recently by Egyptologist Arne Eggebrecht of the Hildesheimer Museum in Germany—used copies of the object (the original is housed in the Iraq Museum of Baghdad) to prove that it *can* create an electric current. With the help of a copper sulfate solution, the battery designed by so-called barbarian nomads emitted .5 volts of electricity.

There are clues that the ancient Egyptians also knew how to produce electrical power. Many monuments built during the time of the pharaohs are filled with rooms and passageways that have no apparent light source. No trace of soot from torches, candles, or petroleum lamps has ever been found, according to Professor Helmuth Satzinger of the Kunsthistorisches Museum in Vienna. Could the builders of the great Egyptian edifices have worked by the glow of electric lights?

Located on the shore of the Nile opposite the city of Qena, the ancient Egyptian temple of Dendera may hold the answer to that question. Inside, strange wall reliefs show human figures beside objects that look like giant light bulbs with serpents—or symbols of filaments—undulating inside. Perhaps it is more than coincidence that Thoth, the Egyptian god of science who illuminated the night with his light, is shown nearby.

The walls of the temple are covered with other illustrations and hieroglyphs that Egyptologists have been unable to fully decipher. But Dr. John Harris, a British scientist at Oxford, who studied the reliefs, concluded that they appear to be the ancient equivalent of technical writing used by today's scientists. Austrian scientist Walter Garn, who has extensive experience as an electrical engineer, agrees that the temple of Dendera holds technical information—specifically, directions on how to produce electricity.

Garn interprets the "serpents" in the bulblike pictographs as electrical arcs; he suggests that the men shown kneeling opposite each other beneath the bubble are symbolic of opposing electrical currents. He also notes that a fluted column that seems to support the "bulb" looks remarkably like a modern high-voltage insulator.

Death Star

When scientists from the University of California analyzed the ages of the earth's largest impact craters, a startling pattern emerged. The craters, created when comets slammed into the planet, appear to have been formed every 28 million years—a time frame that coincides exactly with the mysterious mass extinctions of animals that once roamed the planet.

But what could bring comets into the earth's path at such precise intervals? The researchers say the earth is at the mercy of an uncharted "death star" that brings comets—and catastrophic destruction—to the earth as it regularly passes by this part of the solar system.

Physicist Richard Muller, working with Princeton physicist Piet Hut and Berkeley astronomer Marc Davis, has come up with a theory that explains how the "killer star" operates. A small, cool dwarf, it has an elliptical orbit that takes it as far as 2.4 light years away from the sun—right into a part of space where a comet cloud containing 100 billion comets is located. Whizzing through the cloud, the star picks up some of the comets and later, as it soars past the solar system every 28 million years, it tosses some of the asteroids toward the earth.

"The earth is a small enough target that you'd expect about two dozen of those to hit it," Muller points out. "But they would do it in a relatively short period."

When the meterorites smashed into the planet in the past, Muller theorizes, they created a cloud of dust that blocked sunlight and prevented photosynthesis. That, he says, would explain why dinosaurs were suddenly wiped out about 65 million years ago, after ruling the earth for 140 million years—dust storms plunged the planet into months of cold and darkness and caused the creatures to die of cold and hunger.

The scientists say there's every reason to believe that the "death star" will pay the earth another terrifying visit. But this time, we'll know when it's headed our way: It's due back in about 15 million years.

Ancient Greek Use of Solar Energy

Around 214 B.C., the story goes, Greek mathematician and inventor Archimedes figured out a novel way to stop the Roman forces who were attacking the Sicilian port city of Syracuse—he used solar energy to roast them alive.

Archimedes reportedly instilled a giant concave mirror on the shore. The reflective surface magnified the sun's rays and focused them back on the Roman ships, which caught fire in seconds.

To find out if this tale is simply a myth or if it could be historical fact, a present-day Greek engineer, Ioannis Sakkas, reenacted the event in 1973. Theorizing that Archimedes actually used hundreds of soldiers' mirrored shields instead of one huge curved mirror, Sakkas linked up seventy Greek sailors along the seashore, each holding a five-by-three-foot bronze-coated mirror. Then he signaled the group to angle their mirrored shields in the direction of a plywood boat that floated about 160 feet out in the ocean. The result? The boat burst into flames within a few minutes.

Sakkas noted that Archimedes probably had even greater success with his solar energy assault—the Romans' ships were more flammable than his model, and, while the men participating in the experiment stood at sea level, the Syracusans probably had the advantage of being elevated on a wall. "Archimedes," Sakkas concluded, "would have operated under better conditions."

The Balloonists of Nazca

History books say that the first manned hot-air balloons didn't get off the ground until the eighteenth century. But there's evidence that an ancient people living in what is now Nazca Valley soared above the bleak Peruvian plains centuries earlier. In fact, their aerial talents could explain how the Indians were able to draw giant abstract designs and figures that stretch in straight lines for miles—creations that are visible only from the sky.

In 1975, a travel-oriented organization called the International Explorers Society, based in Coral Gables, Florida, began studying the possibility that the Nazcas were balloonists. The group's members theorized that while Nazca workmen laid out gigantic linear designs on the ground, they were guided from above by observers who hovered over them in hot-air balloons.

Their research came up with a picture on a Nazca ceramic pot that appears to illustrate a hot-air bag. They also learned that textiles recovered from desert graves proved that the Nazcas had the materials needed to make a balloon's envelope.

In addition, they discovered a reference in a document at the University of Coimbra in Portugal that could be an important clue. According to this source, a Brazilian-born Jesuit missionary named Bartholomeu de Gusamão visited Lisbon in 1709. There he demonstrated a model of a balloon that, when filled with smoke and hot air from glowing coals contained in a clay pot, lifted off his hand and drifted upwards. This event was surprising not only because it occurred nearly seventy-five years before France's balloon pioneers, the Montgolfier brothers, flew their first balloon over Paris but also because it is believed that de Gusamão's balloon was modeled after one used by South American Indians.

The International Explorers Society tested their flying Nazcas theory by building the Condor I, a replica of what they believe a Nazca balloon may have looked like. The contraption featured an eighty-eight-foot-high envelope made from fabrics similar to the materials recovered from Nazca graves, as well as lines and fastenings woven from native fibers and a gondola made from the reeds that grow in Peru's Lake Titicaca.

On its maiden flight, the Condor soared to an altitude of 600 feet in just thirty seconds. But, caught up in strong winds, it crashed back to the ground briefly, dumping its two pilots. Then it was off again, rising to 1,200 feet and flying over two miles in eighteen minutes before it gently landed on the desert plain.

Although the experiment got off to a bumpy start, Michael DeBakey (son of the famed heart surgeon and a director of the International Explorers Society) insisted that the flight of the Condor had achieved its goal. "We set out to prove that the Nazcas had the skill, the materials and the need for flight," he stated. "I think we have succeeded."

Monkey See, Monkey Communicate

Animals have long been known to communicate with one another—sounds and body movements, perhaps instinctive, are used as warnings, as aids in pack hunting, and as a means of meeting other basic needs. In recent years, scientists have found that some animals can be taught to communicate directly with humans. For example, the famous gorilla Coco has learned to recognize and react to human words and even to construct her own sentences through the use of sign language.

One incident, however, has caused some to wonder if a group of monkeys could use their own *spoken* language to tell each other about a tragic event and to seek revenge.

After a youth cruelly stoned a baby monkey to death at the Penang Botanical Gardens in Malaysia, about sixty monkeys began attacking joggers and visitors in the area. "Several of us saw a large group of monkeys coming toward us," one jogger was quoted as saying in the *New Straits Times*. "Initially, we thought they were just coming for food and tried to chase them away. We had to run away when they started charging at us."

What was most remarkable about the monkey-human confrontation was that the animals went after only the people who were wearing the same color clothes as the youth who killed the baby monkey—yellow.

Krause, the Miracle Mule

Everybody knows that the mule, which is a cross between a female horse and a male donkey, is incapable of reproduction. It's a scientific fact. But obviously no one ever informed a mule named Krause.

Krause's owners, Bill and Oneta Silvester of Champion, Nebraska, noticed that their mule was gaining weight. "Her mother was a Welsh pony and they have big stomachs," Oneta comments. "So we just thought she was getting fat." It wasn't until Krause delivered a foal that the Silvesters realized they had a very unusual mule on their hands.

According to geneticist Oliver Ryder of the Zoological Society of San Diego's Center for the Reproduction of Endangered Species, there have been other reports of mules apparently giving birth. But in the past, whenever researchers were able to investigate, the claims always turned out to be inaccurate. "The supposedly fertile mule would sometimes prove to be a mulish-looking horse," Ryder notes. "Or she was indeed a mule, but the foal wasn't her own; she had 'adopted' the foal of another horse or donkey."

However, when Ryder investigated Krause and her offspring, named Blue Moon, he found that chromosome testing and a blood analysis showed the mule had definitely given birth to the foal.

"Based on the available evidence, it has always been safe to conclude that mules of both sexes were completely sterile," Ryder explains. "Horses have sixty-four chromosomes and donkeys have sixty-two. Mules inherit sixty-three chromosomes that 'get along' with each other quite well as far as forming a mule; it is only when the mule tries to produce reproductive cells that the incompatibilities are manifest."

But, inexplicably, Krause was somehow able to do what is scientifically impossible for mules to do—reproduce. "To my knowledge, this is the first case of alleged mule fertility that has stood up to complete scientific analysis," Ryder concludes.

Modern-Day Neanderthals

The hairy, low-browed Neanderthal became extinct thousands of years ago. Or did he? According to archaeologist Myra Shackley of Britain's University of Leicester, numerous eyewitness reports suggest that a small band of Neanderthals is still living in caves, high in the mountains of Outer Mongolia. The wild men are called Almas by other residents of the desolate area that stretches between the southern USSR and China.

Shackley, who published her research in the prestigious archaeology journal *Antiquity*, states that "the idea that modern man can be the only surviving hominid species is outmoded biological arrogance. It seems impossible to deny the existence of the Almas."

Shackley notes that responsible citizens, including scientists, have reported spotting the living Neanderthals. While doing fieldwork in Outer Mongolia, Shackley came across possible traces of the Almas herself—stone tools that looked like those known to have been made by Neanderthals. Hoping to discover the origin of the artifacts, she traveled along the edge of the Gobi Desert and the Altai Mountains, asking local herders who made the objects. The answer was always the same, she says—they were made "by people who used to live in the area." These people, the archaeologist was told, now live in mountain caves and hunt for food.

The Mongolians expressed surprise that Shackley was interested in the Almas. "To the Mongols, they were common knowledge," she notes.

The Woman Who Attracts Lightning

Does the thought of lightning striking from out of the blue scare you? Then you'd be wise to steer clear of Betty Jo Hudson of Winburn Chapel, Mississippi—a woman who seems to attract the flashing bolts of electricity.

It all started when she was a child and lightning struck her head and face. Then her parents' house was repeatedly hit by lightning. In 1957, a jolt finally destroyed the home.

In recent years, Betty Jo and her husband, Ernest, have witnessed lightning strike all around their residence in the rural community of Winburn Chapel. Not only was their house hit three years in a row, but their neighbor's home was also damaged by lightning. Other bolts from the blue killed the Hudson's dog, zapped a tree and a pump, and carved out deep ruts in their yard.

So far, Betty Jo has escaped serious injury, but she has had several close calls. For instance, one summer the Hudsons were shelling butter beans on their porch when dark clouds gathered and a summer storm erupted. The couple retreated to their front bedroom only minutes before a bolt of lightning crashed through a window in another bedroom. "If we had been in there," says Betty Jo, "we would have been hit."

UFO Snapshot

Dave and Hannah McRoberts were driving on British Columbia's Vancouver Island when they decided, at about noon, to pull over into the Eve River Rest Area. Off in the distance the couple could see a rugged mountaintop set off against the sky by a white cloud—just the scenic view that Hannah thought would make a pretty snapshot.

Hannah focused her camera and took a single photo. A few weeks later, in October 1981, the film was developed. The mountain scene came out clear and scenic. But there was something odd about the photo, something the McRobertses didn't remember seeing when the picture was taken—a silvery disc flying through the sky.

The McRobertses quickly contacted the Canadian National Defense office at Comox about the UFO they had inadvertently captured on film. The army wasn't interested. However, friends and neighbors were fascinated by the photo, and the McRobertses were soon having copies of the picture made and distributing them to anyone who wanted one.

A copy of the snapshot came to the attention of psychologist Richard Haines in Pasadena, California. Haines, president of the North American UFO Federation, decided to find out more about the photo. He visited the McRobertses at their Campbell River home, examined and tested their camera, and then investigated the area where the photograph had been taken.

In July 1984, Haines told an audience at the Rocky Mountain UFO Conference at the University of Wyoming that, based on his investigation and a computer analysis of the photo, he had come to believe that the saucer-shaped object was real.

He noted that a blowup of the UFO revealed a clear dome on top of the disc. But there's still no explanation of exactly *what* Hannah McRoberts accidentally caught on film. "It remains unidentified," Haines concludes.

Out-of-Body Poll

With all the attention paid to the out-of-body experience (OBE) in recent years, psychiatrist Fowler Jones and two colleagues from the University of Kansas have set out to see whether the phenomenon is real. Toward that end, they questioned 420 randomly selected people from thirty-eight states and three foreign countries. Their findings? A large majority of those polled said they had experienced at least one out-of-body excursion—and some said they had taken a mind-over-matter trip *hundreds* of times.

"Healthy, intelligent people, many of whom attend church on a regular basis, reported these experiences," Jones noted. He points out that OBEs are not drug-altered states of consciousness, nor are they simply dreams.

Whatever the experiences are, Jones adds, they are described as pleasant by 85 percent of those surveyed. "People who have such experiences feel they're quite real. They describe them in various ways, but the common denominator is that the mind, the *I* part of the personality, the thinking-feeling part, is no longer located inside the physical body but is deposited somewhere else in the environment," Jones relates. "It is as if they have a mobile center of consciousness located just a few feet, or several miles, from the physical body."

When the mind leaves the body, it can apparently glimpse events that later turn out to have actually taken place. For example, one man interviewed for Jones's research pointed out that an OBE saved his life. When his mind left his body, it traveled to a room filled with co-workers who were planning to murder him. After returning to his body, Jones relates, the man confronted one of the plotters. She was so frightened by his knowledge of the planned assassination that she confessed on the spot.

UFO-Caused Automobile Accidents

In the summer of 1979, two teenaged boys watched unexplained lights pass over their car. Then some sort of energy pinned them to their seats. When the youngsters were finally able to drive away, they found their car racing out of control as if it had a mind of its own.

A couple of weeks later, at 1:40 A.M., a Minnesota policeman saw an unusual light in the sky and felt his car being blown across the road by an unseen force. Then he blacked out. When he came to, the officer found that his windshield had been shattered and his antenna bent; his clock was inexplicably fourteen minutes slow.

According to the Center for UFO Studies in Evanston, Illinois, these incidents are not unique—there have been 440 cases reported around the world of UFOs provoking car accidents or near accidents. The UFOs appear to initiate "electrochemical events" that can stall engines and break or block radios with static.

Most of the incidents have no scientific explanation, says astrophysicist Mark Rodenghier, who has studied the reports. He points out that the Ford LTD driven by the Minnesota policeman was examined by Ford engineers, who insisted that no known phenomenon could cause the automobile to behave in such a strange way.

Elvis Makes a Comeback

In late 1980, about a hundred miles from Memphis, a truck driver noticed a strange glow coming from some nearby woods. Then he saw a hitchhiker walk in front of the light and turn toward the highway. Stopping to offer the traveler a ride, the trucker noticed that something about the polite young man seemed familiar. But it wasn't until they reached the bright lights outside Memphis that the truck driver recognized his passenger as someone who had died three years earlier—Elvis Presley.

According to psychiatrist Raymond Moody, the trucker's experience isn't unique. As he documents in his book *Elvis After Life* (Peachtree, 1987), since the King of Rock 'n' Roll's death, reports of his ghostly appearances have popped up all around the country. "A psychotherapist, who met Elvis when she was a youngster, claims he unexpectedly stopped by her office one day—after his death—and counseled her on the emptiness of her life," Moody says. "Another woman told me that Elvis materialized in the delivery room to help her with a difficult childbirth."

Moody notes that in addition to ghostly visits, Elvis has also been linked to other paranormal experiences. One fan had a precognitive dream the night before Presley's death in which the singer announced "this is my last concert." Another repeatedly witnessed one sleeve of a jacket once owned by Elvis move up and down by itself.

Goose Falls

Hundreds of geese were swarming over Norfolk county in England in early January 1978 when these masters of flight began falling from the sky. Before long, 136 dead pink-footed geese were found in an area forty-five kilometers long. Another 105 fell near Wicken Farm, Castleacre. Others were discovered in various areas, in groups of two to as many as fourteen.

The goose deaths were not the result of hunters shooting for the sport of it; there were no signs of gunshot wounds. Autopsies also ruled out the possibility of the birds being struck by lightning. Instead, some birds had lungs with blood clots and signs of hemorrhaging, while others had ruptured livers.

Some researchers finally speculated that the geese, traveling across the area, met with an advancing meteorological cold front that carried strong tornadoes. The unsuspecting geese apparently were caught in the vacuum cleaner-like winds and were swept up into higher atmosphere. At such great heights, the birds' lungs then hemorrhaged, causing their sudden death in the air, and they fell to earth over a long strip of land.

Cobweb Storms

Anyone who's seen *The Wizard of Oz* is familiar with the image of a tornado picking up everything in its path and carrying it for miles. But while tornadoes and whirlwinds leave grave damage in their wake, people are often amazed at what they find in the aftermath.

Even small whirlwinds, for instance, have deposited hay on telephone and electrical wires. And ordinary air currents have transported and then dropped cobwebs to Earth. Charles Darwin, for instance, observed a rain of cobwebs while on board the *Beagle*, sixty miles from land. After landing, Darwin reported, many of the spiders formed another web and took off once again.

Today scientists know that some spiders migrate by clinging to an airborne strand of cobweb. In fact, floating cobwebs have on occasion deluged an area as they fell to the ground. In Milwaukee, Wisconsin, during October 1881, for example, webs well over two feet long came in from over a lake, descending from a great height. In a similar case in Green Bay, Wisconsin, webs floated in off the bay; this time, though, strands were up to sixty feet in length and could be seen high in the sky. No one in either of these instances saw any spiders at all.

Yet other cobweb sightings include wads and patches of white material known as "angel hair." Soaring through the sky, reflecting sunlight, a mass of such material might easily resemble a fleet of UFOs.

Manna from Heaven

The biblical story of the Israelites' exodus from Egypt tells the tale of manna that fell to earth in great quantities and prevented the people from starving during their long trek. Scientists have always disagreed on the nature and source of that food.

There have been other reports of manna from heaven, however, occurring in more recent times. In 1890, for example, a shower of manna fell in Turkey, covering an area approximately ten kilometers in circumference. Composed of small spheres that were yellow on the outside and white within, the "manna" was examined by botanists, who determined that it was a member of the lichen family. A plant made up of alga and fungus, desert lichen grows on such solid surfaces as rocks and pebbles; some have suggested it as the source of the Israelites' heavenly food.

Manna, however, has more than one possible source. In a 1927 research expedition organized by Jerusalem's Hebrew University, scientists determined that the manna phenomenon is well known around the world. In many cases, the food source is a clear, sweet excretion from a plant known as the *Tamarix nilotica*. The fluid is ingested by the plant lice and other insects that live on the desert shrub. The dry desert climate causes the syrup to crystalize, producing whitish grains that cover the branches or fall to the ground.

The Lost Fleet of Alexander the Great

The appearance of Greek words in American Indian and Pacific island languages is an intriguing mystery. The first white men who came to Delaware and Maryland found a river that the

Indians called *Potomac*," a soundalike for the Greek word *potomos*, meaning "river."

When the Spanish conquistadores invaded the Aztec Empire of Mexico, they noted that the pyramid temples (where the Aztec priests tore out the hearts of sacrificial victims and threw the bodies down the pyramid steps) were called *Teocalli*. This is a combination of two Greek words, *theos* and *kalias*, meaning "dwelling (of the) god." The meaning in Nahuatl (Aztec) is identical.

While it is possible that ancient mariners of different nationalities reached the Americas through the southern Gulf Stream, Greek words in Hawaiian and related Tahitian are even more striking. Here are a few:

English	Hawaiian	Ancient Greek
eagle	aeto	aetos
come/arrive	hiki	hikano
think/learn	manao	manthano
sing/melody	mele	melodia
thought/intelligence	noo-noo	nous

Where did the Hawaiians get these Greek words? Could it have been from Greek metal-and-horsehair war helmets that the Hawaiians copied in wood and feathers? But where could the Hawaiians have seen the helmets? Could the Greeks have crossed the Atlantic eighteen hundred years before Columbus and *then* crossed the Pacific as well?

There may be a simpler, though equally intriguing, explanation. This concerns Alexander the Great, the conquerer of most of the ancient world. Alexander, after conquering the Persian Empire, pushed eastward into the Indian peninsula, and northward into what is now the USSR, looking for new worlds to conquer. Meanwhile, his fleet of eight hundred vessels, under Admiral Nearchus, explored the coast of India. Most of this fleet was recalled to the entrance of the Persian Gulf in 324 B.C. to take part of his now tired and disaffected troops back to Greece.

But part of the fleet never returned. Had it gone beyond the coast of India, the Malay peninsula, and then continued out into the currents of the Pacific? Perhaps some of the ships reached islands like Tahiti and Hawaii, where life was pleasant, the maidens attractive, and strangers from the sea, with their superior armor and weapons, would probably be treated like visiting gods.

Earthquake Hair

The earthquake roared through eastern Siam, wreaking havoc. The rivers rippled and bubbled, turning white. During the shock, the earth split open, throwing out everywhere what seemed to be human hairs. Long and upright, they remained firmly planted in the ground. Burned, they even smelled like human hair. Reporting on the 1848 quake, the *Singapore Free Press* suggested the hairs were produced by electric currents. Later explanations theorized that some natural material, perhaps tar, shot out through the earth's pores into fine strings. Congealing as it encountered cooler temperatures, the substance resembled hairs.

The appearance in Siam of earthly hairs is not a solitary incident. Chinese who have collected such hairs after earthquakes for thousands of years believe they may belong to a subterranenan animal whose sudden movement causes the earth to shake and the rivers to bubble.

Breathing Earth

For three weeks the islands that constitute the Moluccas were covered by a sulphurous fog. Then on November 1, 1835, a violent and destructive earthquake shook the tiny region to its roots.

Incidents of sulphur released into the atmosphere—along with water, sand, and other material—are not uncommon in early earthquake reports. Indeed, modern scientists have detected an increased emission of gases contained within the earth. The discharge of radon by hot springs and in mines, for example, has been linked to subsequent earthquakes. A significant amount of helium was also discovered along the fault line formed by the 1966 Matsuhiro quake in Japan. In this case, it was suggested that molten rock deep in the earth released the helium that then rose upward and through the earth's crust.

In a 1978 paper published by the prestigious magazine *Nature*, West German biologist Helmut Tributsch proposed that gases forced out of the earth prior to an earthquake are electrically charged, forming ion clouds. The flow of ions, he suggested, would explain the animal agitation, human physiological effects, and atmospheric phenomena that have been reported prior to many big quakes.

Indeed, earthquake lore throughout history is filled with stories of bizarre animal behavior that may have forewarned people of the impending destruction. Five days before the great earthquake that destroyed the Greek city of Helice in 373 B.C., for example, citizens observed mice, weasels, snakes, and other subterranean creatures vacating their underground abodes and making a mass exodus.

Long before humans detect anything, birds, fish, and mammals all seem to sense something unusual is afoot. Cows have been seen bracing themselves by setting their forelegs apart, sheep continually bleat, dogs howl, wolves bark, and cats run frantically about.

During the 1930s, the Japanese studied catfish and found that they showed signs of unrest up to a full six hours before an earthquake registered on seismic instruments. Placed in an aquarium, the normally placid catfish were unresponsive during normal periods when scientists knocked on the glass or on the table. When a quake was impending, however, the same action caused the fish to jump or swim around in a highly agitated state.

Scientists have often tried to tie this mysterious phenomenon to subaudible sound or electromagnetic field changes. Now, thanks to Tributsch, ionized air has also made the list.

Solitary Monster Waves

The Italian ship *Michelangelo* sailed westward through gale winds on April 12, 1966. Proceeding at a cautious, steady speed, six hundred miles southeast of Newfoundland, it headed toward New York—through twenty-five- to thirty-foot waves. Suddenly, a wall of water rose from the sea, towering above all the other waves, and smashed into the ship. Steel superstructures collapsed, heavy steel on the bow was torn off, bridge windows were crushed, and the bulkhead under the bridge was bent back at least ten feet. Three people were killed and twelve injured.

Almost every sailor has a tale of a monstrous wave that appeared suddenly out of nowhere. Measurements vary: In 1921, a giant wave in the North Pacific was estimated to be seventy feet high; a later one about one hundred miles off Cape Hatteras, Virginia, was about one hundred feet high. As far back as 1826, French scientist and naval officer Captain Dumont d'Urville encountered sudden waves eighty to one hundred feet high, an estimate supported by three colleagues. Admiral FitzRoy, first director of the Meteorological Office, reported that he himself had measured waves as high as sixty feet, adding that bigger waves were not unknown.

The cause of these giant waves is still unclear. Some scientists say they are caused by severe storms that generate large waves that then reinforce each other and create an even bigger wave. Yet many giant solitary waves appear in calm seas and can't be attributed to the winds at the time. Could they be the result of underwater earthquakes or volcanic eruptions? Oceanographers continue to study the phenomenon, but the mystery is still there.

Fog Guns

W. S. Cooper was sailing on the Gulf of Mexico, about twenty miles southeast of Cedar Keys, Florida. The water was calm, the sky cloudless. There was a light fog and no breeze. Shortly after sunrise, however, he heard the sound of a gun or distant cannon repeated in five-minute intervals. His companion, who lives on the coast, told Cooper that on still mornings the sounds were often heard.

In a similar account, one A. Cancañi reported that in Italy the sound is longer than that of a cannon shot, and not unlike distant thunder, although more prolonged, and comes at various intervals. In the East Indies, another report adds that several noises, sounding like a foghorn, occur every few seconds, lasting one or two seconds each.

Modern investigators of such mysterious explosive sounds along the coasts of North America and Europe have generally dismissed them as sonic booms. The problem with this explanation is that the foghorn bleats have been reported throughout the world in areas near seacoasts for at least a century.

According to another hypothesis, the shots are caused by the eruptions of natural gas beneath the sea. The discovery of pockmarks in many of the continental shelves at the oceans' bottoms supports the idea of natural gas frequently being released.

Holistic Healing

Some religions teach that we can send a healing force over considerable distances. This belief, which pervades many world cultures, was recently put to a scientific test.

The experiment was designed by Dr. Robert Miller, a well-known scientist, engineer, and inventor. Working with the Holmes Center for Research in Holistic Healing in Los Angeles, California, Dr. Miller wanted to see if people could be healed of their afflictions even if they didn't know a psychic healing effort was going on.

Working on the project from 1976 to 1979, Miller began by recruiting eight healers: four were Science of Mind practitioners, two were psychic healers, and the others were Protestant ministers. The healers were asked to treat high blood pressure patients, who were not told they were part of the experiment.

The patients were secretly selected by several physicians known to Dr. Miller. The healers never met the patients but were provided with their locations, initials, and a few other personal facts. Each healer treated six patients located randomly in the United States. Forty-eight patients were treated during the course of the project, while another forty-eight patients served as the control group. Not even the physicians knew which patients were selected for the psychic treatment and which weren't. The doctors were asked merely to monitor their patients' diastolic and systolic blood pressure readings, heart rate, and weight.

The healers were instructed to treat the patients in any manner they wished, and most of them "healed" by visualizing the subjects in perfect health.

According to the researchers, the experiment was a modest success. More than 92 percent of those receiving distant healing showed a reduction in their blood pressure readings, though 75 percent of those in the control group improved as well.

Children and the Near-Death Experience

Rushed to a hospital emergency room after nearly drowning in a community swimming pool, a seven-year-old girl sank into a deep coma. "I was dead," she related after regaining consciousness three days later. "I was in a dark tunnel. It was dark and I was scared. I couldn't walk."

A woman named Elizabeth materialized to escort her to heaven, the small girl said. Once there, she encountered her dead grandparents, a dead aunt, and "the heavenly Father and Jesus." When asked if she wanted to see her mother, the girl said yes and awoke in the hospital.

Reported by pediatrician Melvin Morse in the *American Journal of Diseases of Children*, the incident was the first juvenile near-death experience to appear in medical literature. Morse later interviewed other children who related similar tales after traumatic accidents. One recalled being scolded in heaven; another was carried on a beam of light through a long, dark tunnel.

Although these children were probably raised in religious households, Morse believes their experiences may be more than mere fantasy. The children, he suggests, may have been glimpsing the hereafter or, more likely, recalling the archetypal images that haunt the outback of human consciousness for us all.

Einstein and the Watchmaker

Albert Einstein's theories changed our concept of time, space, energy, matter, and the universe itself, but the physicist remained silent on the subject of religion—except in one instance. Pressed for his thoughts on the existence of God, Einstein replied that he had always been impressed by the mechanics of the universe. Everything from atoms to galaxies functioned as precisely as clockwork, he said, much like a gigantic cosmic watch.

"Someday," he added pensively, "I should like to meet the watchmaker."

Martian Pyramids

For generations, scientists have suspected the existence of life on Mars. Theories about the form of life there have included everything from simple organisms to humanoids who built cities and dug canals. Italian astronomer Giovanni Schiaparelli first described and mapped Martian "canals" in 1877. With the development of more powerful and sophisticated telescopes, observers downgraded the former waterways to natural riverbeds ranging in width from seven to twenty feet. Many believe there may still be water—in the form of ice—on the red planet.

And while satellite photographs have so far failed to reveal any life-forms, some Mars watchers believe there is evidence that Mars may have once supported life. One area—dubbed "Pyramid City" by astronomers—hosts structures that resemble the Egyptian pyramids; the Martian versions, however, are 3,000 feet wide at the base of each side, compared to 612 feet at the base of each side of the Cheops pyramid. Images of an enormous rock or statue depict a partially shaded face, measuring about one mile wide; the visible eye, nose, mouth, and forehead bear a greater resemblance to human features than do those of the Great Sphinx in Egypt. And at the Cofrates depression, possibly a former sea, there is a series of forms that could be the ruins of an ancient port, with square constructions that might have been docks, streets, or buildings.

Further exploration will eventually prove whether these are mere illusions or real artifacts—like the towers and walls of Babylon and Troy—that are unrecognizable until after excavation on and under the surface of Mars.

The Precognition of Nostradamus

Between 1547 and his death in 1566, Nostradamus foretold such future events as plagues, wars, revolutions, earthquakes, massacres, and the development of modern warfare. Anyone who is familiar with history and nature, of course, can make predictions involving wars and natural catastrophes that occur with a certain regularity. Nostradamus, however, was very specific, indentifying individuals by name hundreds of years before they were born.

The sixteenth-century prophet foretold, for example, the rise of Hitler, describing his nationality, rise to power, and successful invasion of France. Uncannily referring to the German leader as "Hister," he added that "the greatest part of the battlefield will be against Hister."

Nostradamus dramatically foretold the fates of numerous historical figures, including Napoleon, England's Edward VIII, Winston Churchill, and Franklin Delano Roosevelt. He often referred to them by nicknames, but occasionally named them exactly, as in the case of Louis Pasteur, who, he said, would be "celebrated as a godlike figure." Writing of Spain's future Franco, as well as Primo de Rivera and his followers, Nostradamus said: "From Castille, Franco will bring out the assembly" and "Rivera's people will be in the crowd."

Recording his prophecies 223 years before the French Revolution, Nostradamus seems to have been most exact in his predictions concerning the fate of France's Louis XVI. The seer referred to the king as the "chosen Capet," the actual royal family name, and as "Lui," capitalizing the French pronoun meaning "him," which sounds like the French name "Louis."

There are also significant similarities between Nostradamus's predictions and actual events during the French Revolution, which took place more than two hundred years *later*. He wrote, for example, that "a conflict would pass over the tile"; in fact, the French word *tuile* refers to the Tuileries Palace, invaded by the revolutionaries. Later, Louis's attempted escape from France, according to Nostradamus, would be thwarted by "two traitors." He named one of these "Narbon," similar in sound to Count Narbonne-Lara, the French minister of war who betrayed Louis. The other, whom Nostradamus named "Saulce," turned out to be the historical Saulce, proctor of Varenne, who stopped the ruler's coach along the escape route and sent the royal family back to Paris.

The deaths of Louis XVI and his queen, Marie Antoinette, Nostradamus also said, would cause "tempest, fire, blood, and slice"—this last referring to the guillotine, not yet invented in Nostradamus's time.

Indians Who Traveled to Europe by Canoe

During the reign of Augustus Caesar two thousand years ago, when the Romans ruled much of Western Europe, a long, narrow, hollow seafaring vessel washed ashore from the North Sea. Speaking a strange language, the copper-colored travelers it carried frequently pointed to the craft and then to the west. Unable to understand the barbarians, Roman soldiers took them hostage and escorted them to the Roman proconsul, Publius Metellus Cellar, who enslaved them.

The travelers would have disappeared into the shadows of history except for a carved likeness of one of them, a bust resembling a Native American. Apparently, the Indians became lost off the North American coast, and the canoe was carried by the upper, easterly Atlantic current—all the way to Europe.

Columbus, who also used the Atlantic current—the lower, westerly stream—during his voyages to the New World, may have been aware of Publius's slaves. A dedicated student of earlier Atlantic crossings, he once described the story of two dead men, dark in color and perhaps Chinese, found floating in a long, narrow boat washed up on the western shore of Ireland, near Galway.

A Portentous Game

Before the arrival of Europeans in the New World, the pre-Columbian people in Central America, Mexico, and some parts of the southwestern United States were *tlachtli* enthusiasts. The object of *tlachtli*, a game similar to soccer or basketball, was knocking a small, hard rubber ball through a hole in a stone above the players' heads. The rules allowed the use of elbows, hips, legs, and the head, but prohibited the hands from touching the ball.

Apparently more than just a sport, *tlachtli* seems to have been a religious ritual as well. Losers not only forfeited their garments and accoutrements, but often their lives. Aztec priests, for example, are known to have ripped out the hearts of players stretched spread-eagle across a sacrificial altar.

The most portentous *tlachtli* match was played between the Aztec emperor Montezuma and Nezahualpilli, ruler of Tezcoco. The purpose was to determine the reliability of Tezcoco's astrologers, who had predicted that strangers would one day rule Mexico. The stakes in the game were three cocks against the Tezcoco kingdom. When Montezuma lost, with a score of 3 to 2, Tezcoco kept his kingdom and won the cocks.

This fateful game of *tlachtli*, in fact, aided the Spanish conquest of Mexico. Montezuma became so depressed by the prophecy of losing his kingdom that he found himself unable to oppose the strangers when they arrived.

Profanity Prohibited by a Royal Saint

Leading the seventh Crusade (1248–1254) to free the Holy Land from the infidels, Louis IX was captured by the Moslems. After his ransom and release, he spent much of his reign imposing his religious views on his subjects.

Louis, the only French king to be canonized after his death, believed it was his responsibility, for example, to eradicate the use of profanity. To cure speakers of the expletives *pardieu* (by God) and *cordieu* (God's Body), he ordered hot irons applied to transgressors' tongues.

It soon became fashionable to utter such expressions as *parbleu* (by blue) and *sacre bleu* (damned or sacred blue), which resembled the forbidden words. (Besides sounding like *dieu, Bleu* was also the name of Louis's favorite dog.) The inoffensive oaths eventually survived the Middle Ages and are still part of the French language today.

To Beat the Devil

The day before Halloween 1987, an unusual lawsuit was brought in Little Rock, Arkansas. The suit was filed by Ralph Forbes, formerly a candidate for the U.S. Senate, who sought to bar public schools in the state from celebrating Halloween, classifying the holiday as an "observation of the rites of Satan."

Whether or not the complaint had some redeeming value (outlawing Halloween would probably curb children's tendencies to throw eggs, splash paint, "wrap" houses, tip over farm outhouses, and so forth, every October 31), one of the principal defendants named was obviously a disruptive and eerie character. His name is well known to everyone—"Satan," aka *the devil*. Another defendant, of considerably better reputation, was the Russellville School District. The suit was filed on behalf of Ralph Forbes, Jesus Christ, and minor children.

Ancient Brazilian Semites

When the Portuguese discovered Brazil in 1500, they had no difficulty in naming the place. They had, after all, found what they had sought: the iron ore-rich land called Brazil that, according to ancient legends, lay across the South Atlantic. In several Semitic languages, as well as modern Hebrew, for example, *Brazil* (or B-R-Z-L) means "iron" or "land of iron."

It is a fact that many stone tablets, inscribed in Phoenician and other Semitic languages, have been found along the Amazon. A number of them, some describing the fate of expeditions, were initially considered forgeries. Practical jokers, however, would have been hard-pressed to carve them and then deposit them in the deep Amazonian jungle. If they are, in fact, genuine, then it's also possible that ancient Semites not only traveled to the Brazilian shores long before the Portuguese arrived there and before Columbus's discovery of the Americas, but also named South America's biggest nation almost two thousand years before it was officially discovered.

The Man They Couldn't Hang

Convicted of theft and the murder of a police officer in Sydney, Australia, Joseph Samuels was condemned to die by hanging in September 1803. Still protesting his innocence, he was forced to stand in the execution cart, a noose around his neck. But when the horses were whipped forward, Samuels hung briefly from the rope and then fell out of the cart. In the second attempt to hang him, this time with his hands tied together, the rope suddenly unraveled and Samuels was left strangling slowly, but still alive. On the third try, the rope snapped as the wagon moved out from under him, and Samuels fell to the ground with the noose still around his neck.

After three unsuccessful attempts to hang the convicted man, the crowd, believing that Samuels must be innocent, had become unruly. Rather than try once more, the executioners returned Samuels to his jail cell.

Later, Isaac Simmonds, having made himself conspicuous by jeering at Samuels in the death cart, was found guilty of the crimes and condemned to death by hanging. This time the execution was successful on the first try.

Rats, Cats, and History

Between 1346 and 1350, seventy-five million people died from the Black Death that decimated Europe as it spread across the continent. The great bubonic plague is believed to have originated in Kaffa. According to the theories, ships from the Middle East carried rats infected by plague-carrying lice, and the lice spread the disease to humans.

As the plague progressed, all sorts of remedies, penances, and prayers were used for cures and prevention. Superstition led to an attack on supposed witches and their accomplices, cats. Periodic massacres of the cats, however, only made matters worse since there were fewer rat catchers.

Still, when the plague abated, and the devastated villages and towns recovered, cats returned to their rat-catching duties and regained their places on the hearths.

Film Debut of a UFO

During the 1972 filming of a television commercial on the roof of San Juan's Hotel Sheraton in Puerto Rico, the crew witnessed the sudden approach of a large UFO. Viewing it on the monitors, they could tell that the brightly glowing object was not a plane, a blimp, or a helicopter. It vanished as quickly as it had appeared, but not before it ruined the commercial, which had to be reshot.

That year, there were more reports of UFOs (unidentified flying objects, *not* necessarily extraterrestrial in origin) in Puerto Rico than anywhere else in the world. So the Sheraton incident was no different than a host of other sightings—with one exception. The film footage of the large, glowing UFO was sold to Creative Films, a movie company that needed a shot of a UFO in a film it was making at the time.

Dissecting Relatives

The new medical students seemed nervous as they faced their first set of cadavers in anatomy classes at the University of Alabama. But, according to a letter printed in the *Journal of the American Medical Association*, one of the female med students was horrified when she looked over the corpses. There among the bodies awaiting dissection was her recently deceased great-aunt.

Her relative, it turned out, had been shipped to Alabama by the state anatomical board in Florida, where the woman had passed away. When University of Alabama doctors realized that a med student was faced with watching the body of someone she knew being dissected, they immediately moved the body to another laboratory and instituted a new policy. Now the names of cadavers are checked with incoming students.

"That student [who recognized her great-aunt] quickly recovered from the trauma of the situation," notes psychiatrist Clarence McDanal, a cosigner of the letter.

Ironically, it may have been the med student who was responsible for her dead aunt's body being in an anatomy lab in the first place—before her relative's death, the young woman had talked to her about the merits of body donation.

Dream Headlines

Around 3:00 A.M. on January 29, 1963, Mrs. John Walik of Long Beach, California, suddenly bolted upright in bed—awakened by a terrifying nightmare that seemed unusually vivid.

She had dreamed of an airplane flying low over water. It seemed to level off as it approached a landing strip a hundred feet away. But suddenly it dropped, bounced off the water, and veered into the ground, exploding into flames.

The details of the dream haunted Mrs. Walik. She had clearly "seen" that the plane was a big four-engined Constellation—the same kind of plane her husband flew as a navigator for Slick Airways.

Was the dream a warning that John Walik was in danger? As soon as the Slick Airways office opened that morning, Mrs. Walik called to see if her husband was safe. She was assured that no planes had crashed and that John, who was flying on a plane that was delivering freight to the West Coast, would be home in just a few days.

But Mrs. Walik wasn't reassured. As she told friends, neighbors, and family—anyone who would listen—over the next few days, there was something different about this dream, something frightening. It seemed *real*.

On February 3, 1963, Mrs. Walik decided to check on her husband's safety one more time. Again, the airlines insisted there had been no problems with his plane and John would be landing at the San Francisco International Airport later that morning.

As soon as Mrs. Walik hung up the phone, the details of her dream came rushing back. The plane in her nightmare had crashed near water, she remembered. And to land at San Francisco International Airport, her husband's plane would have to fly over the bay.

Quickly she redialed the Slick Airlines office. But before she could finish explaining her concern, her terrifying dream had come true. Her husband's plane crashed beside a runway and began to burn. Five crew members were killed. Four others—including John Walik—survived.

The next day, the *Long Beach Independent Press* ran a story emblazoned with the headline "Mate's Plane Crash Seen in Wife's Dream." The crash of the ill-fated Constellation was, the newspaper noted, the same disaster Mrs. Walik "had seen in her dreams five days before it happened!"

The Humming House

Back in the 1960s, the family of truck driver Eugene Binkowski of Rotterdam, New York, came down with a host of unexplained ailments. Their heads, teeth, ears, and joints hurt. But why?

The family wondered if a faint humming noise they heard day and night in their house could be related to their aches and pains. The local police and technicians from a nearby General Electric plant were called to the house, but they were baffled by the Binkowski family's claims that they heard a constant hum.

Finally, Eugene wrote to President Kennedy, asking him to get to the bottom of the mystery. A few days after his letter reached the White House, six air force sound experts arrived at the suburban Binkowski home, armed with complex instruments used to detect high frequency sound.

Although they did not identify sounds that could be causing the family's problems, the researchers did make a startling discovery: the entire Binkowski household possessed unusually acute hearing and they were physically able to hear what they claimed to hear. In fact, even six-year-old Terry Binkowski could detect sounds well above the normal hearing range of most humans. The only explanation the air force sound specialists could offer for the constant humming the family experienced was that it might be related in some way to three nearby radio stations.

As word leaked out about the humming house in Rotterdam, hundreds of visitors stopped by to listen for the mysterious noise. Most reportedly heard the hum or said their heads began to feel stuffy. Whatever caused the odd sensations, the Binkowski family finally decided they had to escape the constant drone—so they packed up and moved into a nearby garage.

Ancient Russian Mummies

According to the Russian newspaper *Trud*, in the mid-1980s a group of Soviet cave explorers unexpectedly came across an eerie sight: caves filled with so many ancient mummies that they were soon dubbed the "city of the dead."

But why dozens of men, horses, and wild animals entered the caves in the first place—and how they became mummified—remains a mystery.

Soviet experts speculated in *Trud* that the people could have been fourth-century B.C. nomads trying to hide from the invading troops of Alexander the Great. Emory University historian Thomas Burns agrees that "refugees trying to escape that conquering army could have gotten up to where the mummies were found" in the central USSR. He also theorizes that the people "could have been holing up in a cave because of a family feud."

Brad Shore, professor of anthropology at Emory, says that the doomed nomads could have been turned into mummies by a quirk of nature. "It's unusual, but certainly not unheard of," he notes, "to find people preserved like this after being trapped by a mud-slide or a landslide."

Just how the mummies in the Russian "city of the dead" met their fate may never be known, but the local mountain people have long dubbed the caves where they were found unlucky. According to *Trud*, area residents believe that the black plague originally came from the mite-infested caves. In fact, the Russian speleologists noted that they left the caves with painful body sores—evidence of the biting insects that still share the caves with the mummies.

Sleep Language

When Gene Sutherland of Mesa, Arizona, went to bed, it wasn't unusual for his wife Wilma to find she couldn't get a full night's rest—her husband would often wake her up by talking in his sleep. Usually Wilma would make out a word or two and then drift back off to her own dreams. But one night, Gene's babbling sounded strangely different.

Gene seemed excited and agitated, Wilma recalls, and he was speaking in what seemed to be a thick, foreign accent, using sounds like "ski" and "vich" repeatedly.

Sensing this was not Gene's ordinary sleep talk, Mrs. Sutherland quickly grabbed a tape recorder to document the odd gibberish. When she played the recording back to her husband, he was baffled by his outbursts. But Wilma couldn't get the impression out of her mind that whatever her husband had said in his sleep sounded like Russian. She called the foreign language department at Arizona State and asked Professor Lee Croft to listen to the tape.

Croft not only agreed that Mrs. Sutherland had recorded her husband speaking Russian, but he was able to recognize eight or nine Russian terms, including the words for "a drunk" and "excuse me, it's evident."

Gene Sutherland, however, insisted that he didn't know how to speak Russian. His only exposure to the language had occurred during World War II, when as a United States Army serviceman he met up with Red Army allies at the Elbe River.

Croft theorizes that somehow the experience of hearing Russian left an impression on Sutherland's subconscious, enabling him to speak in Russian as he slept. After word leaked out about Gene's odd talent, however, the Sutherlands soon heard from a host of people with other possible explanations—including reincarnation and demonic possession.

Tasmanian Monster

It's not unusual for dead animals to wash ashore after a fierce storm. But the creature that turned up on a Tasmanian beach in July 1960 after a particularly violent gale was unlike anything that had ever been seen before.

Rancher Ben Fenton and some of his workers were rounding up cattle not far from where Interview River empties into the ocean when two of Fenton's men found the "monster"—a large, circular mass, about twenty feet in diameter and six feet thick at the center, covered with short, coarse hair.

Fenton called local authorities to report the strange find, and soon a government naturalist and other interested scientists were at the remote location to take a look at the mysterious animal.

The thing's inch-thick skin was so incredibly tough that taking tissue samples turned out to be almost impossible. After hacking away with sharp axes for over an hour, however, two scientists were finally able to cut out a segment of the beast's white fibrous interior.

But scrutiny in the lab raised more questions than it answered. Researchers were not able to say what the animal was—only what it *wasn't*. According to scientists who examined the evidence, the creature was not part of any known species on Earth.

Two years passed, but the Tasmanian monster was not forgotten. The Australian Parliament expressed interest in getting to the bottom of the mystery and, once again, a group of government scientists descended on the remote beach where the hairy creature still baked in the sun.

After twenty-four hours of examinations and consultations, the group released an official statement. Their conclusion? The beast remained a baffling enigma, unrecognizable to the world of science.

Angels' Wings

Summoned before the Spanish Inquisition in the sixteenth century, the painter El Greco was interrogated not because of suspected heresy, witchcraft, or a relapse of faith. The Church officials were offended by the way he painted the wings of angels.

According to the inquisitors, El Greco's angels were in opposition to canon law and the Holy Scriptures: They weren't painted so that the wings represented real angel wings at all. However, unlike other victims of the Inquisition, El Greco was able to successfully defend his actions. He presented his theories of form, purity, and grace so convincingly that the judges acquitted him and set him free. Perhaps under their black cowls, the representatives of the Church harbored an appreciation of art—as long as it wasn't too openly paganistic.

Ancient Roman Lead Poisoning

Two Roman cities destroyed and buried during the eruption of Mount Vesuvius in A.D. 55, Pompeii and Herculaneum, are archaeological time capsules, valuable for studying what people were doing at the time of the calamity. The more prosperous

Pompeii is better known because more people escaped. Throughout the Middle Ages, in fact, Italian noblemen had mineshafts dug into the buried city and excavated a number of ancient art masterpieces. Some centuries after the eruption, however, a new city was built on the site of the buried Herculaneum, a situation that still makes research difficult, although not impossible.

Archaeological exploration of Herculaneum during 1988, in fact, unearthed parts of the city and a number of corpses. Study of the preserved human remains has revealed the diseases that plagued the ancient Roman citizens, particularly lead poisoning.

The source of the lead, it's believed, was soldered wine and food containers. Scientists suggest that the ingested lead affected the minds and the reproductive ability of the Romans. Unable to replenish the old Roman stock, the people would have been defenseless against the invading barbarians (who didn't use lead in their utensils). Mental aberrations and instability, not only among the general population but also among such emperors as Caligula and Nero, would encourage the further decline and eventual collapse of the empire.

Frasier's Youthful Old Age

In 1971, southern California's Lion Country Safari attempted to breed twelve young lionesses. Five young male lions were sent in to sire cubs, but the lionesses rejected each of them. One male was even badly mauled.

Later, the safari received an old lion named Frasier from a bankrupt Mexican circus that could no longer afford to feed the animal. Having spent most of his life in a cage, Frasier was scarred, bleary eyed, toothless, and lame. Yet the twelve lionesses found him irresistible, vied for his favor, and even chewed his food for him. With his new harem, Frasier eventually sired thirty-five cubs in sixteen months, after which he died, presumably quite happy and content with his active old age.

Mystery of the Dead Scientists

In August 1986, the body of underwater torpedo guidance systems checker Vimal Sajibhai was found under a bridge near Bristol, England. But that was only the beginning of a mysterious wave of deaths. Nine other scientific researchers working on British defense projects suffered strange and seemingly unconnected deaths. In each case, the death was classified as either a suicide or "unexplained."

Several months after Sajibhai's death, a noose was placed around the neck of Ashhad Sharif as he sat in his car. With the other end of the rope tied to a Bristol park tree, Sharif's neck was broken as the car sped away.

This was followed by the January 1987 death of computer designer Richard Pugh, whose body was found in his East London home. During the same month, the body of Royal Armaments Research and Development Establishment computer expert John Brittem was found in his garage, seated in his car with the motor still running. Metallurgy expert Peter Peapul and computer engineer Trevor Knight were also victims of carbon monoxide poisoning.

The list goes on: Computer expert David Sands, the trunk of his car filled with gasoline, crashed into an empty restaurant and burned to death. Computer specialist Mark Wisner suffocated when a plastic bag was somehow placed over his head. Victor Moore presumably died of a drug overdose. And Russel Smith, of the ultrasecret United Kingdom Atomic Energy Authority, was found dead in his car after it plummeted over a cliff.

The British press has suggested that the deaths may have been a series of planned murders. The purpose: To impede antisubmarine warfare and other defense programs. Members of Britain's House of Commons found the deaths suspicious enough to have called for an official investigation.

Rasputin's Miraculous Cures

The Russian czar Nicholas II and his czarina were greatly influenced by the mysterious Siberian monk Rasputin, whom the czarina referred to as "our Friend." The source of Rasputin's power over the royal family stemmed from his hypnotic ability to stop the internal bleeding attacks of their son Alexis, the hemophiliac heir to the throne. Through his power over the czar and czarina, Rasputin was able to enrich himself with munitions contracts, influence the appointments of his friends to government posts, interfere with military tactics, and live a generally depraved life-style, often involving ladies of the court. Moreover, his increasing influence destroyed public trust in the government and weakened the country's military efforts during World War I.

Although suspected of espionage by some historians, Rasputin has never been proved to be a German spy even though his actions certainly aided the enemy. The Germans reasoned that as long as Rasputin reigned within the palace, the Russian war efforts were doomed anyway. They therefore did everything possible to keep the monk firmly in power.

German agents often bribed Russian soldiers to feign unconsciousness until the arrival of Rasputin, who frequently visited the wounded in Russian army hospitals. When the monk stopped to bless a German plant, the soldier would suddenly sit up, calling out that he had been cured and giving thanks to God, the saints, and Rasputin for the apparent miracle. Such "cures" inflated Rasputin's fame among the Russian people and his influence with the royal family.

Finally, in December 1916, Prince Felix Yusupov contrived to rid Russia of Rasputin. Taking advantage of the monk's interest in attractive noblewomen, the prince invited him to a tryst, got him drunk, fed him poisoned cakes, shot him, and then drowned him in the ice-covered Riva Neva.

It was too late, however. Rasputin's influence and actions had so greatly impugned imperial prestige that the February 1917 revolution, already in the works, would mark the end of the Romanov dynasty and its empire.

Versailles Time Warp

Annie Moberly and Eleanor Jourdain, two British teachers, visited the royal palace at Versailles during a trip to France in 1901. Having explored the main palace, they walked through the world-famous gardens on their way to Petit Trianon, Marie Antoinette's small palace. Since they didn't know the ground plan, they requested the assistance of two men dressed in eighteenth-century garb who they thought were caretakers. The men waved them straight ahead, and as the women moved on, they saw a woman and a young girl also wearing old-fashioned costumes standing in a cottage doorway.

The schoolteachers continued walking until they came to a wooded area. There they encountered a dark man with a malevolent expression sitting in front of a *temple d'amour* (temple of love), a pavilion with a round roof supported by columns. A young man emerged from behind some rocks along a weeded path. He spoke a French dialect unfamiliar to the women, but with the assistance of gestures, directed them toward Petit Trianon, across a wooded bridge over a small gulley. On the other side was the front lawn of the palace.

During their walk, Miss Moberly said later, "everything looked unnatural. . . . Even the trees seemed to have become flat and lifeless. There were no effects of light and shade . . . no wind stirred the trees. . . . It was . . . intensely still."

As they looked ahead at Petit Trianon, Moberly noticed an attractive and obviously aristocratic lady sketching the bordering woods. She was wearing a large hat, a long-waisted green bodice, and a short white skirt. Noticing the teachers, the noblewoman stared at them, as if startled.

Suddenly, the eerie stillness seemed to lift and the surroundings returned to normal. A modern guide appeared and escorted the ladies on a tour of Petit Trianon. The aristocratic artist was no longer anywhere to be seen.

The two teachers did not speak to each other of their experience for several days, and not until 1911 did they jointly but anonymously publish their story in a small but successful book. By that time, they had thoroughly researched what they had seen and concluded that they had walked through a summer day in 1789.

The "gardeners," they declared, were Swiss guards. The dark, menacing man was most likely the Count de Vaudreuil, who was visiting Trianon at the time. The woman and the young girl in the cottage doorway, according to old palace records, could have been peasants living on the palace grounds. The memoirs of Marie Antoinette's dressmaker mentioned making several green bodices and white skirts for what turned out to be the queen's last summer.

There was no mention, however, of a wooden bridge over a gulley in any available records. That missing piece to the puzzle caused the teachers' account to be generally ridiculed—until the royal architect's original plans, which included the gulley and the bridge, were eventually found in the chimney of an old building in a nearby town. The plans had been hidden there long before, perhaps for safekeeping.

Nevertheless, the incident on the grounds of Versailles remains unresolved. Had the Misses Moberly and Jourdain truly seen and talked to ghosts from a summer's day in 1789? Or had the ladies somehow traveled back in time as visible, talking apparitions themselves?

The Widow's Dream

When Ruth Ammer fell asleep on a hot August afternoon in 1962, she was the wife of Syrian-American shoe repairman Joseph Ammer. But by the time she woke up, she had a terrible feeling that she was a widow.

Ruth had experienced a prophetic nightmare. As she later recounted to the police, she dreamed that her husband was in his shop when an assailant attacked him, striking him over and over with a hammer.

When Mr. Ammer failed to come home for lunch as he always did, Ruth began to worry even more about the dream. So she decided to pack Joe's lunch and take it to his shop a few blocks away.

When Ruth arrived, she saw her nightmare come true. She found her husband bound with cobbler's twine, beaten to death. The murder weapon, a hammer, lay nearby.

Although she gave the police a description of the man she had seen in her dream, the officers were not particularly interested—until they learned that a man who answered Mrs. Ammer's description, down to the clothes he was wearing, had been spotted washing his bloody hands in a rest room shortly after Joseph's murder.

Although her dream was not admissible as evidence at the murder trial of William Edmonds, Ruth Ammer did have the satisfaction of knowing that her husband's murderer—the same man she had seen in a nightmare—was found guilty and sentenced to life in prison.

The Socialite Who Dreamed of Murder

Sir Henry Wilson, chief of the British general staff during World War I and a member of Parliament, spent a jovial evening with his old friend, socialite Lady Londonderry, and several other people in June 1922. The group joked and talked at the London socialite's home until close to 2:00 A.M. Then Lady Londonderry went to bed, but it was a fitful sleep. When her husband woke her up, she was screaming and wet with perspiration.

In a terrifying dream, she told her husband, she had watched Sir Henry die. She described how her friend took a taxi through the streets of London, stopping in front of his home. Then Sir Henry paid the driver and walked up to his front door. As he started to unlock it, two assassins approached him, whipped pistols from under their coats and shot him at point-blank range. Then the gunmen raced down the street.

There was one detail of the dream that didn't seem to make sense. Lady Londonderry had "seen" Sir Henry in his full-dress military uniform, but the gentleman's customary attire was civilian clothes.

A little more than a week after the socialite's dream, however, Sir Henry Wilson was asked to unveil a war memorial at Paddington Station. For the occasion, he wore his full-dress uniform. After the dedication, he took a taxi home, where, a few minutes after he paid the driver, two armed murderers shot him to death—a tragedy Lady Londonderry had previewed in her terrible dream.

Impossible Rain

Every school kid knows that clouds and rain go together. But there have been unexplained instances of rain pouring from the sky when there wasn't a cloud in sight.

Mrs. R. Babington arrived home on the clear and sunny afternoon of November 11, 1958, and noticed that water was coming down on her grass and her home's roof. It definitely wasn't raining, so she assumed the neighbor's sprinkler was accidentally aimed toward her house and yard.

But closer inspection revealed no one nearby was watering grass. No pipes had burst and no outside faucets were turned on. The water had to be coming from somewhere. But where?

Soon dozens of people, including the managing editor of the *Alexandria Daily Town Talk*, Adras LaBorde, were watching rain fall on an area about one hundred feet square over Mrs. Babington's house—but no place else in the neighborhood. The downpour kept up for hours and officials at the weather bureau and at England Air Base were unable to come up with an explanation for the phenomenon.

Nearly a century before, a similar event was reported down in Dawson, Georgia. Although there were no clouds in the sky on that

September day in 1886, it rained for more than an hour on an area a mere twenty-five feet in diameter.

A month later that same year, two areas in South Carolina were inundated by cloudless showers. According to the *Charleston News and Courier*, one house and lawn in that seaport town were drenched for hours by a mysterious isolated shower. And as reported by the October 24, 1886 *New York Sun*, for two weeks a small section of Chesterfield County, South Carolina, was saturated by a steady rain that poured from a clear, sunny sky.

The Lifesaving Hunch

Mrs. Hazel Lambert of Pennsbury Heights, Pennsylvania, gave a co-worker a ride home from the Cartex Corporation at about ten o'clock on Christmas Eve morning, 1958. Then she decided to pick up a few things at a nearby food store. But as she drove toward the market, Mrs. Lambert was overcome with the need to step on the gas and race down Franklin Street—a road she had never been on before.

What was behind this strange compulsion? Mrs. Lambert never figured that out. All she knows, she later told reporters, is that she had to follow her strong feelings, which took her to Hillside Street. Suddenly, the woman glanced over at a nearby canal and saw a child's hands, covered in red mittens, holding on to the inside edge of a hole in the ice.

Speeding through the intersection and right over the ice, Mrs. Lambert felt the car slip through the frozen water. The doors jammed as the car settled in four feet of water, so she pressed down on her horn and yelled for help.

The commotion brought George Taylor and his teenage son to the scene to help the trapped driver and the child hanging on to the ice. The younger Taylor quickly used a pole to maneuver himself out on the ice and rescue Carol Scheese—a two-year-old girl who most certainly would have died if Mrs. Lambert had not given in to an odd compulsion.

Bizarre Blackouts

The electricity went out, suddenly and unexpectedly, when the power between two of the main stations serving Denver went down for nearly an hour and a half around midday, February 14, 1963. The outage caused an overload of current, which also zapped relay lines to Cheyenne and Boulder out of commission. To keep the turbines of the Cherokee plant from being damaged, the facility had to be closed down.

What caused the blackout? Engineers sent out to check for line breaks, damaged equipment, and other possible explanations were baffled when everything appeared to be in perfect working order. Then, as mysteriously as the region's electrical power had gone off, it came back on again. "We may never know what happened," a state official was quoted as saying by a local reporter.

There are some, however, who think there may be a link between UFOs and similarly inexplicable power shutdowns. One example was researched by Dr. Olavo Fontes of Brazil and recounted in *The Great Flying Saucer Hoax*, written by Carol Lorenzen, director of the Aerial Phenomena Research Organization.

On an August night in 1959, four automatic keys in the huge electric power station at Uberlândia, Minas Gerais, turned themselves off, shutting down power to all trunk lines. Technicians scurried to find out what was going on. Nothing seemed amiss except that the keys had broken the circuit.

Immediately, a worker from a substation placed a call to the chief engineer at Uberlândia and told him an incredible story: A UFO had soared low over the power station, he said, causing the keys at the substation to kick themselves open.

The chief engineer dismissed the man as a drunk and got back to work. He turned on two of the main keys and found they were still not working. Then he turned the third key and suddenly they all popped open. At that moment, workers at the Uberlândia station began yelling and pointing at the sky. A glowing disc-shaped object was passing overhead on a path right over the power lines. As soon as the "flying saucer" passed out of view, the electric power station began working normally once more.

The Moving Memorial

It's not unusual for a memorial to be moving, in the emotional sense. But there's a memorial in the eastern corner of a Marion, Ohio, cemetery that *literally* moves. And no one knows how or why.

The tapered white granite column, set off by a black granite sphere three feet in diameter, marks the graves of Charles Merchant and six of his relatives. Erected in 1897, it didn't create much of a stir until July 1905. That's when a workman noticed that the heavy black ball topping the monument had been moved several inches, exposing a rough spot on the bottom of the orb where it had once fit.

If pranksters were behind the incident, they must have been incredibly strong—or they must have brought heavy equipment with them. Since the sphere weighs hundreds of pounds, it took a block and tackle to budge it.

Determined that no one would disturb the Merchant memorial again, cemetery officials poured lead cement on top of the granite column to tightly hold the sphere in its original position. But two months later, the black ball had moved again. This time it was ten inches away from where it was supposed to be resting.

Curiosity seekers and scientists, including a geologist, offered possible explanations, but none of them panned out. In fact, the big black ball is said to be restless still—moving from time to time, as if it has a mind of its own.

The Ghost Ships and the Destroyer

The Navy destroyer *Kennison* had two ghostly encounters at sea—events dutifully recorded in the ship's log.

The first took place in 1942 not far from the Golden Gate Bridge while the *Kennison* searched for Japanese submarines. The fog was so thick that the crew had to rely on radar to keep from running aground on the Farallon Islands. But a couple of sailors, a lookout listed as Tripod, and a torpedoman first class named Jack Cornelius, spotted something in the dense mist that the radar never picked up—an ancient-looking, unmanned, two-masted sailing vessel passing within a few yards of the *Kennison*'s stern.

The men yelled over the intercom for the rest of the crew to take a look. The ghostly ship, however, had vanished in seconds. But Tripod and Cornelius gave identical descriptions of the strange craft they had seen plowing across the water.

In the spring of the next year, the *Kennison* was patrolling the coast about 150 miles out from San Diego. The log notes that the sea was smooth and the night sky was clear and starry. Sailors Carlton Herschell and Howard Brisbane were on lookout duty on the flying bridge. As they looked through binoculars, they both saw a freighter heading toward the destroyer. They quickly warned the radarman, who failed to see anything on his scope.

Herschell and Brisbane put down their binoculars. They could now see the freighter with their naked eyes. It was about seven miles away and still coming toward them. Then it simply disappeared.

Time Warps in the Bermuda Triangle

For many years the Bermuda Triangle, an area between Bermuda, the east coast of Florida, and Puerto Rico, has been the scene of hundreds of disappearances of ships from the sea and planes from the sky, or sometimes just the crews suddenly vanish from their ships. Only a few inconclusive last messages have been received. Little wreckage has been recovered. The many theories for the disappearances are varied and speculative:

—Sudden giant seiche waves or eruptions of underwater volcanoes. If wreckage surfaces it may be carried up the coast and farther out in the ocean by the Gulf Stream.

—Human error, compounded by known frequent failure of electromagnetic equipment, including that used for radio communication and motor power.

—Whirlpools and "holes in the ocean" that swallow ships and planes.

—Hijackings by modern pirates or drug traffickers or both.

—Disassociation of matter by sound resonance (a suggestion from the USSR).

—Small, dense, compact fogs on the surface or in the sky, where craft enter but do not exit.

—Selection of human beings and their artifacts by collectors from outer space entering through the Triangle, an area that perhaps allows easy electromagnetic access, functioning as a "hole" in the sky.

—Sudden release of subsurface gas deposits through seismic action causing temporary lack of buoyancy on the sea and whiteouts and loss of horizon by aircraft, which results in their plunging into the ocean.

—Giant sunken pyramids, built by Atlanteans as power sources, that may still function sporadically and interrupt the controls and communication systems of ships and planes.

Besides disappearances, there have been a number of very unusual *appearances*, also without any logical explanation, that may put into question our acceptance of time, space, and matter:

—An oceanic investigative party on the yacht *New Freedom*, in July 1975, passed through an intense but rainless electromagnetic storm. During one tremendous burst of energy, Dr. Jim Thorpe photographed the exploding sky. The photograph when developed showed the burst in the sky, but it showed, too, a square-rigged ship on the sea about one hundred feet away from the *New Freedom*, although a moment before the sea had been empty.

—John Sander, a steward on the *QE-I* saw a small plane silently flying alongside his ship at deck level. He alerted another steward and the officer of the watch while the plane silently splashed into the ocean only seventy-five yards from the ship. The *QE-I* turned around and sent a boat over, but no indication of anything was found.

—Another "phantom plane" silently crashed into the ocean at Daytona Beach on February 17, 1935, in front of hundreds of witnesses, but an immediate search revealed nothing at all in the shallow water by the beach.

—A Cessna 172, piloted by Helen Cascio, took off for Turks Island, Bahamas, with a single passenger. About the time she should have arrived, a Cessna 172 was seen by the tower circling the island but not landing. Voices from the plane could be heard by the tower, but landing instructions from the tower evidently could not be heard by the pilot. A woman's voice was heard saying, "I must have made a wrong turn. That should be Turks, but there's nothing down there. No airport, no houses." In the meantime the tower was frantically giving landing instructions, which were not heard. Finally the woman's voice said, "Is there no way out of this?" and the Cessna, watched by hundreds of people, flew away from Turks into a cloud bank from which it apparently never exited since the plane, the pilot, and the passenger were never found.

The plane had been visible to the people on Turks, but when the pilot looked down, apparently she saw only an undeveloped island. Had she been seeing the island at a point in time before the airport and the houses were built? And where did she finally go?

101

The Boy Who Lived Before

Indian businessman Parmanand Mohan died in Moradabad on May 9, 1943. About ten months later, in Bisauli, India, a baby boy was born to college professor Bankey Lal Sharma and his wife. From the age of three, the child, who was named Pramodh, insisted that *he* was Parmanand—he even described how his previous life had ended. "My tummy got wet and I died," he told his father. "Now I have come to Bisauli."

When his son was five, the professor took him to Moradabad, a town the child had never visited before, to see if his tales of life as Parmanand had any basis in fact. The boy quickly led his father and other relatives to a shop where he had been employed in his former lifetime—pointing out in detail how the carbonating machine Parmanand had operated worked. A confrontation with the late Parmanand's wife and sons seemed even more convincing. He identified them by name, talked to them about intimate matters, and even pointed out how their home had been remodeled after "his" death. The visit left both Parmanand's family and Pramodh in tears.

The trip resulted in an explanation for one of the youngster's first assertions concerning his former life. "My tummy got wet and I died" proved to be an accurate, if childlike description, of Parmanand's demise. The man, suffering from an undiagnosed abdominal discomfort, was given a hot bath just before his death.

The Dreams That Saved Josiah Wilbarger

Schoolteacher Josiah Wilbarger of La Grange, Texas, set out one morning in 1838 with four other men to visit his friend Reuben Hornsby, who lived on a farm not far from what is now Austin. But soon after starting the trip, the companions were attacked by a band of Indians. Two of the men immediately fell, mortally wounded. Josiah, shot in the throat, stripped of his clothing, and scalped, was left behind by the two companions who managed to escape with their lives. Josiah must be dead, his friends reasoned—and if it weren't for a woman's dreams, he would have been.

Freezing as he lay naked in the brush, Wilbarger woke up after spending several hours unconscious. Blood streamed from his throat and head. But he was alive and determined to make it to the Hornsby house, about six miles down the trail. Dragging himself a quarter of a mile in that direction, he finally collapsed and drifted in and out of consciousness. Then his sister appeared to him.

"Brother Josiah, you are too weak to go on by yourself," the dreamlike figure said. "Remain here where you are and friends will come to take care of you before the setting of the sun." Then his sister smiled sadly and moved in the direction of the Hornsby's home. Only later was it learned that the woman had died in Missouri twenty-four hours before she appeared to comfort her injured brother.

That evening Mrs. Hornsby, who had been told by Wilbarger's companions that her friend was dead, had a frightening dream. She saw Josiah lying beneath some small cedar trees. He was bloody, naked, and scalped, but still alive.

Mrs. Hornsby woke up from the nightmare and assured herself it was merely a dream. But when she fell asleep again, it returned with the same terrifying vividness. The next morning, due to her insistence, her husband and Wilbarger's companions set out to search for Josiah.

Following the man's bloody trail, they soon found him leaning against a scrub cedar, barely alive. The men cleaned his wounds, wrapped him in warm blankets, and carried him to his friend's farm where he eventually recovered.

The story of Mrs. Hornsby's dreams was not forgotten. The state of Texas eventually erected a monument to the woman whose nightmares helped save a schoolteacher named Josiah.

The Barren Grave

In the early nineteenth century, young Englishman John Davies came to the Welsh town of Montgomery to work for a local widow on her farm. It was the biggest mistake of his short life.

While walking down a road one day, two local men accosted him, demanding money. Davies refused the thugs' request and a fight broke out. Not only was Davies beaten up, but his muggers carried him to Welshpool, where they insisted that *he* had tried to rob *them*.

It wasn't long before the Welsh authorities, never particularly fond of Englishmen, had sentenced Davies to die on September 6, 1821, for highway robbery. Seconds before the noose was put around his neck, he held up his right hand and declared that an innocent man was being sent to his grave: "I die praying to God that He will let no grass grow on my grave and that He will so prove my innocence."

John was buried in the Montgomery parish churchyard alongside rows of other graves—all of which were covered with grass. But Davies's plot remained barren. Local authorities tried topping the grave with green sod, but it immediately turned brown and died. Next, grass seed was tried. None ever sprouted.

Thirty years after Davies's execution, the cemetery was relandscaped. All the graves were covered with two feet of fresh soil and grass seed was planted. Soon the area was covered with a thick, grassy lawn—except for one lonely, brown rectangle that neither seed nor fertilizer could turn green. It was the grave of John Davies. Eventually, a fence was placed around the plot, which remains a barren, mute testimony to one man's innocence.

Who Really Discovered America?

It was back in 1921 that Elwood Hummel found the strange stone. He was fishing along the Susquehanna River near Winfield, Pennsylvania, when he spotted, under the clear water, the small flat object covered with odd markings. On examination, Hummel found it was not a rock after all; instead it was some kind of baked clay tablet. Whatever it was, it didn't seem particularly important to the fisherman, so he just stuck it in the pocket of his fishing coat. It wasn't until thirty-seven years later, when his grandchildren asked about the peculiar object they'd found mixed in with his fishing gear, that Hummel decided to send it to the Field Museum's curator in Chicago.

There scholars pored over the markings and finally translated its message. The clay tablet gave details, they said, about a loan made by an Assyrian merchant in Cappadocia about 1800 B.C. What they couldn't explain was how an ancient Assyrian document got into a river in Pennsylvania.

That mystery has never been solved, but the out-of-place object is just one of many found in the United States which indicate that the New World had a host of visitors long before Columbus—or even native Americans—set foot there.

For example, in Bradley County, Tennessee, J. H. Hooper came across a stone marked with odd symbols. The farmer wondered if there were other strange rocks on his property, and he soon found several more—plus a long stone wall covered with indecipherable signs, numerals, and pictures of animals. A report by the New York Academy of Sciences indicated that the markings on the wall included numerous Oriental characters, which the baffled researchers decided must be "accidental imitations."

The Australian Astronomers and the UFO

When a "flying saucer" is spotted by a couple of teenagers or a tired truck driver, it's easy to brush off the incident as a case of overactive imagination. But when three highly trained astronomers spy a UFO at the same time, that's a different story.

On May 30, 1963, the headlines of the *Melbourne Herald* in Australia declared: "Three Astronomers See Flying Saucer." The article itself noted that the incident was "the best authenticated so far." Professor Bart Bok, a world-renowned authority on the Milky Way; Dr. H. Gollnow, a senior astronomer at the Mount Stromi Observatory; and assistant astronomer Miss M. Mowat, the newspaper reported, had spotted a glowing, reddish orange object around 6:58 P.M. almost directly over the observatory.

The three astronomers tracked the object for one minute as it traveled west to east below the clouds at speeds far too fast to be a balloon. The observers also ruled out a meteor, since the UFO moved slower than those celestial bodies and left no visible trail.

Since the thing was moving under cloud cover, it was far too low to be a satellite, the astronomers reasoned. Besides, a check of satellite charts indicated that none was over the area where the UFO was seen. The Civilian Aviation Control Center also confirmed that there were no planes in the vicinity at the time.

The three scientists concluded that the object, which they noted was self-luminous and did not reflect sunlight, "was definitely man-made!" But just what sort of "man" made this flying craft, which was not a satellite or an airplane, was never explained.

Deadly Warnings

Does death give some people a warning when it is near? In countless cases, the answer seems to be yes.

In February 1958, for instance, twenty-three-year-old Eugene Bouvee found that he couldn't get his seventy-year-old uncle Eugene off his mind. There was no reason to be worried about the old gentleman—he wasn't ill as far as anyone knew. In fact, when young Eugene called one of the elderly Eugene's neighbors the next day, he was told his uncle was feeling healthy and happy. Still, the nephew couldn't shake the feeling that something was terribly wrong.

The young man drove to his uncle's home in Flint, Michigan, but he couldn't get in. The door was locked and smoke was wafting out from around it. He quickly kicked down the door, only to be driven back outside by thick smoke and flames. The fire department arrived shortly afterwards, but it was too late—Uncle Eugene's body was found on the bathroom floor.

In a similar incident, Mr. and Mrs. Richard Ryan of Sheboygan, Wisconsin, received a warning from their son, airman Lawrence Monk, that his death was near. He told his mother he was sure he would die soon and he wanted her to keep his Bible. "I won't be needing this anymore, Mom," he said. "You'll never see me again—but you'll hear about me."

Two days after their son's visit, the Ryans received the tragic news: Their son had been killed, along with sixty-six other passengers, in a United Airlines plane crash in Wyoming.

Not all deadly premonitions turn out to have dire consequences, however. Sometimes they *save* a life. Take the case of thirty-year-old Fred Trusty of Painesville, Ohio, who in 1958 experienced what he called a "strange feeling." It made him drop the tools he was using to build some steps on a hill near his house and compelled him to glance toward a nearby pond. He saw nothing unusual, just some rippling water probably caused by the muskrats who lived in the pond. He picked up his tools again, but the odd feeling returned. Once more he looked over at the pond. This time, he saw a little boy's cap in the water.

Running down the hill, Trusty dove into the pond just in time to save the life of his own two-year-old son, Paul.

The Lost Arms of Venus de Milo

The Venus de Milo was officially found in 1820 on the island of Milos. Now enshrined in the Louvre in Paris, it is one of the most famous and most beautiful of the world's statues. However, seeing that it lacks its arms, art lovers and admiring tourists have long wondered how the arms originally were positioned and what the goddess Venus (or Aphrodite in Greek) was holding in them.

When Venus was first found, she had her arms in place. A Greek peasant living on Milos found her complete, in an opening under a field, perhaps part of an ancient house or temple. He brought the statue to his barn and hid her. He would often go alone, after his day's work, to admire her beauty. He spent so much time this way that his wife suspected he was meeting another woman in the village. She enlisted the aid of a priest. When the priest discovered that the beautiful rival was made of stone, the wife was satisfied, but the secret was out and news of the ancient statue spread far and wide.

Turkish occupation troops who wished to take the find to Constantinople arrived at Milos at the same time as a French frigate sent by King Louis XVIII, who wanted the statue for the prestige of France. A fight started between the French and the Turks. Meanwhile the Greeks were trying to get the statue out to sea, and, as they fled in a small boat followed by the French and the Turks, the statue lost its attached arms, which fell into the sea. The French got to the small boat first, seized the statue, and transported it to Paris, where it now stands in the Louvre as a wonder of the ancient world.

The mystery of the arms' position was not a mystery when the statue was found on Milos. The arms were still in place and a drawing had been made of the statue before the French-Turkish-Greek confrontation. The goddess's right hand was gracefully holding up her robe, already hanging halfway down her body, while the left hand held out an apple, the golden Apple of Discord, connected in legend with Helen, Paris, and the Trojan War.

To find the arms and reunite them with the body of Venus would be an archaeological triumph. Jim Thorne, a deep-sea diver and archaeologist, led an expedition in the 1950s to the area of the coast where the arms were thought to be. On his first dive he found what seemed to be long, lovely white arms reaching up from the bottom. On his second dive he found that they were the graceful and whitened branches of a tree. He never did find the arms.

The lost arms of the world's most famous statue are doubtlessly still lying on the sea bottom not too far from the harbor of the island of Milos.

The Mysterious Demise of Jimmy Sutton

Around 8:30 P.M. on October 12, 1907, Mrs. James Sutton, Sr., told her husband she had just experienced a frightening premonition. "I heard a terrible roaring sound and felt a smashing blow on my head," she exclaimed. "Then I felt stabbing pains in my body and my senses reeled. I don't know why, but I just know that something has happened to Jimmy. Something terrible!"

At 2:30 the next morning, a phone call confirmed Mrs. Sutton's ominous prediction. Her son, U.S. Navy Lieutenant James Sutton, was dead. Navy officials told the family that the young man had committed suicide in Annapolis after getting into a drunken argument with two fellow officers at a Naval Academy dance.

But, according to Mrs. Sutton, as soon as she heard this news an apparition of her son appeared to her and insisted he had not killed himself. "Mama, they beat me almost to death," the grieving mother heard her son say. "I did not know I was shot until my soul went into eternity."

Four days later, the ghostly vision returned, this time to deny published navy reports of how the young man died. Mrs. Sutton claimed that her son gave details of his death that would prove it was not a suicide. For example, Jimmy claimed there was a bruise on his forehead and a lump on his left jaw—facts that directly conflicted with evidence presented at the navy inquest.

Mr. and Mrs. Sutton demanded that their son's body be exhumed and, at a second inquest directed by a nongovernment physician, it was confirmed that Jimmy had indeed died with a large bruise on his jaw and another on his forehead. The doctor also concluded that there was no way the young lieutenant could have killed himself because of the path of the bullet—it had entered from almost the top of the victim's head. In addition, it was learned that the bullet retrieved from Jimmy's body had not been fired by the deceased man's gun, as the navy had claimed.

The second inquest concluded that Jimmy Sutton had not committed suicide. Someone had beaten and then shot him—just as his ghostly apparition had claimed.

Séance for a Murder

Fall was in the air in 1921 when medium Dr. O. A. Ostby and several friends met in Minneapolis to hold a séance. Soon Ostby informed the group that a young girl was in their midst. The spirit, he said, was crying and asking for a favor. She called herself Edna Ellis. It seemed, the medium continued, that Edna wanted someone to write a letter to the St. Louis police department explaining that she had been murdered. She did not want her parents to continue to think that she had run away to lead an immoral life.

The next day, following the ghost's request, Ostby wrote to the chief of police, Martin O'Brien, in St. Louis. O'Brien replied that Edna Ellis had indeed been murdered and that her boyfriend, Albert, was serving a life sentence at the Missouri State Penitentiary for the slaying.

When Ostby and his group met for another séance, the young woman again appeared and thanked the medium. Then she requested that he send O'Brien's letter to her parents in South Dakota. Ostby was confused by one detail in the apparition's story, however. The girl spoke of the lover who had killed her as George, but the police called him Albert Ellis. Edna's spirit explained that her boyfriend's full name was George Albert, although she had always referred to him as George.

In November 1922, the Supreme Court of Missouri reviewed Albert Ellis's case and decided he had been unfairly convicted. The man was released from prison, but four years later he died in an accident. Edna Ellis apparently held no bitterness toward her killer. On July 16, 1928, the spirit of Edna Ellis dropped by another séance being conducted by Dr. Ostby to inform him that she and George were happily together at last.

The Two Mr. McDonalds

A person *can* be in two places at the exact same time. At least that's the decision reached by a New York City jury on July 8, 1896.

The strange verdict came at the end of a burglary trial. William McDonald was charged with burglarizing a house on Second Avenue. Although the defendant insisted he was innocent, six people testified that he was definitely the man they had surprised as he packed up stolen articles inside the home. After a fight, the accused burglar escaped. McDonald was arrested soon after based on witnesses' accounts.

But at McDonald's trial, another witness gave surprising testimony in the accused burglar's defense. According to Professor Wein, a medical doctor who performed public hypnotism experiments from time to time, McDonald was hypnotized in front of several hundred people in a Brooklyn theater at the exact time the burglary was under way.

Wein testified that he was sure McDonald was the volunteer he had put in a trance. He remembered him clearly because the man had been an unusually good hypnotic subject.

111

"He was . . . very responsive and quick to execute the instructions," the doctor told the courtroom. "I considered him to be in a cataleptic state—that is, deprived for a certain time of all sensations other than those I imposed on his will."

"Was it possible," a lawyer asked, "for this man's spirit to wander while his physical body was in a hypnotic trance and in full view of the audience?"

The professor answered, "Yes. Quite possible."

After hearing this testimony and that of the six eyewitnesses to the burglary, the jury acquitted William McDonald. They decided that everybody was telling the truth—McDonald had been on a theater stage and, at the same time, in a house five miles away.

UFO Landing Strips

If extraterrestrials decide to make their presence known on Earth, they may choose to land at areas built by UFO enthusiasts especially for visitors from outer space.

In 1973, a retired marine officer drew up plans for some fake flying saucers that could be used as decoys to lure alien pilots. His funds ran out, but in the 1980s a group called the New Age Foundation was able to create a similar landing strip designed to attract UFOs. The group christened the fifteen-acre site, near Mount Rainier in Washington State, Spaceport Earth.

Farther south, in Lawson Valley, near San Diego, California, UFO buffs have constructed another saucerport. It's owned by Ruth Norman, head of the Unarius Education Foundation, who believes extraterrestrials will soon be parking their spacecraft in the area.

The Living Dead

Most of us assume that zombies are fictional creatures who dwell only in horror films. But in Haiti, the living dead are taken seriously. In fact, that country's penal code states that turning someone into a zombie is equivalent to murder. And the chief of psychiatry of Haiti, Lamarque Douyon, says he's personally examined three of the creatures. "I am absolutely convinced that zombies exist," he states.

Douyon spent twenty years trying to prove voodoo and related phenomena were fakery. Then he had face-to-face encounters with zombies. Douyon learned that they were real people who had been brought to a state of apparent death by drugs—probably a poison derived from flowers of the genus *Datura*. "These people are pronounced dead and publicly buried," Douyon explains. "Then they are exhumed and reanimated by the voodoo sorcerers who administered the drugs in the first place."

The sorcerers enslave most of these zombies for life by giving their victims small amounts of the drug each day. Some of the living dead have managed to escape however. Two are under study at Douyon's Port-au-Prince clinic, where the psychiatrist is working to unravel the secrets of the real-life zombies of Haiti.

Monkeying Around with Evolution

If you go by the fossil evidence, humankind and monkeys haven't been close family members for at least 20 million years. On the other hand, researchers have discovered that only 4.5 million years ago, the DNA in both people and monkeys was pretty much alike. Two British science writers, Jeremy Cherfas and John

Gribbin, have proposed an explanation: Men didn't evolve from monkeys; monkeys *descended* from man.

Gribbin and Cherfas's theory states that a race of walking apes split into two groups about 4.5 million years ago. The group who lived on the plains in time evolved into primitive man. The other walking anthropoids "de-evolved"—they frolicked in trees and eventually became today's apes.

Do Cherfas and Gribbin really think it's time to monkey around with the theory of evolution? Maybe, and maybe not. "We simply want to show how many gray areas there are in fossil evidence," Cherfas comments. "We'd like paleontologists to consult the molecular clock and then reconsider their findings."

Chesapeake Bay Monster Movie

Loch Ness isn't the only body of water in which a dinosaurlike creature has been spotted. One American sea creature, nicknamed Chessie, is said to live in Chesapeake Bay, where it has been videotaped gliding through the water.

It was nearing sunset on the evening of May 31, 1982, when Bob and Karen Frew and their dinner guests first saw a dark object moving in the bay. Bob quickly picked up his video camera and began filming what looked like a thirty-foot-long serpent with humps on its back.

Several Smithsonian Institution scientists agreed to look at the three-minute tape soon afterwards. George Zug, who heads the vertebrate zoology department at the Smithsonian's National Museum of Natural History in Washington, concluded that whatever was in the movie couldn't be dismissed as simply a submerged log or optical illusion. "It was most interesting," the scientist says, although he refuses to speculate on exactly what it was.

Mike Frizelle and Bob Lazzara, members of a Maryland organization called Enigma, which looks into unexplained phenomena, have decided to compare past sightings of Chessie with new reports, including the Frews' videotaped sighting. If they can find out just where the animal is most likely to be seen, Lazzara suggests, then they can go out and look for it.

"We didn't take 'Chessie' so seriously before," Frizelle adds. "But the Frew tape elevated it to a legitimate phenomenon."

Is There Intelligent Life in the Universe?

Even if there are not any intelligent aliens roaming the universe right now, they could exist "within a cosmic eye blink," according to paleobiologist Dale Russell of Ottawa's National Museum of Natural Sciences.

After studying the fossil record of the earth to find out how much brain size and intelligence have increased over the epochs, Russell has concluded that Earth's creatures are quickly developing bigger and better brains. On other planets, the same process could be going on. "Intelligence in the universe may be like a yeast cake," Russell says, "coming up fast."

Russell disagrees with other researchers who think there may be only a few other intelligent creatures in the galaxy. "Their estimates are based on the erroneous assumption that such civilizations will exist for a while, then simply die out. But biology just doesn't work this way."

In fact, Russell points out, even if the humans of Earth become extinct, the planet could still give rise to even more clever species. "It's possible for man to be replaced by an entirely different creature," he explains. "Already the parrot, elephant and dolphin are as large-brained as some of man's ancestors and closest relatives."

He adds that there's no reason to think that earthlings are the only brainy inhabitants of the galaxy. "We haven't yet detected extraterrestrials. But the universe is still evolving and is most likely full of civilizations."

Apparently there is no intelligent life on Earth.

The Constitutional Rights of Extraterrestrials

In an era of odd legal claims and lawsuits of all kinds, an unusual incident took place in 1983. The Pentagon was served with a writ of habeas corpus in the United States District Court of Washington, D.C., by Larry Bryant of Alexandria, Virginia, ordering that there be produced within sixty days the bodies of "one or more occupants of crash-landed UFOs of apparent extraterrestrial origin."

The extraterrestrials in question were allegedly found in three so-called flying saucers that crashed in New Mexico, where a huge radar installation had apparently interfered with the UFO control mechanism. Each flying saucer, as stated in the writ, was manned by three humanoid bodies, dressed in metallic clothing. The writ of habeas corpus was issued under the legal right of citizen's arrest and, according to the complainant, the bodies were kept at Wright-Patterson Air Force Base in Ohio. Bryant further stated that if the extraterrestrials were still alive, keeping them against their wills was depriving them of their constitutional rights.

Nothing since has been released to the public concerning this action, which has been described by Henry Catto, a Pentagon spokesman, as a writ of "habeas corpus extraterrestrial."

The Heavy Fate of Dinosaurs

John Ferguson, an aerospace engineer based in Surrey, England, thinks the earth's gravity has undergone changes as the solar system has passed celestial bodies on its travels through the

Milky Way. Those long overlooked gravitational shifts, he says, probably spelled disaster for the dinosaurs that once ruled the planet.

"During high-g periods everything would weigh more, while during low-g periods everything would weigh less," Ferguson theorizes. Creatures that developed in the sea during a high gravity period, he adds, couldn't live on land until a lower gravity period came along—then they could crawl out of the water.

"Dinosaurs evolved under weak gravity conditions and declined as gravity increased," Ferguson says. Because the massive creatures weighed so much, life became impossible when the pull of gravity was intensified. In addition, the researcher explains, increased gravity must have resulted in the sun generating more energy; otherwise, it would have collapsed under pressure from the earth. With the sun releasing more high-energy, ultraviolet rays and less warm, low-energy infrared light, the climate cooled.

That, says Ferguson, was probably the final death blow to the dinosaurs: Tropical food sources died out and ultraviolet light, raining down on the giant reptiles, caused a cancer epidemic.

Solar-Powered Suicide

When the sun is used as a symbol, it is usually associated with happiness and hope. But one day in the mid-1980s an unemployed Seattle man turned the sun into a vision of death. By rigging up a solar-activated suicide machine, he transformed the warmth of spring sunshine into death rays.

Robert Saylor, who had studied electronics through a correspondence course, called his estranged wife and warned her that he was going to die. He said he'd locked himself in a hotel room; he wanted to see her and their young daughter just one more time. At the meeting, he told the woman that he had created a "foolproof" suicide machine made out of a solar cell, a battery pack, and explosives.

The following day, Saylor called again. This time when he said he was about to kill himself his wife called the police. Just after midnight, the police burst on the scene and tried to talk Robert out of his plan.

According to King County, Washington, police spokesman Dick Larson, the officers thought they had convinced the man to come out of his barricaded room. Instead, as the sun began to rise, a muted explosion was heard. When the police hurried inside, they found Saylor's lifeless body.

He was sitting in a chair with his legs stretched out on a bed. Saylor had put a photosensitive receptor in the hotel room window: It was connected to a battery pack, which was wired to a bomb.

"We'll never know if he really intended to come out," Larson comments, "or if he was just waiting for the sun to rise."

The Satellite from Another World

In July 1960, a *Newsweek* article noted that the number of manmade objects known to be orbiting the earth didn't jibe with the actual number of satellites that had been sent into space. The National Space Surveillance Center said the United States had eleven in orbit and the Soviet Union had two. But according to the *Newsweek* article, several scientists claimed at least one other spacecraft was circling the planet. Where did it come from?

"This satellite, the scientists suspect, is a visitor sent by the beings of another star within our own Milky Way—a sort of United Stellar Organization perhaps—interested, for archaeological and anthropological reasons, in how things are going in this part of the galactic neighborhood," *Newsweek* reported.

Could the alien satellite have been the same UFO spotted on December 18, 1957? That evening, around 6:00 P.M., Dr. Luis Corrales of the Communications Ministry in Caracas, Venezuela, snapped a photo of the Soviets' Sputnik II. When Dr. Corrales developed the picture, he was startled to find that he had captured another object on film, too.

Alongside the Russian satellite was a UFO, which showed up as a streak of light because of the short time exposure Dr. Corrales had used. When researchers examined the photo, they concluded that the object wasn't a meteor or star. Instead, they determined that it was an unrecognizable kind of intelligently controlled craft that was able to deviate from the path of the Sputnik II, and then return to its side.

The Woman Who Slept over a Bomb

It's hard to understand how until recently Zinaida Bragantsova ever got a good night's sleep. Since 1941, the woman's bed rested over a bomb that had crashed into her apartment in the Soviet town of Berdyansk and made a hole in her floor. It wasn't that she didn't think about the danger—she simply couldn't find any help for her explosive problem.

Unable to convince anyone that the bomb was real, Bragantsova just moved her bed over the patched hole in the floor where the bomb rested. According to the newspaper *Literary Gazette*, other people in her town made fun of her claims and teasingly called her "the grandmother with her own bomb." Soviet authorities accused her of making up the story just so she could get a new apartment.

In recent years, however, the woman's plight got some attention. When new telephone cables were installed in her neighborhood, demolition experts began searching for buried explosives from World War II. This time when she asked officials to look into her problem they reluctantly complied.

"Where's the bomb, grandma? Under your bed?" an army lieutenant said sarcastically to the seventy-four-year-old lady. "Yes," she answered.

The demolition experts were startled to find that Bragantsova was telling the truth. A five-hundred-pound explosive was discovered and, after two thousand people were evacuated, it was detonated. Bragantsova's home was destroyed by the blast but, the *Literary Gazette* noted, the grandmother finally received a new, bomb-free apartment.

Spacecraft Propulsion Systems

UFO skeptics are quick to point out that there's no way a spaceship could travel the tremendous distances between solar systems without breaking the laws of physics.

Freeman Dyson, a former consultant to NASA who now works at Princeton's Institute for Advanced Study, says that's simply not true: "I think it's quite likely that there are other species zipping around, exploring the far reaches of interstellar space."

Just how extraterrestrials—or humans—could accomplish such a feat is no longer a mystery, according to Dyson. In fact, he says there are several practical spacecraft propulsion systems that could zoom spaceships to the stars. These include systems that would propel a spaceship by shooting either a high-velocity laser beam or solid pellets of light into a kind of "sail" and an orbital electromagnetic "generator" that would launch an interstellar craft by flinging it into space at incredibly high speeds.

By propelling a spaceship at half the speed of light, Dyson predicts, these propulsion systems could probably have a crew of space explorers from our nearest star system neighbor setting down on Earth in less than nine years.

The Mystery Man Who Toasts Poe

Since Edgar Allan Poe wrote about the mysterious and the macabre, it seems appropriate that the anniversary of his death each year is associated with some strange goings-on. Indeed, someone has placed roses and cognac on Poe's grave in the Westminster Churchyard in Baltimore each and every January 19 since 1849.

On a recent birthday of the author, Jeff Jerome, the curator of Poe House, decided to do some detective work to discover the mysterious visitor's identity. After staking out the grave for hours, Jerome and four other Poe fans suddenly heard the cemetery gates rattle at about 1:30 A.M. When they shined a flashlight across the graveyard, the intruder fled—but not before Jerome and his friend Ann Byerly caught a glimpse of him.

Byerly describes the mysterious stranger as a man with blonde or brown hair who was wearing a dramatic-looking frock coat. "He was clutching a walking stick with a golden sphere on its end—like the one Poe carried," Jerome adds. "Before vanishing over the wall, he raised his cane high in the air and shook it at us triumphantly."

Chinese Ape-Men

Chinese citizens have repeatedly reported encounters with seven-foot-tall wild ape-men in the mountainous region of Hubei. The creatures, who are said to swing through trees and eat leaves and insect larvae, are covered all over with brown hair. One witness said he made peaceful contact with a female ape creature who was accompanied by a child. Another man says he ran into a violent ape-man, whom he finally stabbed.

In recent years, Chinese scientists Yuan Zhenxin and Huang Wanpo have proposed that the creatures could be descended from *Gigantopithecus*. Writing in the Chinese journal *Hua Shi*, they note that many fossilized remains of that primate, long believed to be extinct, have been found throughout Hubei.

An ancient myth provides another possible explanation for the origin of Chinese ape-men. According to legend, during the rule of Emperor Ch'in Shih Huang Ti around 200 B.C., a group of people refused to work constructing the Great Wall of China. Fleeing to the mountains, they eventually reverted into primitive beings—"de-evolving," the story goes, into hairy, apelike creatures.

Fossil Dream

As nineteenth-century scientist Louis Agassiz recounted in his book, *Recherches sur les Poissons Fossiles*, a persistent dream directed him to one of his most important discoveries.

The zoologist had tried for weeks to figure out how to transfer a vague outline of a fossilized fish from an ancient hunk of rock. Nothing worked, and Agassiz finally put the stone on a shelf and went on with other work.

But a couple of nights later, he dreamed of what the fossilized fish looked like when it was alive. When he awoke, Agassiz found he couldn't shake the image. So he studied the fossil-bearing slab again. However, he still couldn't see anything other than a vague image.

That night the dream came back. Once more, in the morning, the scientist turned to the stony outline to see if he could make out the prehistoric fish's shape—but he was no more successful than before.

Would the dream return? Suspecting it might, the zoologist put a pencil and paper by his bed. Then he went to sleep and again saw the fish in a dream. Rousing himself to consciousness, Agassiz woke up and in the darkness drew what he had seen.

The next day, the scientist was surprised to find that his drawing contained details that he had never spotted on the fossil. Using the sketch as a guide, Agassiz decided to chip away at the fossilized rock, in hopes that it might reveal additional details of the fish's body.

As he worked slowly and carefully, the scientist found that the fossil had not been completely uncovered. When he removed a paper-thin layer of stone, the image of the fish became clear. This time the prehistoric creature could be seen in sharp relief—it was a previously unknown fish that matched, in every detail, the animal Agassiz had seen in his dream.

A Dream from Prehistory

Anthropologist Joseph Mandemant dreamed it was night and he was standing at an opening of the Bedeilhac cave in France. Inside, a group of Magdalenian hunters, clad only in animal skins, gathered around a campfire. Mandemant could see hunting scenes drawn on the roof of the cave. He also noticed that a young man and woman were sitting apart from the others.

The couple soon got up and went into another of the cave's rooms which contained a ledge. They began to make love in the dark. But the idyll—and the anthropologist's dream—came to an abrupt end when the roof of the cave suddenly crashed down, sealing off the area where the young couple had gone for privacy.

The dream was so detailed and clear that Mandemant wrote it down and set off to visit the actual cave located at Bedeilhac. Everything seemed just as the scientist had dreamed it, except that the main "room" had a wall on the right made of solid limestone.

Could this slab of stone have concealed the room where the lovers retreated for their tryst? Mandemant tapped on the limestone with a mallet and found that it was hollow—another room *was* behind the limestone.

For several days, workmen hacked through the rock. Finally, there was a hole large enough for the anthropologist to climb through. On the other side was the room, just as Mandemant had dreamed it, including the ledge.

There were no signs of the young man's and woman's skeletons, however. Mandemant's detective work showed that when the stone originally fell from the roof of the outer cave, it left an opening just big enough to have provided an escape passage for the young couple.

Despite the fact that much of his dream had been verified by his inspection of the cave, Mandemant still had no tangible proof that while sleeping he had somehow transcended time and space. Then he remembered another detail of his dream—the hunting scenes on the roof of one of the cave's rooms. Following the drawing he had made of the images from his dream, the scientist found the same ancient illustrations he had somehow "seen" when they were new, thousands of years ago.

The Prime Minister Who Dreamed His Own Death

In the spring of 1812, a wealthy Englishman named John Williams had an unusual dream that returned, three times in all, on the evening of May 3. Although he wasn't interested in politics, Williams repeatedly dreamed that he was in the cloakroom of the House of Commons watching a small man in a dark green coat shoot Prime Minister Spencer Perceval in the chest. The dream was so disturbing that Williams thought about warning the prime minister. But when his friends scoffed at the idea, he put the odd nightmare out of his mind.

Prime Minister Perceval, however, learned about the nightmare firsthand—he had the identical dream seven days later. As he told his family on the morning of May 11, he dreamed that while walking through the lobby of the House of Commons, he was shot by a crazed man. The assailant wore a dark green coat set off by brass buttons.

Although Perceval's family urged the prime minister to heed the dream's warning and stay home that morning, he headed off for the day's session of the House of Commons, determined not to let anything so silly as a dream interfere with his official duties. As the prime minister was walking through the lobby, a man whom he had never seen before, wearing a dark green coat with shiny brass buttons, shot Spencer Perceval to death.

Mick to the Rescue

Percy the chihuahua today romps happily around his home in England. But if it had not been for the inexplicably keen senses of another dog, Mick the terrier, he would have been buried alive.

Percy's owner, Christine Harrison, took her pet with her when she visited her parents in Barnsley. The tiny dog refused to stay in the yard and, when he raced into the street, was hit by a car. "We couldn't detect a heartbeat, and his eyes were fixed and staring," Christine recalls.

Sure her beloved Percy was dead, she had her father put him in a heavy paper sack. Then the dog was buried, two feet under, in the garden.

Mick, Christine's parents' dog, refused to budge from Percy's grave. After Christine returned home, she was shocked when her parents reported that Mick had dug up her pet's body and dragged him, still in the burial sack, to her parents' house. Incredibly, the terrier had somehow known that Percy was still alive.

"My dog had come back from the dead," Christine says. Although unconscious, the little canine had a faint heartbeat. He was rushed to a veterinarian, who deduced that the animal had managed to survive because of air trapped in his burial sack. The vet also said that Mick had helped Percy recover by giving him a lick massage that boosted his circulation.

Mick was recognized for his bravery by the Royal Society for the Prevention of Cruelty to Animals. But Christine says she doesn't understand why the terrier saved Percy. "Those two dogs hate each other," she notes. "They always have, and they still do."

Red Army Wonder Woman

In the closing days of World War II, teenage Red Army soldier Nina Kulagina was wounded in the front lines by a German artillery shell fragment. Hurt and sent home, she felt her frustration mounting. While her recovery dragged out, friends and countrymen were dying in the struggle against Hitler and his troops.

"I was walking toward a cupboard," the aggravated Kulagina said later, "when suddenly a jug moved to the edge of the shelf, fell, and smashed to bits."

Lights started turning off and on in her presence. Doors swung open and shut for no apparent reason. Dishes danced on tabletops. Kulagina first suspected a poltergeist, or "noisy ghost," but soon came to recognize the mysterious force as her own. From that realization followed months of concentration and practice, until Kulagina was able to move objects at will.

Edward Naumov became the first Russian scientist to actively investigate Kulagina's psychokinetic abilities. A series of successful experiments conducted by various authorities followed, more than sixty of which were filmed. In the most dramatic of these, an egg was broken and slipped into a saline solution behind glass. Standing several feet away, Kulagina directed her attention toward the egg in the aquariumlike tank. Slowly she separated the egg white from the yolk, moving the two apart with her mind. At the time of the experiment, Kulagina was wired to several instruments, which showed her to be under extreme mental and emotional stress. Her electrostatic field was monitored by Dr. Genady Sergeyev, who reported a four-second pulse cycle as Kulagina separated the egg.

Sergeyev equated the pulsations with magnetic waves. When they occur, he said, "they cause the object she focuses on, even if it is something nonmagnetic, to act as if magnetized. It causes the object to be attracted to her or repelled."

The Wonder Girl from Georgia

A thunderstorm in Cedartown, Georgia, kept fourteen-year-old Lulu Hurst and her cousin, Lora, from falling asleep one summer night in 1883. Then the girls noticed strange rappings and popping sounds that seemed too close to be thunder.

Lulu's parents at first thought the odd commotion was related to the severe electrical storm. But the next evening, it was obvious some other phenomenon was involved—their daughter's bed was thumping so strongly they could feel it, and over a dozen witnesses heard wall-shaking noises in Lulu's room. Observers discovered that the sounds seemed to answer questions. One rap apparently meant "yes"; two knocks were "no."

No one realized, however, that whatever was going on had a connection with Lulu until four days later. That's when a visiting relative was thrown across the room after she touched a chair handed to her by Lulu. Four men who grabbed on to the gyrating piece of furniture found themselves in an exhausting wrestling match with an invisible force that finally broke the chair to bits.

Lulu ran screaming and crying from the scene, terrified by her new powers. But within two weeks she was performing baffling feats in front of live audiences.

The first show by "the wonderful Lulu Hurst," as she was dubbed by the newspapers *Atlanta Constitution* and *Rome Bulletin*, was in a hall in Cedartown packed with curious spectators. Judges, lawyers, bankers, state politicians, and doctors sat on the stage to watch the small, frail teenager's talents up close.

A solidly built man in the audience volunteered to test the girl's powers. He was given a closed umbrella, which he held with both hands across his chest. Told to keep the umbrella still, he braced his feet. But when Lulu simply touched the palm of her right hand against the umbrella, the object jerked violently from side to side. The man began writhing up and down and ended up flung into the laps of the onstage observers.

For the next two years, Lulu demonstrated her powers as she toured the United States. She appeared before the faculty and students of the Medical College at Charleston, South Carolina, an audience that the *Charleston News and Courier* called "notable and critical." After watching the small girl toss people around the stage by simply touching them, the newspaper concluded, "There was not a man in this distinguished and learned array who could explain the mysterious phenomenon."

Nonetheless, twenty scientists from the Smithsonian and Naval Observatory staffs eventually joined Alexander Graham Bell in studying the teenager. They suspected she possessed some kind of electrical force. But their studies failed to solve the puzzle of the amazing Lulu—and when she married and retired a couple of years later, the source of her powers remained as mysterious as ever.

The Strange Trance of Molly Fancher

Molly Fancher of Brooklyn, New York, seemed like a normal and healthy twenty-four-year-old until she suddenly became dizzy and fell unconscious one day in early February 1866. Her mother thought Molly had simply fainted. But when physician Samuel F. Spier came to examine the young woman, he found her in a trancelike coma—the likes of which he had never seen before.

Months passed, and Molly failed to wake up. Dr. Spier examined her clammy body and found that she hardly appeared to breathe at all. Her body temperature was subnormal and her pulse was extremely weak; it sometimes seemed to disappear altogether. Numerous other physicians were called in for their opinions but no one could offer any help.

Dr. Spier was still caring for his comatose patient nine years later when he made two remarkable observations. The records showed that in all the time she had been in a near-death state, Molly had lived with almost no sustenance. Over the years she had only eaten, Spier said, "about the amount a normal person would consume in two days!" In addition, she had developed what the doctor called "supernatural" abilities.

Dr. Spier invited several scientists, including two noted neurologists and the famed astronomer Dr. Richard Parkhurst, to witness Molly's strange talent. "Gentlemen, this girl can fully describe the dress and action of persons hundreds of miles from here, just as they are this instant!" he told the group. "Furthermore, she can read unopened letters and books!"

To test Dr. Spier's implausible claims, the two brain specialists put a message inside three sealed envelopes and had it sent by courier to Dr. Spier's office several miles away. Then Dr. Parkhurst asked Molly what was in the envelope. To his amazement, she answered correctly. "It is a letter," she whispered. "In three sealed envelopes, written on a sheet of paper are the words, 'Lincoln was shot by a crazed actor.'"

To test her powers further, they asked Molly where neurologist Peter Grahman's brother was and what he was doing. Miss Fancher quickly said that Frank Grahman was in New York. He was wearing a coat that was missing a button on the right sleeve and he had left work early because of a headache. A telegram soon confirmed that everything the young woman had said in her trancelike state was true.

Molly outlived her mother and Dr. Spier. For forty-six years she remained in a coma. But in 1912, she woke up as suddenly and mysteriously as she had become unconscious. She lived until March 1915, when she died peacefully in her sleep at the age of seventy-three.

Blind Sight

When European explorers first reached the Samoan Islands, they heard remarkable tales of blind natives who could see through their skin. While this sounds like a fable, it may have been based on fact—there are numerous documented accounts of people who could somehow see without the use of their eyes.

French physician Jules Romain studied this ability in both blind and sighted people for several years after the end of World War I. He found that some people had areas of skin that were photosensitive. So, he theorized, certain nerve endings in the skin could be the pathways by which sight without eyes is possible.

One man who claimed to have this ability was Ved Mehta, an Indian who became totally blind when he was three years old, following an attack of meningitis. In his book, *Face to Face*, published in 1957, Mehta explained that he never needed a cane to get about. In fact, he could maneuver a bicycle through crowded streets with no problem. His secret? Mehta insisted that he possessed "facial vision"—he somehow "saw" through the skin on his face.

Sometimes the sighted claim to have this talent as well. Teenager Margaret Foos of Ellerson, Virginia, was so skilled at "seeing" when her eyes were blindfolded that her father took her to the Veterans Administration Center in January 1960 for special testing. Not only did the fourteen-year-old point out the location and colors of objects while her eyes were taped and bandaged, but she also read newspaper articles aloud.

Syndicated newspaper columnist Drew Pearson, who wrote about the testing of the girl's abilities, said that one psychiatrist noted, "It's conceivable that some new portion of the brain may have just been discovered."

Brains That Baffled Medicine

The brain is so complicated that scientists are constantly working to discover just how it works. It is well known, however, that even seemingly minor injuries and shocks can sometimes cause damage to the brain—and result in anything from a loss of sensation to seizures. On the other hand, medical literature cites cases of severe brain damage that didn't seem to affect patients at all.

In September 1847, twenty-five-year-old Phineas Gage, a foreman on the Rutland and Burlington Railroad, became one of these lucky people. While tapping some gunpowder into a hole, preparing to blast it, the iron rod Gage was using hit a stone. That touched off a powerful explosion that rammed the rod into Gage's skull.

Still conscious, Gage was carried by fellow workers to a doctor's office where the metal was removed—along with pieces of his skull and brain tissue. The two physicians who treated him never expected him to survive, much less endure such a head injury without permanent aftereffects. But, with the exception of losing the sight in his left eye (which was forced almost out of its socket by the accident), Gage soon recovered completely.

A woman working in a mill in 1879 suffered an equally ghastly on-the-job accident. A machine threw a huge bolt that landed four inches deep in the woman's skull. Pieces of her brain were lost during the impact and more brain substance was destroyed when physicians took the bolt out of her head. The woman recovered and lived another forty-two years—without even suffering a headache from her ordeal.

According to the 1888 edition of *The Medical Press of Western New York*, about one-fourth of a man's skull was destroyed when he was caught between a bridge timber and the superstructure of the ship he was working on. The sharp corner of the timber clipped off part of the deckhand's head. Doctors who closed the wound found that the man had lost a substantial amount of brain matter, as well as blood. But as soon as the victim regained consciousness, he talked and dressed himself as though he felt perfectly fine. Except for a few dizzy spells, he was healthy despite the loss of part of his brain, until twenty-six years later when a partial paralysis and unsteady gait developed.

For twenty-seven days, a baby born a St. Vincent's Hospital in New York City in 1935 appeared to be a typical infant—it cried, ate, and moved. Only after its death did doctors discover during an autopsy that it had no brain at all.

In a report prepared by Dr. Jan W. Bruell and Dr. George W. Albee which was delivered to the American Psychological Association in 1957, the physicians noted they had been forced to perform drastic surgery on a thirty-nine-year-old man. Although they removed the entire right half of the man's brain, the patient survived. And, the doctors concluded, the operation inexplicably "left his intellectual capacity virtually unimpaired."

An even stranger case was recounted by the German brain expert Hufeland. When he autopsied a paralyzed man who had been fully rational until the moment of his demise, he found no brain at all—just eleven ounces of water.

The Case of the Murder-Solving Mentalist

When Royal Canadian Mounted Police Constable Fred Olsen entered the home of farmer Henry Booher of Mannville, Alberta, in 1928, he was faced with a rare crime—mass murder. Henry and his twenty-one-year-old son, Vernon, had discovered the bodies of Mrs. Booher, her son Fred, and two hired hands. All had been shot to death.

Whoever committed the bloody deed had carefully retrieved all the cartridge cases, except one. Found where it had fallen in a dish of soapy water, it came from a .303 rifle, the kind of gun that had been stolen from a neighbor not long before. There were few other clues to the murderer's identity. But Constable Olsen was suspicious of the glaring looks of hatred and sneering contempt that young Vernon directed in the Mountie's direction when he thought the officer wasn't looking.

Olsen soon learned that Vernon's mother had caused the breakup of his affair with a pretty woman in Mannville and he accused the young man of murdering his mother and the others in a fit of revenge.

"Have you found the rifle?" Vernon calmly asked. When the constable admitted he hadn't, the young Booher added, "You will certainly never get a confession out of me, you know."

Olsen was positive he had discovered the murderer, as was his fellow officer, Inspector Hancock. They even arrested Vernon. But they had no proof that would stand up in court. Desperate for a lead, Hancock finally contacted Maximillian Langsner, who claimed he could solve crimes through his ability to read the minds of criminals. The mentalist, who said he had studied telepathy in the Far East, agreed to tune in to Vernon's thoughts in order to find out where the murder weapon was hidden.

"If he thinks about it, I can pick up the impulses sent out by his brain and interpret them for you," Langsner assured Constable Olsen.

For four hours Langsner sat outside Vernon's cell, staring. Finally, the suspected murderer began to crack. "Get away from here, damn you!" he screamed. "Get away, I say!"

But Langsner didn't budge. He just kept staring. Another hour passed and Booher was clearly exhausted from the mental strain. It was the opportunity the mentalist had been looking for to gain access to the dark recesses of the mass murderer's mind.

"He told me mentally where that gun is hidden," Langsner explained to Constable Olsen. Then he sketched the exact location—under some bushes not far from the Booher farmhouse.

Constable Olsen, Inspector Hancock, and Langsner were soon on their way to the area. The mentalist immediately recognized the spot he had "seen" with his telepathic powers. Running ahead of the others, he fell to his knees by the bushes and began scooping up earth with his bare hands. The murder weapon was soon exposed.

Faced with this evidence, Vernon promptly confessed to the killings and was sentenced to death by hanging.

Although mental telepathy wasn't a usual tool of the Canadian Mounties, Inspector Hancock decided to make Langsner's role in solving the crime public knowledge. He discussed the facts of the case with newspaper reporters and dutifully recorded in the official Royal Canadian Mounted Police files how a mentalist had read the mind of a mass murderer.

Arthur Price Roberts: Psychic Detective

Born in Denbeigh, Wales, in 1866, Arthur Price "Doc" Roberts possessed unusual talents even as a child—he used extrasensory perception to locate lost objects and missing persons. As an adult he became a psychic detective who helped the police as well as private citizens solve mysteries.

For example, Duncan McGregor of Pestigo, Wisconsin, disappeared without a trace in July 1905. Months later, his distraught wife turned to Doc Roberts for help. Unable to come up with an immediate mental impression, Doc went into a trancelike state and soon told Mrs. McGregor not only that her husband had been murdered but exactly where the body was located. Police followed the psychic's directions and found the corpse just where Roberts said it would be—in the Menominee River, trapped under sunken logs by tangled clothing.

Doc also solved the case of wealthy Chicago businessman J. D. Leroy's missing brother. The man had been murdered, Roberts informed Leroy; Doc's psychic impressions told him the body was in a particular area of Devil's Canyon in New Mexico. The victim was found just two hundred feet from a spot described in detail by the psychic detective.

While a guest at the Fond du Lac Hotel, Doc Roberts was approached by local police who asked for help with a two-year-old unsolved murder. Closing his eyes, the psychic "saw" the murder victim and described him accurately. The next day he asked the officers to show him photographs of known criminals. As he flipped through the mug shots, Roberts suddenly stopped and pointed. "There's your killer, gentlemen!" he exclaimed. "You will find him in British Columbia—working for the Mounted Police Service!" Doc's mental detective work proved accurate, as usual.

Roberts was skilled at predicting the future as well as psychically delving into events that had already transpired. According to the *Milwaukee News*, Doc made some astounding prophecies on October 18, 1935. He warned the Milwaukee police to be prepared for bombings. "I see two banks blown up and perhaps the city hall. Going to blow up police stations. Then there's going to be a big blow-up south of the river [Menominee] and then it'll be over!"

Eight days later dynamite exploded in the village hall, killing two children and injuring many others. The next day, bombs went off in two Milwaukee banks and a couple of police stations.

Milwaukee police detective English turned to Roberts for information about the violence. "On Sunday, November fourth, there'll be a big one south of the Menominee. And that'll be all!" Doc predicted.

On November 4, a blast rocked Milwaukee with such power that people eight miles away heard it. As Roberts predicted, it was the final explosion. The police found the scattered remains of the bombers, twenty-one-year-old Hugh Rutkowski, and his nineteen-year-old friend Paul Chovonee, amid the debris. The two had accidentally blown themselves to bits while building more bombs to terrorize the community.

Arthur Price "Doc" Roberts made one of his final predictions at a dinner party in his honor. It was November 1939, and the seventy-three-year-old psychic detective thanked his friends for coming to the get-together. "I am afraid that I won't be present at the next one. As much as I would like to remain, I won't be with you beyond January 2, 1940."

Once again, Doc was right. On January 2, 1940, he died at his home in Milwaukee.

Gladstone's Gift

It was a cold December night in 1932 when off-duty Royal Canadian Mounted Police constable Carey decided to visit a small theater in Beechy, Saskatchewan, for some entertainment. A tall, handsome man who called himself "Professor Gladstone" was on stage performing a mind-reading act.

Constable Carey laughed along with the rest of the audience as hypnotized volunteers performed silly antics under Gladstone's direction. Then the mood changed as the mentalist stood before rancher Bill Taylor and cried, "I have it! You are thinking about your friend Scotty McLauchlin! He was brutally and wantonly murdered!"

Then he pointed at Constable Carey. "That's the man. He is the one who will find the body," Gladstone exclaimed. "And I'll be with him when he does!"

The Mountie knew that Scotty McLauchlin had mysteriously disappeared nearly four years earlier. But the case remained unsolved. Carey approached the mentalist privately and asked how he knew what had happened to McLauchlin. Gladstone explained that he psychically "felt" that Scotty had been murdered.

Detective Corporal Jack Woods of the Criminal Investigation Bureau in Saskatoon decided to question the mentalist further. Gladstone assured him that he didn't know who killed Scotty, but he would know the murderer when he saw him.

The two officers and the mentalist set out to visit people who had known Scotty McLauchlin before he disappeared on January 16, 1929. They stopped by the house of a man named Ed Vogel, questioning him about reported threats made against Scotty in his presence. Exploding in anger, Vogel insisted the Mounties' information was "a bunch of lies."

Suddenly Gladstone pointed at Vogel and began to recite what had happened on the night in question. "You were sick in bed. Schumacher [an acquaintance] pushed through the door and told you he had had a quarrel with McLauchlin and swore that he would kill that damned Scotty," the mentalist said.

Vogel turned white and admitted Gladstone was correct.

Heading to Schumacher's farm, the officers were asked to slow down by Gladstone. He claimed he smelled something foul. The body of Scotty McLauchlin was somewhere in the vicinity, he said.

The officers soon found Schumacher and drove him back to town for questioning. The suspect insisted that he and Scotty had been amiable partners on the farm; when the missing man said he was leaving town, Schumacher had purchased his share of the land.

Gladstone's psychic impressions, however, said the man was lying. "It's the barn!" the mentalist exclaimed. "Now I can tell you how you did it! Scotty left the house. . . . You followed him. You forced him into a quarrel—there was a fight! . . . Scotty fell. . . . But you kept striking and striking until you knew he was dead! Then you buried his body near the barn under some rubbish!"

Schumacher denied the charges. The next day, officers Woods and Carey, accompanied by Gladstone, brought the suspect back to his farm. They were heading toward the barn when the mentalist walked up to a frozen manure pile and announced, "Scotty McLauchlin is buried under there, gentlemen."

The corpse of the long-missing man was soon exhumed, and Schumacher broke down, confessing that the slaying had happened just as "Professor Gladstone" had pictured it in his mind.

The Talking Pencil

Legend holds that King Arthur and Queen Guinevere were buried at Glastonbury Abbey. There are even those who claim that Jesus was a visitor there around A.D. 27. Despite its historical significance, however, the abbey was destroyed by Henry VIII, who plundered the libraries and then blew up the buildings with gunpowder. A thousand years later, the spot dubbed by some the "holiest spot in Britain" was nothing but crumbling ruins.

In 1907, archaeologist-architect Frederick Bligh-Bond began digging at the site, searching for two long-vanished chapels described by early chroniclers of the abbey—one was dedicated to the martyr King Edgar, and another was the Chapel of Our Lady of Loretto. As he noted in his 1933 book *The Gate of Remembrance*, his greatest clues for the excavation project came unexpectedly from a "talking" pencil.

Bligh-Bond first heard about "automatic writing," a method of receiving paranormal written messages from another dimension, from his friend Captain Bartlett. Curious about the phenomenon, Bligh-Bond decided to try it himself. Holding the pencil lightly, he asked, "Can you tell us anything about Glastonbury?"

Following more questioning, the pencil began to move, spelling out, in ancient Latin, details concerning the Chapel of Edgar the Martyr. It described how the structure had been revised and drew a map of the way the abbey once looked, including one of the long-sought chapels.

An entity who identified himself as a monk named Gulielmus noted that Edgar's chapel had extended thirty yards to the east and had windows made of blue glass. Using the directions provided by the "talking" pencil, Bligh-Bond's work crew soon uncovered the ruins of the chapel—including blue glass fragments.

When the archaeologist tried using automatic writing to reveal the location of the Chapel of Our Lady of Loretto, this time he received a message written in early sixteenth-century English. It informed Bligh-Bond that he would find the ruins in the hard bank of earth on the abbey's north side. But only one wall would be uncovered, the writing continued, because looters had removed the rest for private buildings. Digging in the area showed, once again, that the "talking" pencil was correct.

Disembodied entities, one claiming to have been Johannes Bryant, who died in 1533, provided more historical details about Glastonbury. Another spirit, who wrote he was "Awfwold ye Saxon," told Bligh-Bond to dig in a place where evidence of a thousand-year-old wattle-work hut would be found. The archaeologist followed the instructions and once again made the predicted find.

For a decade, Bligh-Bond and his friend Bartlett kept records of the information they received through automatic writing—messages that provided such exact directions on where archaeologists should dig that they were often accurate within a fraction of an inch.

Revolutionary Prophecies

The Duchess de Gramont of France planned a pleasant garden party in the summer of 1788. Among the witty and brilliant guests were the outspoken atheist Jean La Harpe and an eccentric poet named Jacques Cazotte. When Cazotte began uttering strange prophecies, La Harpe wrote them down. Fanatically skeptical of anything supernatural, La Harpe was sure he could use the predictions to ridicule believers. He was destined to use the material—but in a far different way than he dreamed of at the time.

Cazotte's predictions began after Guillaume des Malesherbes, minister of Louis XIV, proclaimed: "A toast to the day when reason will be triumphant in the affairs of men—although I shall never live to see the day!"

Cazotte approached the minister. "You are wrong, sir!" he cried. "You *will* live to see the day—for it shall come within six years!"

Next, Cazotte turned his gaze to the Marquis de Condorcet and told him, "You will cheat the executioner by taking poison!"

The prophet continued moving through the crowd of guests,

stopping by Chamfort, the king's favorite, to tell him he would slash his wrist twenty-two times with a razor. "But it will not kill you," Cazotte said. "You will live a long life thereafter."

The predictions became even more gruesome as he told the famed astronomer Bailly that he would be executed by a mob.

Guillaume des Malesherbes tried to bring back some levity to the evening. He bowed in front of the poet and asked with mock piety, "Can you also end my breathless concern about my own fate?"

"I regret to inform you, sir," Cazotte answered, "that your fate shall be the counterpart of that that awaits your friend Chamfort. You too shall die as a public spectacle."

Skeptic Jean La Harpe had had about enough of this hocus-pocus. "And what of me, sir?" he asked sarcastically. "You do me ill by neglecting my neck. I beg to be permitted to join my friends that we may hiss at the mob together! Surely you can grant me this last favor?"

The atheist and the poet were known to hate each other, so the guests found this exchange hilarious. Cazotte did not smile, however.

"Monsieur La Harpe," he responded, "you will escape the executioner's axe—only to become a devout Christian!"

The crowd roared with laughter. Trying to keep up the renewed good spirits of the evening, the duchess pretended to pout and asked Cazotte why future executioners seemed to spare the ladies.

The poet-turned-prophet held both hands of his hostess. "Alas, my good friend, the executioners have poor regard for the finest of ladies," he said sadly. "It is a day when it will be fatal to be noble. You will die like the king himself, after riding to the scaffold in a woodcutter's cart!"

Five years later, the "impossible" predictions of Jacques Cazotte all came true during the French Revolution. And Jean La Harpe's eyewitness account of the poet's prophecies was willed to the monastery where he had become a devout Christian—just as Cazotte had foreseen.

Dream Translation

Born to poor parents in Cornwall, England, in 1857, E. A. Wallis Budge hardly seemed likely to receive even the most rudimentary education, much less to become the foremost linguistic scholar of his time. But thanks to an extraordinary affinity for Oriental languages—and a mysterious dream—that's exactly what happened.

Prime Minister William Gladstone, who was a master of classical languages, heard of the twenty-one-year-old Budge's natural talent in that field and arranged for the studious young man to attend Christ's College at Cambridge as a charity student.

In order to continue his education, Wallis knew he needed a scholarship for graduate study. So he decided to participate in an upcoming competition that would be conducted by one of the greatest living experts on ancient languages, Professor Sayce. Each student vying for the scholarship would be required to answer four difficult questions at length.

The night before the fateful examination, Budge found he had studied so hard his mind seemed blank. Mentally and physically drained, he quickly fell asleep. Soon he was having a most peculiar dream.

He was taking the examination but he wasn't in a classroom. Instead, he seemed to be in a shed. A tutor entered and handed him the exam. For some odd reason, the questions were written on green paper. Budge easily answered the first part of the test. But when he was asked to translate complicated Assyrian and Akkadian cuneiform characters, he became frightened and woke up.

Drifting off to sleep again, the same dream returned, three times in all. He finally got up and looked at the clock. It was just past 2:00 A.M. Instead of going back to bed, Budge turned to the book *Cuneiform Inscriptions of Western Asia* by Rawlinson. It seemed to him that the difficult passages he had dreamed about were included in the text. For the rest of the early morning hours he pored over the book.

At 9:00 A.M., Budge went to the examination hall but was told the room was full. He was directed to a room he had never seen before. Not only did it look like the shed he saw in his dream, but he also recognized the scarred table and dingy skylights as details he had "seen" while asleep.

The coincidences continued. The tutor who opened the door was the same man Budge had dreamed about. And he presented the young student with questions on *green* paper—the identical questions about cuneiform characters that Budge had studied for hours because of his strange dream.

As Wallis Budge's good friend Sir Henry Haggard recounted in his 1926 book, *The Days of My Life*, Budge won the scholarship and became a renowned scholar, best known perhaps for his translation of the Egyptian Book of the Dead. For a man born to poverty with little hope for such a career, it was a dream come true—in more ways than one.

Somnambulist Theft

In Monroe County, Indiana, in 1881, a local newspaper reporter named D. O. Spencer started dabbling in mind reading. He dubbed himself "Colonel" Spencer and performed his act, which combined some hypnotism with sleight-of-hand magic, around town. Spencer never claimed to have any paranormal powers, but one day he found himself drawn into *real* mind reading—and he solved a mystery in the process. As the *Indianapolis News* wrote, "After that, Mr. Spencer was known as somewhat of a wizard!"

Spencer was performing in a school auditorium. In the audience were Mrs. Harmon and her adult children, three daughters and a son. The family was being torn apart because their savings, about four thousand dollars hidden in five separate places, had disappeared. Since only the family members knew where the money had been stashed, it was clear that one of them was a thief. But which one?

John Harmon rose from his seat and asked if Colonel Spencer

could use his mental powers to find out. Spencer had never been confronted with this kind of request before, and he quickly acknowledged that solving a crime would be an experiment for him. "I'll try if you like," he told the Harmons, adding that "the spirits" would expect 10 percent of anything he found.

The next day, a crowd of about three hundred curious people milled around the Harmons' yard, hoping to catch a glimpse of Colonel Spencer solving the mystery of the missing money. The mind reader found Mrs. Harmon and her daughters sitting nervously in the sitting room. Explaining to the crowd of onlookers that he needed quiet, Spencer began hypnotizing each member of the family and asking them to take him to the money.

Nancy Harmon began to cry, so Spencer turned to her sister Rachel. The young woman was quickly hypnotized, but she was so lethargic that the colonel gave up on getting any information out of her. Next, he tried Rhoda. She was soon in a deep trance.

"You are now going to go straight to the place where the money is hidden," he ordered. "You will walk slowly, following me, straight to the hidden money. If I make a wrong turn you will stop. Now, walk to the money!"

With his hand pressed against the girl's head, Spencer walked backwards as the girl led him toward a corncrib built of logs about a hundred yards from a barn.

"Dig here, men," Spencer told the crowd. "This is the spot!"

Buried in a shallow hole beneath the logs was a roll of yellowed newspaper. Inside was the missing money.

As soon as Rhoda was awakened from her trance, she fainted at the sight of her family's retrieved savings. Colonel Spencer theorized that the woman had stolen the money while sleepwalking and didn't remember her crime.

Spencer changed his mind about "the spirits" taking 10 percent of the recovered money. He also changed his mind about being a professional mentalist and no longer performed his mind-reading act after the Harmon case. There are those who think he may have discovered that there were powers of the mind he didn't understand—and didn't want to tamper with.

Psychic Pill

According to British parapsychologist and researcher Serena Roney-Dougal, people may one day pop psi-pills in order to read minds or peer into the future.

Although that sounds like a scenario out of a science fiction movie, Roney-Dougal says that the drug probably already exists—it's harmaline, derived from the plant genus *Banisteriopsis* in the Amazon. Primitive peoples used the substance for generations to produce mystical changes in consciousness. Because harmaline is chemically similar to a natural substance, melatonin, produced by the pineal gland, Roney-Dougal suspects that harmaline somehow increases psi powers by stimulating the pineal gland and the synthesis of melatonin.

"All these factors seem to point to the pineal gland's being in some way connected with psi, possibly as an organ that stimulates a psi-conducive state of consciousness," Roney-Dougal notes.

The scientist believes that harmaline, considered an experimental drug, should be approved for parapsychological studies. Research subjects would be given the substance and then tested for psychic talents. If the results turn out positive, she thinks other ancient procedures for activating the pineal gland should also be tried in hopes of increasing a person's ESP.

"What is needed," Roney-Dougal says, "is experimental verification of anthropological evidence."

Water Apes

Mankind's apelike ancestors didn't all swing through the trees. About 3.5 to 9 million years ago, some of the anthropoids lived in the sea. That theory, explained by British author Elaine Morgan in her book *The Aquatic Ape*, explains why human bodies have adaptations that aren't found in other land-bound mammals.

Morgan says that when these missing links emerged from the oceans to live on land again after their aquatic evolutionary detour, they were "naked" compared to other apes. This loss of hair has usually been chalked up to the sweltering heat of the open savanna. But Morgan insists if that were the case, then other hunters like the lion and the hyena would also have hairless bodies.

Man lost his hair, she says, for the same reason whales and dolphins lost theirs. "Because if any fairly large aquatic mammal needs to keep warm in water," she notes, "it is better served by a layer of fat on the inside of its skin than by a layer of hair on the outside."

Morgan adds that our aquatic ape ancestors developed long and strong hind legs, perfect for walking upright, after eons of swimming. In addition, they learned to talk out of necessity—speech was essential because being in the water made it difficult to communicate through eye-to-eye contact and facial expressions.

Morgan also points out that while humans are the only weeping primates, seals and other sea mammals cry. "If we view man as a land animal, he is unique and inexplicable," she concludes. "If we view him as an ex-aquatic, he is conforming to the general pattern."

The Boomerang-Shaped UFO

On several nights from March 17 through March 31, 1983, hundreds of Westchester County, New York, residents witnessed a dazzling sight—a boomerang-shaped craft that hovered over them soundlessly, displaying bright rays of light. The multiple reports were unusual, as J. Allen Hynek, director of the Center for UFO Studies in Evanston, Illinois, pointed out, because most UFO sightings are isolated occurrences. "But this UFO was seen in a relatively urban area over a number of days," he stated, "with a broad spectrum of witnesses."

Meteorologist Bill Hele was the first to spot the strange check mark–shaped object with rows of multicolored lights as he drove down the Taconic State Parkway. He saw the lights blink off for a moment; then they came back on—this time flashing a brilliant green. Hele reported that the craft, which hovered one thousand feet in the air for two or three minutes before it drifted out of view to the north, was almost one thousand yards across.

Within a few days, other sightings were pouring in and the Center for UFO Studies launched an investigation headed by Westchester science teacher Phil Imbrogno, coinvestigator George Lesnick, and Hynek himself. The team interviewed a host of witnesses—including doctors, nurses, lawyers, business executives, housewives, and a group of striking Metro-North trainmen—and used an Apple II computer to cross match the information they came up with. The results? All the descriptions of the UFO closely matched Hele's.

But the investigators also came up with some contradictions. Since sightings occurred in towns miles apart at the same time, could multiple UFOs have been in the sky? The evidence pointed to that possibility. However, reports of hundreds of sightings in five Connecticut towns a month after the Westchester incidents seemed to point to a hoax—the witnesses there heard engines and saw maneuvers that could have been performed by small planes flying in formation.

Nonetheless, the investigators declared, this latter event differed substantially from the genuine UFO sightings of a boomerang-shaped craft over New York. Stated Imbrogno, "Single-engine planes cannot hover soundlessly, make ninety-degree turns, or shoot down dazzling beams of light."

How Quick-Frozen Mammoths Taste

The mammoth, the modern-day elephant's hairy ancestor, has been extinct, it is presumed, for thousands of years. Yet everyone from tourists to scientists in Siberia have reportedly sampled flesh from the huge pachyderm: Frozen for eons, it has been fried and roasted and served up for modern man.

Russian scientists are rumored to get together occasionally for "mammoth banquets." And a group of Soviet construction workers got into hot water with paleontologists when they fed mammoth meat to their dogs.

Geologist Robert M. Thorson of the University of Alaska in Fairbanks hasn't tasted mammoth meat yet, although he is currently excavating one of the partially preserved beasts. However, he has snacked on a sample of thirty-thousand-year-old frozen bison. "The piece I ate tasted pretty bad," he notes. His colleagues, who have sampled mammoth meat, say that that wasn't very tasty either—although no one has been known to get sick from eating the ancient fare.

There may be more mammoth to eat in the future, and not just the frozen kind. At a recent symposium on mammoth tissue, held in Helsinki, some scientists suggested that the mammoth may still be alive in remote areas of Siberia. And Soviet zoologist Nikolai Vereshchagin has proposed cloning new mammoth herds from the frozen cells of a long-dead beast.

UFOs and Altered States of Consciousness

Lorraine Davis, a researcher at John F. Kennedy University in Orinda, California, conducted a study under the university's consciousness studies department which she says may show that UFOs have an explanation most people have overlooked. Instead of being spaceships from other galaxies, they could be psychic phenomena related to the bright lights some people see before they die.

Davis came up with the idea after attending a seminar on near-death experiences (NDEs) led by University of Connecticut psychologist Kenneth Ring. Davis noted striking similarities between the altered state of consciousness described by near-death survivors—including seeing an almost blinding light and glimpsing long-dead relatives—and the experiences reported by UFO contactees. Using an NDE questionaire developed by Ring, Davis contacted 261 people who said they had been in contact with UFOs.

When she analyzed the ninety-three replies she received, Davis found that a remarkable pattern stood out. Like people who had been revived from clinical death, those who had seen a UFO consistently said they, too, had undergone three profound changes: Their attitudes toward themselves and other people became less egocentric and their personal religious beliefs moved from atheism or sectarianism to a kind of universal spirituality. They also reported that their psychic abilities had notably increased.

Davis thinks that UFO sightings and NDEs are both examples of altered states of human consciousness. "The UFO participant was thrust into this psychic state by a precipitating event," she says, "just as the NDE subject was transformed by the nearness of death."

This does *not* mean, she emphasizes, that people who see UFOs are just imagining the experiences.

"If the UFO experience does take place in an altered state of consciousness, perhaps a nuts-and-bolts machine *is* materialized for a few minutes," she says. "Who knows? It's certainly possible to perceive and experience in other states of consciousness, sometimes with an even greater sense of reality than that which we experience on a day-to-day basis."

Cigar-Shaped UFO over New Mexico

About an hour before sunset on December 8, 1981, Dan Luscomb watched a huge cigar-shaped object sail across the sky near Reserve, New Mexico. Luscomb, who owns the Whispering Pines Resort seven miles south of Reserve, said the UFO was "as big as four 747s linked together." He also saw a jet pursue the strange object. "But every time the plane got close," Luscomb recalls, "the object slipped away."

The director of the Center for UFO Studies, J. Allen Hynek, learned about Luscomb's sighting from an article in the *El Paso Times*. A few months later, in April, he decided to visit Reserve to investigate the case personally.

Hynek found nine local people who insisted they, too, had seen the same cigar-shaped object at about the same time that Luscomb spotted it. Lance Swapp, an employee at Jake's Grocery Store in nearby Luna, said he saw a bright light while driving home from work. "When I got home, my brother was hollering at me to look up in the sky," he recalled. "There was a large object over our heads, with a jet on its trail."

Housewife Alma Hobbs reported she saw a red ball rising from the ground as she headed toward Luscomb's resort. A few seconds later, it turned sideways and she noted it was tube-shaped.

Hynek stated that whatever these witnesses saw, it wasn't a missile, which would have made deafening noise—the UFO over New Mexico was silent. He also concluded it was probably not a military test vehicle because "no known technology can make a ninety-degree turn in seconds as this object allegedly did. The feat defies Newton's Second Law of Motion.''

Jules Verne's Amazing Prediction

When science fiction writers prophesy future developments, their predictions are often wrong, but occasionally they're incredibly right.

Writing in the 1860s, the French science fiction writer Jules Verne described a moon-bound trajectory leaving a base on the coast of Florida. He named the ship the *Nautilus*. Its travel time to the moon was 73 hours 13 minutes. By an almost unbelievable coincidence, the real moon shot—the Apollo 11—took 73 hours 10 minutes to reach the location in space from which it was to orbit the moon.

In another time jump, Jules Verne predicted the dimensions of an atomic submarine, which he also called the *Nautilus*, 150 years before the atomic submarine was built. The first United States atomic submarine, gracefully christened the *Nautilus* by the United States Navy, was the first submarine to pass through the icy waters under the North Pole, and it gave its name to a whole class of atomic submarines.

The Nostradamus Program

For five centuries, interpreters have labored to decipher the coded prophecies of the astrologer and mystic Nostradamus. Although he was a Christian who claimed to be inspired by God, Nostradamus feared the wrath of the Catholic Inquisition, so he disguised his predictions with all sorts of mysterious literary stratagems, including word-play techniques such as anagrams and aphaeresis (dropping the initial letter or syllable from a word).

About four hundred interpretations of his predictions have been attempted, but none completely broke Nostradamus's complex code until a computer was put to the task. Jean Charles de Font-brune, a pharmaceuticals manager whose hobby is studying the seer's writings, fed the data he had come up with over the years into a computer network. That allowed him to measure the repetition of letters, words, phrases, and the other linguistic devices Nostradamus employed. Soon it became apparent to de Fontbrune that the mystic had thought in Latin structures and had transposed those structures directly into French—a clue that enabled de Fontbrune to decode six hundred of Nostradamus's eleven hundred verses.

Although he published a book containing his findings in 1980, it didn't create much of a stir. Then someone noticed that de Fontbrune had pointed out that "the year the Rose flourished" would coincide with an uprising of Moslems against the West.

Since the rose was the symbol of the Socialists who took power in France the same year the U.S. embassy in Tehran was seized, people were suddenly interested in what else de Fontbrune's book predicted. Readers discovered that Nostradamus had used his amazing powers to prophesy the death of Henry II in a tournament, the rise of Napoleon Bonaparte, and even the ouster of Iran's shah by "religious zealots."

According to de Fontbrune's interpretation of Nostradamus's verses, Islam will destroy the Roman Catholic Church before the end of the century, when the Arab nations team with the Soviet Union and invade Western Europe. Paris will then swim in blood and the world will be locked in a terrible war. These predictions have created such a stir that some French citizens have reportedly already fled the country.

Future Forms

Physicist Freeman Dyson of the Institute for Advanced Study in Princeton, New Jersey, says that molecular biologists have already begun developing the technology needed to redesign Earth life. One day, he claims, humans will be genetically engineered so that they will be able to thrive in space or alien environments without the need for space suits or artificial life-support systems.

What will these humans of the not-so-distant-future look like? Dyson says they may be noseless ("There's nothing up there in space to smell anyway") and have airtight, crocodile-like skin to protect their greatly reduced internal body pressure from boiling because of a lack of atmospheric pressure. He adds that the new, scientifically altered race of humans could be covered with insulating fur or feathers that would come in handy in the frigid cold of space. The tendency of bones to dissolve during long space flights in zero gravity could also be overcome, he says, by re-adjusting the body's chemical balance.

Ancient Japanese Space Suits

Between 7000 B.C. and 520 B.C., Japanese artisans created small clay statues with pointed heads, slits for eyes, and torsos decorated with intricate patterns of stripes and dots. Known as *dogus*, the objects are usually regarded as representations of ancient Japanese fertility gods. But Vaughn Greene, author of *Astronauts of Ancient Japan*, thinks *dogus* depict just what they look like—humanoids in space suits. In fact, he says, they look surprisingly like they are wearing the extravehicular mobility unit (EMU) suit designed by NASA for space shuttle astronauts to wear outside their ship.

Greene suspects that the top and the bottom of the *dogu* space suit were put on separately, just like the EMU. He also points out that the EMU chest-pack control units are in approximately the same place as the circular knobs found on a *dogu* chest. The stripes around the *dogu* knobs, he theorizes, are not decorations—instead, they are marks used to calibrate the quantity of water or oxygen being released to the creature inside the space suit.

Mystery Cats and Dogs

For the past decade, author Michael Goss has investigated reports of mysterious, flesh-eating creatures in Great Britain that are variously described as either huge cats or dogs.

Goss has documented seventy such sightings throughout the British Isles. Sometimes the animal is described as a tawny, ten-foot-long cat; many of those who have seen carcasses devoured by the creature even say that its eating habits are decidedly feline. However, other eyewitnesses, including a local bus driver and Royal Marine commandos sent to shoot a beast that killed almost one hundred sheep in Stokenchurch, say it resembles a large dog.

One of the mystery beasts was spotted in the summer of 1982, Goss says, east of London in the Fobbing Marshes. A water company foreman working at an isolated storage area one afternoon was startled by the animal. A few days later, a passerby saw what was probably the same creature jump from behind a hedgerow. Neither of the eyewitnesses was sure if he had seen a cat or a dog. On the other hand, in late 1983, three people, one with binoculars, glimpsed an animal just a mile from Fobbing Marshes that they insisted was a large panther.

Some people in Britain, Goss relates, think these reports point to "alien" cats and dogs stalking the country. "If this is a new folklore, we ought to know it," he concludes. "If it is a zoological or paranormal fact, then it is even more essential that we learn what we can."

The Search for Mallory's Camera

On June 8, 1924, while attempting to climb precipitous Mount Everest, George Mallory and Andrew Irvine disappeared without a trace. No one knows how close the two came to being the first conquerors of the highest mountain in the world, but there may be a way to find out. Massachusetts computer engineer Tom Holzel has launched a search for the Kodak Vest Pocket cameras the mountain climbers carried with them.

Holzel learned about the cameras from a small article in the *New Yorker* magazine. He realized if they could be found, they would probably contain undeveloped film that would show how high the explorers got. But finding cameras on the huge mountain, he admits, "is like looking for a needle in a haystack."

However, Holzel thinks it's possible. To help with the search, he had White's Electronics of New England build special, rugged-duty metal detectors specifically designed to tune in to the steel-and-brass bodies of the cameras.

Holzel went looking for Mallory's and Irvine's cameras for three months in 1986. He didn't find what he was looking for, although he did come up with oxygen bottles at what may have been the explorers' campsite.

Why is Holzel, despite enormous odds against his success, determined to continue looking for the cameras and the historic film they contain? He answers in much the same way Sir Edmund Hillary did when questioned about why he was climbing Mount Everest: "Because Mallory's there."

Mallory was found in May 1999,

Bigfoot Hunter

Mark Keller resigned from his job at the post office and announced that he was leaving on a five-month hunting trip. He was going after big game, he said—specifically Bigfoot, the legendary ape creature said to roam the deep forests of the Pacific Northwest.

But when word got out that Keller was planning on bagging a Bigfoot, he received more than one hundred threatening phone calls. Some callers said they would find a way to interfere with Keller's plans. Others threatened the hunter's life.

"Some bow hunters up in Washington called and said if I go out and try to kill Bigfoot they will get me," Keller reported.

Arcata, California, police sergeant Jim Dawson notes that Keller also received several threatening letters. However, the police were unable to find out who was responsible.

But all the people who were so concerned that a Bigfoot's death was imminent were soon relieved to hear that Keller's hunting trip had been delayed—indefinitely. He was spotted, not in the wilds of the Pacific Northwest, but in downtown Eureka, California, where county deputy Rich Walton arrested him.

"He had a rifle with a night-vision scope on it," the officer explains. "So I took him in."

Tomb of Ice

Wesley Bateman of Poway, California, was watching a videotape about UFOs one night when he made a curious discovery. He noticed that an ice-covered object allegedly photographed by Apollo 11 astronauts had the rough outline of a TBM Avenger. "The heaviest part of the plane—the nose—is pointed toward the earth," he explains, "and you can easily recognize the bubble turret and the tail."

But what is a 1945 propeller-driven airplane doing in orbit around the earth? Batemen thinks he has the answer. The plane was one of five TBM Avenger torpedo bombers that left the naval air station in Fort Lauderdale, Florida, on December 5, 1945, never to return.

Less than three hours into that routine mission, the planes and their crew of fourteen vanished. A Martin Flying Boat with thirteen men on board sent out to rescue the crew also disappeared. There has been speculation over the past thirty years that aliens were involved in the mysterious incident—especially since some claimed they heard the flight instructor cry, "Don't come after me; they look like they're from outer space," before his voice faded from his radio.

Bateman says the Avenger orbiting the earth could offer solid proof that extraterrestrials were behind the disappearance of the planes. He thinks that when the Avengers dropped depth charges on their training mission, they may have damaged an alien craft under the sea. "When the UFO rose out of the water to avoid further damage," he says, "its rapid departure created a propulsion vortex, sucking up a lot of seawater and the planes along with it."

He adds that anyone who doubts that a 1945 Avenger is circling the earth several thousand miles up should take a look at the photo of the ice-entombed plane. "I can't imagine anyone looking at this and saying it's *not* an Avenger. This is conclusive proof that UFOs exist."

Dreams of the Dead

Some dreams hold clues about life after death. That, at least, is the conclusion reached by Swiss psychologists Marie-Louise von Franz and Emmanuel Xipolitas Kennedy after studying twenty-five hundred dreams.

The researchers say that many dreams about the afterlife simply reveal a psychological dimension of the dreamer. But other dreams have an almost photographic, supernatural quality that sets them apart and convinces the dreamer there is life after death. "These dreams do appear to be encounters with postmortal souls," Kennedy explains. "After having these dreams, people feel it is the dead they have seen."

When the terminally ill are near death, their dreams frequently take on a similar quality, he adds. The dying may appear rejuvenated in their dreams, Kennedy says, or they may encounter someone who has already passed to the "other side."

"Dreams of the dying seem to confirm for the unconscious that impending death is not an end," Kennedy declares. "The ultimate goal appears to be the union of the individual self with the archetypal self we think of as the godhead. These dreams point to the notion that whatever is unresolved in this life must somehow go on, to be continued after death."

Vision of Murder

When Etta Louise Smith, a Lockheed shipping clerk and mother of three youngsters, heard a radio newscast about a missing nurse one afternoon in 1980, she had a strange feeling that the young woman was already dead. The news stated that the police were conducting a house-to-house search for the woman, but Smith kept thinking, "She's not in a house." Then she had a vision "as if there was a photograph in front of me," she recalls. "The woman was dead."

Smith decided to share her psychic insight with the Los Angeles police. After talking to investigators, she visited the remote canyon site she'd "seen" mentally, hours before. Soon she'd discovered the battered and raped body of thirty-one-year-old Melanie Uribe.

Smith was promptly booked on suspicion of murder and spent four days in jail before a local resident confessed that he and two accomplices had committed the crime. The men were later convicted.

Smith filed suit against the city of Los Angeles for false arrest, and Superior Court Judge Joel Rudolf ruled that the police had lacked probable cause and sufficient evidence to arrest Smith for the killing. The jury awarded her $26,184—according to the foreman, the majority of the jurors believed that Smith did have a psychic experience that led her to the murder victim's body.

Smith, however, isn't so sure she should have acted on her extrasensory vision. "Maybe in the future," she says, "I'll call in anonymously."

The Mystery Plane of the Bermuda Triangle

Finally, there appeared to be a break in the mysterious case of the five navy TBM-3 Aztec Avenger planes and the Martin Flying Boat that all disappeared without a trace after leaving Fort Lauderdale on December 5, 1945, and heading into the so-called Bermuda Triangle. Treasure hunter Mel Fisher's crew discovered what seemed to be one of the missing planes partially covered by mud. It was sitting on the ocean bottom about twenty miles west of Key West.

Although UFO enthusiasts have long suspected that aliens captured the missing planes, the wreckage of the Grumman Avenger found by Fisher's men showed no sign of extraterrestrial contact. It simply looked, said K. T. Budde, a member of the salvage crew, "like it had gotten lost and run out of fuel."

So has the mystery of the vanished planes been solved? Far from it. According to David Paul Horan, Fisher's attorney, navy records have revealed that the recently discovered Avenger was *not* one of the famous five planes. "Instead, it was lost from Key West nearly three months prior to those planes' disappearing," he notes. "One survivor who bailed out has been able to identify this plane absolutely."

Horan, who is also a pilot, says he's disappointed that the mystery of the missing Avengers hasn't been solved by Fisher's crew as they comb the ocean bottom seeking buried treasure. "In fact," Horan points out, "nothing that has been found down there looks like it might be related to that whole incident."

Blue People

Curiously colored creatures—like little green men from Mars—are a staple of science fiction stories. But scientists have documented real blue humans living right here on Earth.

When mountaineer-physiologist John West of the University of California at San Diego's School of Medicine visited an area in the Andes near Aucanquilcha, Chile, he made a startling discovery. Researchers had long believed that humans could not live at altitudes higher than 17,500 feet, but West came face-to-face with a handful of men living at nearly 20,000 feet—and they were blue.

Although scientists have long known that certain diseases can give the skin a bluish cast and that genetic abnormalities have caused some people in the Ozark Mountains to be pastel colored, West found that the Andes men were blue for another reason— their coloration seems to have resulted from an adaptation to the air at the extremely high altitude, which has less than half the oxygen found at sea level.

West explains that the miners appear to produce large amounts of hemoglobin, the oxygen-carrying pigment in blood cells. "The hemoglobin is poorly oxygenated," he says, "and it shows through their skin, giving it a bluish color. I suspect these men increase the depth and rate of their breathing and because they were born and bred at five thousand to twelve thousand feet, that may have given them a head start in adapting. But there's a lot we don't yet understand."

University of Pennsylvania physiologist Sukhamay Lahiri has also seen the blue men of the Andes firsthand. He points out that Tibetan priests who spend time at similar altitudes in the Himalayas also have a bluish tint. "But what's startling about the Andes men," he says, "is that they are living and doing heavy labor at these altitudes."

The Cursed Highway

A lot of people might have second thoughts about traveling down New Jersey's new Route 55, a 4.2-mile project in south Jersey's Deptford Township. Part of the road slices through the archaeological remains of an ancient Indian village, including graves of paleo-Indians who inhabited the area eight thousand years ago. Nanticoke Indian Carl Peirce (also known as Wayandaga), the local medicine man, publicly warned that the desecration of his ancestors' resting places would result in disastrous consequences.

"I told them if they proceeded with that road, my ancestors would take revenge," Peirce says. "I warned them that reciprocation from the spirit world could be expected."

Soon after a press conference at which Wayandaga aired his predictions, mishaps and deaths began to plague Route 55. A worker was killed by an asphalt roller and another collapsed on the job from a brain aneurysm. One worker found his feet turning black from a circulatory disorder while another was injured when he fell from a highway bridge. Still another highway laborer suffered three heart attacks. Then a van carrying five crewmen exploded in flames.

"It got to the point that 'What's going to happen next?' was something commonly asked on the job," notes site inspector Karl Kruger.

Wayandaga insists the cursed road will never be safe for travelers: "Until they relocate Highway 55, there will continue to be deaths."

Glimpses of the Future from the Near-Dead

According to psychologist Kenneth Ring of the University of Connecticut, those who have returned from clinical death frequently report they saw more than their past flash before their eyes—they saw the future as well.

Ring, who has studied the experiences of more than a dozen of these people around the country, points out that one man apparently saw himself as a married adult while near death at the age of ten. The vision, which took place during an appendectomy in 1941, included the subject and his two children. He "saw" himself sitting in an armchair and he noticed something "very strange" behind the wall.

In 1968, the man suddenly realized his near-death vision had come true. "When I sat in a chair, reading a book and happened to glance at my children, I realized that *this* was the memory from 1941," he explains. "And the strange object behind the wall was a forced-air heater, something not in my sphere of knowledge as a child."

Other research subjects told Ring similar tales. But there were also numerous reports that, while clinically dead, they had witnessed the fate of Earth. Almost all of these people, Ring says, have foreseen a disastrous era that they insist will start in less than ten years. Earthquakes, volcanoes, famine, nuclear war, and droughts are among the catastrophes predicted. But the near-death survivors also say that peace will eventually prevail. Following a period of disasters, "decades of worldwide brotherhood" will follow.

Ring doesn't think anyone should panic about the predicted worldwide turmoil. "I'm inclined to think the prophecies are metaphors for the fears and hopes of the subconscious," he says.

UFO Movies

A little after 9:00 A.M. on January 11, 1973, near the village of Cuddington, England, building surveyor Peter Day spotted a glowing orange ball in the sky. He reached for the Super-8 movie camera he had in his car and filmed the object as it moved over treetops about a quarter of a mile away.

When the British UFO Research Association (BUFORA) was given the movie to analyze, it announced that the image Day had captured was both "genuine and puzzling." Another examination by UFO-photography specialist Peter Warrington, working with the Kodak-UK laboratories at Hemel Hempstead, concluded, "There has been no trickery." The film was further authenticated by Kodak-UK's technical-information consultant Peter Sutherst, who declared, "Whatever the film shows, it is a real object in the sky."

However, another research team headed by UFO expert Ken Phillips studied the film and concluded that the object in Day's movie was a United States Air Force F-11 jet that had developed a malfunction after taking off from Heyford Air Force Base and then caught fire. The time and date of the crash? It was at 9:46 A.M. on January 11, 1973.

But not everyone agrees. Photography specialist Warrington emphasizes that his team of investigators studied the film under considerable magnification, "and at no point was an aircraft detected."

Day says flatly that he doesn't believe he filmed an aircraft. "A dozen other people, including a schoolteacher and several schoolchildren, also saw the UFO. They were closer to the object than I was, and their descriptions tally with what is on the film."

Brazilian UFO

Most people were napping on the overnight flight between Fortaleza and São Paulo, Brazil, in February 1982, when pilot Gerson Maciel De Britto made an unexpected announcement: "I see a strange object forty or fifty miles to the left and I need eyewitnesses."

The passengers stirred and discovered that they were bathed in a brilliant light. Looking out the plane's windows for the next hour and twenty-two minutes, they observed the sky turn red, orange, white, and blue.

From his vantage point in the cockpit, De Britto made out a "fast-moving, saucer-shaped disk with five spotlights." When the object failed to establish contact after De Britto sent it radio messages in Portuguese and English, he tried communicating through concentration—attempting to send or receive information telepathically.

As the airliner approached within eight miles of Rio de Janeiro for a scheduled stopover, the pilot noted that the UFO was only eight miles from the plane and moving closer. Although radar failed to pick up the object, the Rio tower asked three commercial pilots flying in the area whether they saw the strange light and were told they did. Brazilian military planes were soon soaring after the craft; the official report of the outcome of that chase remains classified.

After major Brazilian newspapers and magazines carried the story, UFO skeptics began pointing out that Venus had risen in the eastern sky at 3:10 A.M. on the morning in question. Could pilot De Britto and his plane's passengers have been fooled into thinking they saw a UFO by the intense and colorful glow of that planet?

De Britto says that's impossible. He insists he saw Venus *and* the strange object. In addition, he says that the light maintained the same orientation to the plane even after he changed course by fifty-one degrees—which suggests an intelligent force was manning the craft. "If what the pilot says is true, then it could not have been Venus," noted J. Allen Hynek, director of the Center for UFO

Studies in Evanston, Illinois. "If it wasn't Venus, then it was a UFO."

Reactions of the Newly Dead

Bodies can and do move after death, as anyone who has seen a chicken's head chopped off can verify.

Reactions of severed human heads and the bodies from which they came were noted from the Reign of Terror during the French Revolution of 1792 when the guillotine was first used. Great numbers of unfortunate people, first the aristocrats and then other dissenters, were decapitated, one after the other. In full view of interested spectators, some macabre results were noted.

Sometimes a victim's mouth would open and close, as if wishing to speak; sometimes eyes would continue to move in their sockets or would alternately open and close. Bodies would also continue to twitch and move, although without heads they were obviously dead.

Equally frightening was the case of the criminal George Foster, executed by hanging in London in 1803. After Foster's execution, a Professor Aldini applied the galvanic process to the corpse in the presence of medical observers to see what would happen. The results were startling and indicated that some motor nerves were still capable of operation. The legs moved, the right hand was lifted and made into a fist, and one eye slowly opened.

In any case, Foster achieved a partial revenge on society. A surgeon named Pass, who had witnessed the postmortem, died on his way back from the experiment. His death was ascribed to heart failure caused by fright.

Is this true?

The Village That Vanished

It isn't unusual to hear about a missing person, but in 1930 a whole village vanished—and it's still missing.

The village was located near Lake Angikuni, about five hundred miles northwest of the Royal Canadian Mounted Police base at Churchill, Canada. Although it was an isolated spot, the Eskimos who lived there were frequently visited by trappers who swapped furs and joined them for meals of caribou. French-Canadian trapper Joe LaBelle, who had traveled through that part of the Canadian wilderness for about forty years, considered the folks who lived on Lake Angikuni old friends.

But in November 1930, when Joe decided to stop by the village for a visit, he immediately knew something was wrong. First of all, the dogs didn't bark. He shouted a greeting but no one answered. Finally, he opened the doors to several of the low sod huts and yelled for his friends. No one replied.

An hour-long search of the village showed that every inhabitant had disappeared. There were no signs of a struggle—pots of food sat over fires that had been cold for weeks. A needle was still in some clothing that a woman had been mending. Kayaks had been left unattended for so long that waves had battered them. Rifles stood gathering dust. The Eskimos' dogs were found dead from starvation, tied to stumps.

The mystery deepened when LaBelle searched his friends' cemetery where bodies were customarily covered with rocks. One grave had been opened and the body exhumed. Stealing a body, LaBelle knew, was taboo for an Eskimo. Whoever had done the deed had stacked the grave stones in two piles—ruling out any possibility that an animal had uncovered the body.

The Royal Canadian Mounted Police investigated LaBelle's report of the village that disappeared. Despite their reputation of "always getting their man," the Mounties were baffled as to how and why thirty Eskimos, in the middle of winter, had disappeared. Months of detective work, including interviews with other tribes in the area, never turned up a clue to explain the village that vanished.

Desert Ship

The *Arakwe* was a wooden ship with huge paddle wheels, like those of the famed Mississippi riverboats, built in the latter days of the War Between the States. Armed with a few small cannons, it was listed as a gunboat in the United States Navy and sent to the Horn of Aconcagua in Chile under orders to show United States support for the Chilean government by displaying the American flag and showing off its guns.

The *Arakwe*'s captain and crew had little reason to believe they would actually see any action, much less that it would occur on dry land. But because of a freak accident of nature, that's just what happened.

Captain Alexander was in his cabin, when, according to his log, he "noticed that the cabin lamp was swinging fore and aft. I hurried on deck and quickly recognized the nature of the disturbance as a submarine earthquake, since the water was rapidly draining seaward from the bay."

Soon the *Arakwe* was caught up for a wild ride on a powerful tidal wave, which carried the wooden ship, and dozens of other boats, far inland. Finally, Captain Alexander and his men found themselves two miles from the sea at the bottom of a cliff. Although the flat-bottomed *Arakwe* was broken up, she was still in good condition compared to the wreckage of other ships scattered all around.

The remains of the destroyed ships' cargoes were strewn for miles, drawing crowds of looters. Some tried to board the *Arakwe*. Captain Alexander and his crew drew their pistols and ordered the looters to back away. But they simply moved just out of pistol range.

The captain knew he needed more forceful weapons—but the crew couldn't reach the shot to load the cannons. The ammunition had been buried somewhere under the boat's damaged deck. There was only one chance, Alexander reasoned, one possible substitution. Quickly, the crew gathered hard, round cheeses from the galley and loaded them, along with the gunpowder, into the cannons.

Holding his fire until the looters moved within a couple of hundred yards of the battleship, the captain finally signaled for the cannons to be fired. The weapons roared as the cheese knocked over enough of the mob to frighten the rest of the looters away.

The *Arakwe* was never seaworthy again, and she is recorded in the navy's official records as lost in action. But she went out with a unique distinction: the only battleship in all the annals of U.S. military history to fight a battle on dry land—with cheese—and win.

The Tennessee Viking Saga

Around 1874, near some Indian graves and earthworks at Castalian Springs in Sumner County, Tennessee, a nineteen-by-fifteen-inch slab of ancient limestone was uncovered. Engraved on its surface was a vivid depiction of a fierce battle—between Native Americans and Vikings.

There are two distinct groups of people portrayed in the scene. Those with almond-shaped eyes appear to have come from over some hills that are represented by four vertical scallops; they have painted faces and wear animal skins, ankle and wrist bands, and elaborate headdresses.

As for the second group, the eyes are outlined with rays. Researchers Ruth Verrill and Clyde Keeler of the Georgia Academy of Sciences concluded that the rays could represent eyelashes, which would have been more obvious on fair persons like the Norse. The leader of the second group holds a square shield. It looks unlike anything used by American Indians—but it's similar to shields used by the ancient Normans. On the ground is a spear shaped like the Viking weapons documented by Johannes Bronsfed in *The Vikings*. The ray-eyed men wear shoes and one wears a Phrygian or Roman-type helmet with a large crescent-shaped crest.

No one may ever know just what the battle was about, but it was clearly bloody. One ray-eyed person is shown decapitated. There are also hints that women may have played a role in the dispute:

An almond-eyed female, wearing a skirt and shoes, holds onto something—perhaps a wampum belt, as an offering of peace. She is being attacked by a male Indian. Another woman, this one a ray-eyed person, kneels inside a structure that Verrill and Keeler have identified as an Indian medicine lodge. She stares upward, as if appealing to her god and smokes a ritual pipe.

The part of the picture that most convincingly identifies the second group as Vikings is the image of a distinctive Viking boat. Verrill and Keeler noted that the boat has the same single mast and yardarm to carry the sail that Vikings used; other features of the boat match those used by North European traders and explorers up to around A.D. 1200. The ship's commander stands at the prow, wearing the famed Viking horns designating his leadership. Five oarsmen are depicted at the rowing level and the paddle ends of their oars are rounded—a feature identical to the Iron Age rock carvings of a Viking boat discovered in Sweden. At the middle of the boat is a landing hook, and, toward the stern, a mooring line extends out into the water. The slab also clearly outlines a type of anchor known to be used in certain instances by Vikings.

If Vikings landed and fought Indians in Tennessee, how did they get there? Verrill and Keeler concluded that a Viking ship could have entered the Gulf of Mexico and sailed up the Mississippi, Ohio, and Cumberland rivers to Rock Creek and then to Castalian Springs—which would have brought them right to where the ancient stone engraving was found.

The Return of John Paul Jones

In 1773, a young Scotsman named John Paul was captain of a British merchant ship. Fighting a mutinous crew, John Paul shot and killed a man, and when the boat reached the port of Tobago, the British authorities arrested him. Knowing he faced almost certain death, he picked the lock on his prison door and fled to the American colonies.

There he met a family who befriended him and he soon changed his name to theirs—becoming John Paul Jones. It was a name that would one day be so beloved by his new countrymen that in the twentieth century the U.S. government would launch a strange mining expedition to recover his body.

Under the leadership of Admiral John Paul Jones, the struggling American fleet outfought the British ships time and again. After the Revolutionary War, he signed on as a mercenary for the Russian navy under Catherine the Great, helping to defeat the Turks.

The proud soldier could not win his battle with failing health, however, and, at the age of forty-five, he died alone in Paris. The U.S. government ordered that his body be embalmed and shipped back to America.

But, perhaps because of bureaucratic bungling, no one ever called for the body and the great Revolutionary War hero was buried in Paris. John Paul Jones was not destined for obscurity, though. One hundred thirteen years later, the American government decided to retrieve his body. There was just one problem: no one was sure where it was.

The cemetery where Jones was buried had been abandoned decades earlier and was covered with factories, businesses, and hospitals. Finally, a researcher discovered old archives that showed where the body should be.

But how could it be reached?

The only solution was to use miners. A shaft was dug near a large building a couple of hundred feet from where John Paul Jones's body was believed to be. Then the miners tunneled around and under buildings until they found the lead casket, emblazoned with the initials J.P.J.

When the coffin lid was cut away, witnesses noted that the body was so well preserved that it still looked remarkably like portraits of the war hero.

The admiral was soon back in the United States, bestowed with honors and laid to rest among the other heroes at Annapolis. Appropriately enough, John Paul Jones was escorted to his final resting place by part of the American battle fleet that he had helped establish more than a century before.

The Psychic Horse

Soon after a Richmond, Virginia, woman named Mrs. Lord purchased a two-week-old colt in 1925, the animal began to behave in odd ways. She came trotting toward her owners before they called her—as soon as they *thought* about calling her. Several years later the horse, named Lady Wonder, could count and spell short words by maneuvering toy blocks around with her nose.

Lady Wonder used her unusual talents to predict the future with startling accuracy. For example, according to the *Chicago Tribune*, the horse predicted that Franklin D. Roosevelt would be the next president of the United States before he had even been nominated. And in fourteen out of seventeen years, the mare correctly predicted the winner of the World Series. In at least two tragic cases involving the deaths of children, Lady Wonder was also able to supply facts that even the police had been unable to uncover.

In the early 1950s, Lady Wonder was asked by authorities in Norfolk County, Massachusetts, if she could help them find four-year-old Danny Matson, who had been missing for months. The horse "told" police to go to a water-filled stone quarry. The site had already been searched without yielding any evidence connected to the case. But the police decided to give it one more try—and they found the body of little Danny.

In October 1955, another boy, three-year-old Ronnie Weitcamp, disappeared after he left three playmates in his front yard and scooted around his family's central Indiana house. Sheriff's deputies and the Indiana state police, accompanied by an estimated fifteen hundred employees of the local navy depot, combed thousands of wooded acres near Ronnie's home looking for the toddler. But there was not a trace of the little boy.

Had Ronnie been kidnapped or murdered? Was he lost? Leads and fruitless clues poured in to the police department, but no solid evidence developed. Ronnie Weitcamp had disappeared. By October 22, the official search was called off.

Remembering the strange tale of Lady Wonder, journalist Frank Edwards, then news director of television station WTTV at Bloomington, contacted a friend who lived within driving distance of Mrs. Lord and asked him to see if her talking mare could offer any help in finding Danny.

Although already thirty years of age, extremely old for a horse, Lady Wonder was still able to "talk," and Edwards's friend asked several questions.

In answer to "Do you know why we are here?" the horse immediately spelled out "boy," by flipping out large tin letters that hung from a bar across her stall. When asked the youngster's name, the mare turned up the letters R-O-N-E, as if trying to spell Ronnie.

According to Lady Wonder, the boy was dead. He had not been kidnapped and he would be found in a hole more than a quarter mile but less than a mile, from his home.

"What is near him?" the horse was asked. "E-L-M," Lady Wonder spelled out. She also indicated the soil around the boy was sandy, and that he would be found in "D-E-C."

Edwards broadcast the information provided by the "talking" telepathic horse on October 24, 1955. Predictably, the story received widespread ridicule and criticism. Then two teenagers found Ronnie's body.

The child was found near an elm tree in a sandy gully, about a mile from where he was last seen alive. And he was found in December, just as the remarkable Lady Wonder had predicted nearly two months earlier.

The Peculiar Death of Meriwether Lewis

Although almost everyone has heard of the famed Lewis and Clark Expedition, few people know the strange fate that awaited Meriwether Lewis. The national hero was doomed to die under such peculiar circumstances that it's unlikely that even Sherlock Holmes could have figured out exactly what happened.

Just before he was killed in October 1809, Lewis was traveling to Washington, D.C., with United States Army Major John Neely to answer accusations that, as governor of the Louisiana Territory, he had mishandled financial affairs—charges that were eventually dismissed. As they made their way along the foothills of eastern Tennessee, several pack mules carrying Lewis's record books bolted during a thunderstorm. Major Neely took off to bring the animals back.

Governor Lewis kept on riding alone. He was a broken man— thin from malaria, worried about the political charges facing him, and lovesick over the rejection he'd suffered at the hands of Vice President Aaron Burr's daughter. When he finally reached the cabin of Mr. and Mrs. John Griner, he quickly asked if he could stay the night and rest.

The tall stranger didn't identify himself. He simply ate his dinner in silence and retired for the evening. Later, the Griners heard someone talking in his room, although they couldn't tell if their guest was muttering to himself or actually carrying on a conversation with someone else. And if he *was* talking to someone else, why hadn't the dogs barked when another stranger entered the house?

Just before dawn, the Griners were awakened by a gunshot. The couple quickly looked around and found that everything seemed to be in place. Then they heard moans coming from the stranger's room.

Entering the bedroom, the Griners saw that the gaunt man was dying. Blood poured from a wound in his left side as he tried to speak. "I am no coward," he said. "But it is hard to die . . . so young . . . so hard to die." Moments later, it was all over.

When the Griners searched through his leather knapsacks for identification, they found a ledger identifying the deceased man as "Meriwether Lewis, Albemarle, Virginia. Capt., U.S. Army."

Had the famous explorer taken his own life? The Griners were both by Lewis's side within seconds of hearing a gunshot. But they insisted there had been no powder smoke in the room—despite the fact that the gunpowder used in those days always left a strong-smelling white fog. Lewis's rifle was found still standing in the corner of the guest room. It had not been fired. No other pistol or gun of any kind was uncovered in the room.

The governor's traveling companion, Major Neely, did not arrive at the Griners' cabin until midmorning the day after Lewis's demise. Why did it take him so long to round up a few mules, and where did he spend the night?

If Meriwether Lewis did not kill himself, is it possible his political enemies arranged his death—and made sure they would have access to his personal records in case they contained evidence that would incriminate them?

No one has ever been able to answer those questions. The peculiar death of Meriwether Lewis remains unsolved.

The Day the Devil Came to Town

When George Fairly, a baker in Topsham, England, went to work early on the morning of February 8, 1855, he noticed curious tracks leading up to the door of his shop. Since a snow blanketed the ground, Fairly could clearly make out the odd nature of the footprints: Somehow, whatever made the curved marks had walked near the base of a wall, jumped on top of it and walked for a while, and then returned to the ground again before heading toward the bay.

This incident would not be particularly interesting except for one thing. George Fairly was only one of *thousands* of residents from around Devonshire, England, who awoke that snowy winter morn to find evidence that a strange visitor had scampered, walked, or slithered over their roofs, fields, and fences—leaving behind clear U-shaped footprints in an unbroken line.

Rumors soon spread that the U-shaped tracks, which sometimes appeared cloven, were devilish in nature, and near panic ensued as people armed themselves against the unknown creature.

In an article published in the February 16, 1855, *Times* of London, the prints were described as ". . . more like that of a biped than a quadruped. . . . The steps were generally eight inches in advance of each other. The impressions of feet closely resembled those of a donkey's shoe, and measured from an inch and a half to . . . two and a half inches."

Whatever made the tracks managed to cover hundreds of miles in a few hours—its trek must have started after the snow stopped falling at around 7:00 P.M. on the night of February 7 and ended before the prints were discovered the next morning. It was also able to cross two large bodies of water, including the Exe River at Exmouth.

No one ever caught a glimpse of the creature who became known as the "devil of Devonshire" and no other U-shaped marks were ever found in the area. But whatever the thing was, it may have also visited barren Kerguelen Island, near the Antarctic. According to the official records of explorer Captain James C. Ross, a landing party found similar, unexplained footprints in the area ". . . described by Dr. Robertson as being three inches in length and two and a half in breadth, having a small and deeper depression on each side and shaped like a horseshoe."

Could whatever made the bizarre footprints have come out of the sea? Two strange finds off the coast of England point to that possibility. In November 1953 a badly decomposed creature, about two and a half feet long, with feet and legs arranged so that it could have walked like a human, washed ashore at Canfey Island. Then, in August 1954, the Reverend Joseph Overs came across another one of the creatures floating dead in a tidal pool. This one weighed about twenty-five pounds, was over four feet long, and had two short legs. The local police who examined the thing reported that it had large eyes, holes where a nose should be, a gaping mouth, and gills. Instead of scales like a fish, it was covered with thick pink skin.

But it is the shape of the creature's tiny feet, documented by the British bobbies, that reminded some people of an incident that happened nearly a century before—the thing had five little toes on each foot, arranged in a U-shape around a concave arch.

ITT versus Sharks

Some of the interference on overseas telephone calls may be caused by sharks biting the new cables that run at considerable depths across the Atlantic Ocean. Sharks have been indicated as the culprits because shark teeth have been found imbedded in the damaged lines. Since oceanic sharks had not presented a problem to undersea cables until now, the attacks on the new cables are surprising, considering that the new cables, which are under an inch in diameter, are somewhat less noticeable than the old ones, which are as thick as one's arm. The cost to repair each of the shark-damaged cables, which cross both the Atlantic and the Pacific oceans, is at least $250,000.

It has been suggested that the taut suspension of the new fiber-optic cables may cause vibrations that the sharks pick up as a food signal. Sharks react to signals produced by an electronic field and would try to snap at and eat anything that generated such signals (a valuable point to remember for swimmers with electronic equipment).

ITT officials are considering countering the shark attacks with cables wrapped in double layers of steel tape on which sharks would crack their teeth.

The Cannibal Tree

Roger Williams came to the American colonies in 1630. Because of his passionate belief in religious freedom, he was soon thrown out of Massachusetts. But he was destined to become the beloved, outspoken leader of the colony of Rhode Island. While history books recount Williams's life, they leave out one of the most fascinating aspects of his death—how some Rhode Islanders accidentally ate him.

It all started in 1683, when he died and was laid to rest, beside his wife, on their farm. A simple headstone marked the graves, and several years afterwards, local townsfolk decided to erect a memorial worthy of Williams's stature.

A commission was duly authorized to disinter the remains of Roger and his wife so they could be given a more proper burial beneath the new monument. But there was a problem: When the two graves were opened, every trace of Williams and his wife had disappeared.

Although it took a while to figure out who had robbed the graves, the thief was finally caught—it was an apple tree, well known for its particularly tasty fruit.

The tree's roots had grown through the coffins that contained the Williamses' remains and penetrated the areas where the couple's chest cavities once lay. Eventually it had completely absorbed both of the bodies. Curiously, the spreading and branching roots, which were preserved and moved to the Rhode Island Historical Society, had taken on a strong resemblance to the circulatory system of the human body.

It soon became obvious that all who had chomped down on the tree's delicious red apples had inadvertently eaten one of America's most famous colonial figures and his wife.

Eyewitnesses to Life after Death

Thanks to the miracles of modern medicine, more and more people are surviving heart attacks and accidents—and living to tell what it's like to die and visit "the other side."

A group of cardiologists from Denver, Colorado, studied twenty-three hundred heart patients who had been revived after facing clinical death. The doctors' 1980 report concluded that 60 percent of these people had remarkably similar stories to tell: They described visits to a place of beautiful light, where they were met by friends and family members who had died.

According to these researchers and others, the tales rarely vary in substance, although not all the details are the same. The clinically dead frequently find themselves at the site of their deaths—an accident scene or hospital room, for example. Aware they are dying, they feel themselves separate from their physical forms, and they begin to move through the power of thought alone. They may watch people work frantically over their unconscious bodies until, finally, they are pulled into a dark tunnel and toward a point of light.

When they reach the light, they find themselves in an exquisitely beautiful outdoor scene and are overwhelmed by feelings of peace. Family and friends who have died before them usually stand behind a barrier like a body of water, either beckoning the clinically dead to come to them or telling them to return.

Finally, the newly "dead" are once again plunged into inky darkness before they are faced with what near-death-experience researcher James Graves calls "a dazzling pillar of light that overwhelms them with joy. They say the being of light does not identify itself, but you see your whole life in front of you and it asks: 'What have you done with the life I've given you?' "

According to Graves, who started collecting reports of these experiences when he was a psychology instructor at Muskegon Community College in Michigan in the 1960s, many people don't want to return to life. They say the light gives them the greatest happiness they've ever known. "It is the last stage," Graves comments. "Any farther, they don't come back."

Not all near-death experiences are so pleasant, however. Researchers have found that some people go through the tunnel of darkness only to find themselves imprisoned in a gray atmosphere full of anger and depression. They go in circles with other people trapped in despair.

The experiences of the clinically dead who have returned to life have been dismissed by some as simply the result of drugs or lack of oxygen to the brain. That doesn't explain, however, numerous examples of near-death experiences that seem to prove the "dead" person was indeed hovering above his lifeless body.

For example, a patient's heart stopped beating during surgery at a Muskegon, Michigan, hospital. When he was revived, the man was able to give the name of the pharmacist who had supplied a frantic nurse with the medicine needed to save his life. While his eyes were closed and he was in cardiac arrest in an operating room, the patient insisted he had been in the corridor with the nurse as she raced into the hospital pharmacy. "I'd always trusted you," the man later told the nurse, "so when I saw you leave the room I followed you."

Monster Turtles

When most people think of sea monsters, they usually envision something akin to a dinosaur or serpent. But there's another type of sea monster that's been sighted repeatedly in the oceans of the world—gigantic turtles.

As he traveled near the southeast tip of Spain in 1484, Christopher Columbus spotted one of the huge creatures. It was, he reported, "a repulsive sea monster big as a medium-sized whale, with a carapace like a turtle's, a horrible head like a barrel, and two wings."

Nearly five hundred years later, in October 1937, a Cuban fisherman caught a monster-sized turtle. Over thirteen feet long and weighing several hundred pounds, the reptile was estimated by zoologists to be at least five hundred years old.

In March 1955, a man stranded on a raft off the Columbian shore without anything to eat or drink for ten days spotted a similar creature that measured about four meters from head to tail. According to a newspaper account written by Nobel prize–winner Gabriel García Márquez, the man "saw a giant yellow turtle with a tigered head and fixed dumb eyes that resembled two giant balls of glass."

A Miami fisherman named Bruce Mournier claims that while swimming underwater off the Bahamas, he met a giant turtle face-to-face. Mournier says the beast weighed about two hundred pounds and "had a monkey's face with its head protruding out in front. And it rotated its neck like a snake."

If monster-sized turtles are real, where do they originate? The creatures have already been sighted in the Caribbean, near Canada, and off the European coast. All three areas have one thing in common: They lie in the route of the Gulf Stream. The Gulf Stream, then, could prove to be the natural habitat and breeding ground of the giant beasts.

The Number of the Beast

Signs carried by protesters are now a normal occurrence in most parts of the world, but a sign seen in Athens in 1986 suggested something more unusual than concern over politics and international issues. The occasion was a public protest over the distribution of new identity cards. Protesters were urging popular rejection not of the cards but of the bar code number keyed to it, which was 666. To anyone familiar with the last book of the Bible—Revelation—666 represents the "Beast" or the "Antichrist" and suggests the work of Satan.

According to Orthodox Archbishop Afxentios of Athens, the number was placed there by "dark forces" inimical to the Christian religion. Several thousand people carried signs saying "No to 666!" showing that public awareness of Satan's war on true believers is still alive in that ancient city.

In any case, the identification in the Bible is specific:

Revelation 13:18—"Here is wisdom. Let him that hath understanding count the number of the beast: for it is the number of a man; and his number is six hundred threescore and six."

The Final Curtain Call

In November 1986, the actress Edith Webster gave her final performance in Baltimore of the play *The Drunkard*. Her role, which she had successfully played over a period of eight years, was that of an elderly grandmother. As part of the script directions, she would sing the song "Please Don't Talk About Me When I'm Gone" and collapse on the stage. But during her final performance, as she was being loudly applauded by the audience, she actually died, and the audience thought it was part of the play, even during the loud cries for a doctor. It took some time before they realized that the death was not feigned but real. Then the applause stopped and most of the audience joined in prayer.

The Eyes Have It

Monsters with multiple eyes may sound like pure fantasy. But strange cases of misplaced eyes have been well documented—and some are even more bizarre than any myth.

In the 1854 edition of the *Boston Medical Journal*, for instance, an English authority related the case of a four-eyed man from Cricklade. The patient sported a double pair of eyes, one pair positioned over the other. "He could shut any eye independently in its orbit or could turn them to look in different directions, which was most distracting to the onlooker," the journal noted, adding that the four-eyed man was strange in other ways as well. For instance, according to the author of the paper, he sang "in a screeching voice to which I could not listen without disgust."

A man named Edward Mordrake, a member of the British aristocracy, also had four eyes, but his extra pair sat on the back of his head. And they were accompanied by an extra nose, lips, and ears. Mordrake's extra face could laugh and cry and its eyes could see, but it never ate or spoke. Instead, it stared and drooled. Mordrake eventually became insane and died a lunatic.

Science has recorded the existence of a real, one-eyed Cyclops as well. The man, who lived for years in the backwoods of rural Mississippi, possessed a normal-sized eye right in the middle of his forehead. He was frequently offered jobs in sideshows and circuses but chose not to exploit his odd deformity—and he gave a menacing one-eyed stare to anyone who tried to convince him to do otherwise.

Pearl Harbor Warning

The message scrawled in paint on the sidewalk in front of the public grade school in Owensville, Indiana, was, townsfolk thought, an aggravating bit of vandalism. But what did the cryptic message mean? The huge letters spelled out: "Remember Pearl Harbor!"

The citizens talked about the writing that winter morning in December 1939. What did "Pearl Harbor" mean? They never figured out who painted the words, or why. It seemed just a prank or some mindless vandalism, and the incident was forgotten—until the Japanese bombed Pearl Harbor on the exact day, two years later.

The Face in the Pail

Not all portraits are painted by artists. Sometimes unexplained likenesses of people show up in unusual places without any apparent help from human hands. In 1948, in Northamptonshire, England, a portrait mysteriously appeared in a milk bucket.

Mrs. Margaret Leatherland was milking her cows when she was surprised to see a face smiling up at her from the inside of a shiny pail. The image, which sat just above the milk line, was a portrait of her famous circus entrepreneur brother, Sir Robert Fossett.

Mrs. Leatherland summoned her family to see the strange image, and they too recognized it as a picture of Sir Robert. The subject of the eerie portrait never saw it, however. A few weeks after the face appeared in the pail, he died.

Mrs. Leatherland was determined to scour the picture out of her milk pail, but strong solutions of soda and even acids didn't work.

Sometimes the picture seemed to grow dimmer, but it soon came back just as clear as ever.

The story of the strange face in the pail soon spread. A newspaper published a verified photo of the inside of the milk bucket and the Northampton Society for Psychical Research sent a representative to study the phenomenon. He also saw the picture of Sir Robert inside the pail and went away baffled.

As for Mrs. Leatherland, she eventually became so upset she reportedly disposed of the pail. And with good reason. Every time she filled the bucket, she would look inside to see her dead brother's face drowning in milk.

Frog Survival

According to a report in the February 2, 1958, *Salt Lake City Desert News*, four uranium miners were digging for ore in a Utah mine when they made an incredible find. The workers— Charles North, his son Charles, Jr., Ted McFarland, and Tom North—had hacked through eight feet of sandstone until they reached a fossilized tree stuck in the middle of a bed of uranium. In order to get to the ore, they had to blast the tree out of the way.

The explosion opened up a hole in the stony trunk where a tiny frog sat. The creature was grayish brown and appeared shriveled. It had long, unwebbed toes and suction cups growing out of its tiny fingers. The way the rounded hole was shaped showed that the amphibian had once completely filled the cavity—but, through the eons, it had apparently shrunk to a third of its usual size.

The miners reported that the animal was, incredibly, still alive. It appeared to have somehow survived stuck in the fossilized tree through countless epochs. But twenty-eight hours after being released into the twentieth century, it died.

The Unexplained Portrait

English artist Margaret Moyat woke up on a June morning in 1953 after a strange dream. There was something unusually vivid about the images she had seen in her reverie. An elderly man, whom she didn't recognize, had appeared before her. He smiled, and she assumed he was waiting for her to paint his portrait.

The artist couldn't get the vision out of her mind. In fact, she seemed compelled to paint the old man's picture. The portrait, which showed a striking figure with light blue eyes and a snow-white beard, was completed in just two days.

A few weeks later, two women who had once lived in Eythorne for over thirty years came to visit Miss Moyat. Glancing over at the portrait based on a dream, the two ladies gasped. It was, without a doubt, they told the artist, a portrait of a Mr. Hughes—a minister who had lived in Eythorne and who had been dead for twenty-five years.

Other longtime citizens of the town confirmed that the painting clearly depicted Hughes. But just how Miss Moyat came to paint his portrait remains unexplained—the artist had only lived in Eythorne for two years and had never even heard of the Reverend Hughes until *after* she captured his likeness on canvas.

The Footprints on the Tombstone

Salem, Massachusetts, wasn't the only place that became caught up in witch hunting. Bucksport, Maine, also joined in the frenzy, thanks in large part to the founder of the town, Colonel Jonathan Buck—a cruel man who persecuted one old lady as a witch simply because she had a strong chin and eccentric ways.

The woman insisted she was innocent, but Buck countered that she worked for the Devil and ordered her tortured until she changed her story. The woman, despite hours of pain, still refused to confess. The colonel finally ordered her execution.

As she breathed for the last time, the elderly lady cursed Buck. When the colonel died, she warned, evidence would appear to show he had murdered an innocent woman—her footprint would be found on his tombstone.

Clearly concerned about the woman's prediction, Buck left instructions at the time of his death that his tombstone should be "unblemished and without flaws." Honoring his wishes, his relatives placed a huge, snowy white stone monument over his grave.

But soon both the local sexton and the town's minister noted that an image had appeared on the gravestone. Day by day it became more distinct—a woman's footprint. Buck's family immediately had a stonemason scrape it away. After a few weeks, however, the footprint reappeared.

Buck's grave was drawing throngs of curiosity seekers, so his heirs removed his tombstone and replaced it. But soon the new stone too was emblazoned with the outline of a woman's foot—a legacy that seemed to prove that the murdered old lady had carried out her threat.

The Extra Coffin

Henry and Harry Kalabany of Westport, Connecticut, were digging around their family burial plot in Green Farms Congregational Church Cemetery in September 1956 when one of their shovels hit something unexpected. They had struck a coffin in an area of the burial plot where no member of the family had ever been laid to rest.

Curious about this stranger in their family gravesite, the brothers opened the expensive-looking casket. Inside was the body of a ruddy cheeked gentleman they had never seen before. He appeared to be between forty-five and fifty years old and was dressed in a fine blue suit. The Kalabany brothers had to rebury the coffin; since the man couldn't be identified they couldn't get a permit to move his body. Then they set out to discover who the man was and why he was buried in their family plot.

Finally, the following spring, the local police agreed to help the brothers. Once again, the mysterious out-of-place coffin was dug up. But this time, there was no wealthy-looking, preserved body inside. Instead, all that was found was the skeleton of a man who had been dead at least half a century.

Although the brothers argued that this was not the body they had seen, the police reburied the body where it had been found and closed their investigation of the case.

The Kalabanys never learned the identity of the man they had originally seen. Could he have been a murder victim, later moved and replaced by the disintegrated corpse? Or did the body they found rapidly turn to dust after they opened the coffin? Or could Harry and Henry Kalabany have somehow seen the skeleton as it had appeared in life?

An Ancient Giant

In July 1877, four prospectors moved along the hills of Spring Valley near Eureka, Nevada. They cracked open pieces of rock, looking for outcroppings of precious metal. One of the group spotted something sticking out of a ledge of rock nearby and he climbed up to make out the object's identity. What he found wasn't gold ore, though; instead it was evidence of an ancient giant.

Using their picks, the prospectors soon chipped out human leg and foot bones that had been encased in solid quartzite. The black bones, which had been broken off just above the knee, included the knee joint, kneecap, lower leg bones, and a complete set of foot bones. The man who had once walked on this leg was obviously huge—from knee to heel, the bone was thirty-nine inches long.

The men quickly took their find to Eureka, where it was examined by local physicians. The doctors ruled that the bones were human, and extremely old. After the Eureka newspaper wrote articles about the gigantic leg bone, several museums sent archaeologists to look for the rest of the remarkable man's skeleton—but not another trace of the ancient giant was ever found.

The Pilots Who Walked Off the Face of the Earth

Both temperatures and tempers were blazing in the summer of 1924 in the Middle Eastern desert. In the area then known as Mesopotamia, the Arabs were fighting and the British were trying to keep a handle on the situation. On July 24, Flight Lieutenant W. T. Day and Pilot Officer D. R. Stewart took off in their single-engine plane for a routine, four-hour-long reconnaissance flight over the area.

When the fliers failed to return, a search party was sent out after them. The next day their plane was found—in perfect condition. The craft had not been shot down. Moreover, gasoline was in the tank and the engine turned over as soon as it was started. But where were Day and Stewart? And why did they land in an area of barren desert?

Looking for clues, the search party noted boot marks where the officers had jumped out of the plane. Their footprints showed that the men had left the plane and walked along, side by side, for about 120 feet. Then, while still standing next to each other, the men simply stopped—and vanished.

A half dozen patrols of desert tribesmen, soldiers in armored trucks, and search planes never turned up a trace of the pilots, who seemed to have walked off the face of the earth.

Mystery at Sea

It was a clear, quiet night on October 28, 1902, as the steamship *Fort Salisbury* moved through the Gulf of Guinea off the west coast of Africa, heading for the equator. Knowing he had a well-built ship and a trustworthy crew, the ship's captain went to bed and drifted off into a peaceful sleep. The night seemed to be totally ordinary and uneventful. But suddenly, at five minutes past three, the lookout shouted a frantic alarm.

Dead ahead of the *Fort Salisbury*, where nothing was supposed to be, was a huge, round object.

A. H. Raymer, the second officer, rushed on deck and ordered the searchlight to be turned on the thing in their path. It revealed a metallic structure with two small orange-red lights at one end and two blue-green lights near the other. The crew described it as similar to a tremendous airship made out of metal plates. From inside the thing came noises that sounded like machinery working, as well as unintelligible, excited babbling.

As the captain and his men watched the strange object slowly sink beneath the waves, they shouted offers of help. But there was no answer as the giant metal disc slipped out of their sight forever.

A Paranormal Rescue

A religious man, Howard Wheeler was on his knees in prayer in his Charlotte, North Carolina, home about one o'clock Sunday morning on June 10, 1962, when he suddenly stood upright. "I heard an automobile wreck!" he announced to his startled wife, Pat. "I'll be right back!"

Wheeler raced out of his house and jumped into his car. Then he stopped to think for a few seconds. All he had heard was a kind of distant rumble. Where was he going, and why?

Although his neighborhood was crisscrossed with streets, something seemed to guide Howard down Park Road. When he reached Woodlawn, he turned right, down a hill to a shrimp boat. There was no wreck in sight. Then he felt strongly that he should turn around and get back to Montford Drive as fast as he could.

"He went about two hundred yards on Montford, around a curve," the *Charlotte News* reported, "and there was a car smashed against a pole—the engine driven back into the car. He saw no one . . . but a voice said: 'Help me, Humpy, help me!' "

Wheeler soon found an old friend, Joe Funderburke, who had always called him Humpy, trapped in the wreckage. Although Funderburke was badly injured, Wheeler was able to free him from the twisted metal and take him to a hospital. Emergency surgery saved Funderburke's life.

Howard Wheeler could never explain how he heard a car accident happen a half mile from his house, nor how he found it—forty-five minutes before the police or any other passersby discovered the wreck.

Cinque

One of the main participants in the San Francisco kidnapping of Patty Hearst in 1974 had adopted the name Cinque. The original Cinque, who led a slave mutiny on a sailing ship, became famous in the later years of the "Middle Passage," the importation by sea of African slaves.

Cinque, a Mende tribesman captured in 1839 in what is now Sierra Leone, was shipped with others to Cuba, but the slave ship was stopped en route by a British antislavery patrol and sent back to Africa under escort. Once back in Sierra Leone, however, the persistent slavers shipped Cinque and fifty other slaves out again, aboard the bark *Amistad*, its destination Cuba.

When a cook on board, also a Mende tribesman, told the slaves that they were to be killed and their bodies salted for later eating, Cinque decided it was time to act. With a nail, he jimmied the locks of his manacles and those of the other slaves. He found some long knives, and after killing some of the slavers and keeping the others as pilots for the voyage back to Africa, he assumed control of the *Amistad*.

The Africans knew how to plot directions by following the sun but could not orient themselves by the stars. Therefore the captive Spanish pilots steered toward Africa by day but toward Cuba or the southern United States by night. In effect they veered northeast, and when they finally landed, they were on the north shore of Long Island, New York, near Montauk Point. Cinque and others went ashore to look for provisions and brought back dogs and gin. But they were followed by the United States Coast Guard, which had been alerted by duck hunters.

The ship was impounded and the slaves were sent to prison, first in New London and then in New Haven during the subsequent trial.

The affair aroused abolitionists, who formed a "Committee for the Defense of the Africans of the *Amistad*" that included former President John Quincy Adams, Emerson, and Garrison. The committee was immediately opposed by Southerners, who claimed it was interfering with due process.

President Martin Van Buren was alternately petitioned and pressured by abolitionists, slave interests, Queen Victoria through the British ambassador, and the Spanish government. Van Buren decided for neutrality and did not issue an executive order for the slaves' return. Meanwhile the Africans were aided by students from the Yale Divinity School and other sympathizers.

The case went to the Supreme Court. Former President Adams made a plea a hundred thousand words long, including the statement that the slaves "must be considered as free born human beings" and "be discharged at once."

In 1842 the presiding judge ruled that the captives be returned to Africa and establish a Christian mission in Sierra Leone, a project paid for through collections at public appearances and lectures. (They had been taught English since 1839 by Yale students.)

Cinque returned to Africa with the other slaves, but he did not stay long at the mission. He went back to the forest from where there were reports that he had become engaged in the local slave trade on his own.

The *Lusitania* Nightmare

When lecturer I. B. S. Holbourne left the United States in the spring of 1915 after a highly successful lecture tour, he booked passage home to Great Britain on the huge Cunard ocean liner, the *Lusitania*. There was no way for him to know he would soon witness the vessel's violent destruction. But, somehow, on the other side of the ocean, his wife was able to "see" what lay in store for her husband.

Marion Holbourne woke up on May 7, 1915, in an easy chair in her home's library where she had been taking a nap. While asleep, she had experienced a detailed nightmare. She saw a large liner in terrible trouble. The ship was listing badly and lifeboats were being prepared for launching. Although there was no panic, people were very agitated.

In her dream, Mrs. Holbourne appeared on the upper deck as she watched the ship sink beneath her. A young ship's officer approached her, and she asked if her husband was aboard. The officer answered that the professor had already escaped from the ship in a lifeboat.

On awakening, Mrs. Holbourne told her family about the disturbing dream. They laughed at her and dismissed her vision as "just another nightmare."

Later that day, no one was laughing. The news that the *Lusitania* had been attacked and sunk by a German submarine off the Irish coast soon reached England. Many had lost their lives.

But Professor Holbourne, the family was told, had been saved. After helping other people into lifeboats, he had been ordered to leave the ship himself. When he finally arrived home, he was able to confirm that his wife's dream of the *Lusitania* disaster was accurate—including her description of the young man she talked to. The professor remembered him as being the officer who had ordered him into a lifeboat, saving his life.

Auroras at the Surface of the Earth

During the winter of 1917–1918, according to a 1931 issue of *Nature*, workers at a government radio station in the Arctic "were enveloped in a light mist or foglike substance." Their extended hands seemed to be surrounded by a colored fog, and "a kaleidoscope of colors was visible between the hand and the body." Perhaps most surprising, though, was that there was no apparent dampness in this fog or mist. Stooping down, moreover, they could see under it since it hung just four feet from the ground.

Many explorers have told tales of just such ethereal fog, attributing the phenomenon to auroras—the streamers of light created by electrical charges in the sky. Scientists have refuted this explanation, declaring that auroras never descend lower than fifty kilometers and are usually hundreds of miles above the surface.

Reports of low auroras, nonetheless, persist. Floyd C. Kelley observed such a phenomenon in Hartford, Connecticut, where he was attending Trinity College. "The light effects gave me the impression that the atmosphere was filled with fog and someone was illuminating it by playing a searchlight back and forth," he wrote in a 1934 issue of *Nature*. He also heard "swishing sounds" timed to the flickering of the aurora light.

Lightning Pranks

It's sometimes hard to explain the behavior of lightning. In 1891, for example, the Royal Meteorological Society's quarterly journal reported an incident in which a lightning bolt wrecked a County Mayo, Ireland, kitchen. "All objects of glass or china in the room were upset, but only a few of them were broken; a corner was cut clear off a glass ink bottle, without spilling the ink. The most extraordinary occurrence was what happened to a basket of eggs lying on the floor of the room. The shells were shattered so that they fell off when the eggs were put in boiling water, but the inner membranes were not broken."

An 1886 issue of *Nature* reported lightning's effect on a window in Germany during a particularly violent thunderstorm. Lightning apparently broke a hole—the size of a bullet—in the lower pane. A jet of water shot upward through the opening, striking the ceiling, part of which fell and broke a small table below.

More recently, in Scotland, lightning also drilled a circle in a windowpane at the University of Edinburgh's Meteorological Department. According to a 1973 issue of the journal *Weather*, the missing glass disc was found, intact, inside the room.

The Steamship That Cruised Beside a UFO

There is a curious entry in the logbook of the captain of the *Llandovery Castle*—it tells of how, on the night of July 1, 1947, the steamship cruised briefly through the Straits of Madagascar with a UFO.

It was about 11:00 P.M. when some of the passengers first noted a bright light traveling overhead. As the light passed over the ship, it lost altitude and speed and began to descend within fifty feet of the water. The light was cast downwards at first, creating a search beam that reflected off the water. But then the light went out, and the passengers and crew could see the object beside them.

The witnesses described the craft as gigantic (at least one thousand feet long), cylindrical, and metallic. Some said it was shaped like a mammoth steel cigar with its end clipped. About five times as long as it was wide, the thing had no visible windows or portholes. But because the mysterious craft matched the speed of the *Llandovery Castle* exactly, the crew deduced that something intelligent must be guiding it.

After cruising beside the *Llandovery Castle* for about a minute, the enormous object rose silently. When it was about a thousand feet in the air, it emitted streams of orange flames and shot upwards, disappearing into the night skies.

The Day UFOs Visited Hawaii

Unidentified flying objects have been in the news, off and on, since the late 1940s. At first, researchers could find no patterns to their appearances. Later, "flying saucers" seemed to show up most often in the Northern Hemisphere in the spring and summer months. The rest of the year they were more likely to visit the southern half of the world.

In the early sixties, another pattern emerged—UFOs popped up again and again at satellite launchings and atomic bomb tests. They also seemed to be curious about other aspects of human technology. For example, Captain Joe Walker spotted and photographed strange objects that followed him as he made a test flight in the rocket plane X-15, soaring thousands of miles an hour, high in the sky.

While many of these reported UFOs were only seen by one or two people, an incident on March 11, 1963, involved hundreds—and maybe even thousands—of eyewitnesses. A circular, glowing object followed by a hazy white light soared through the sky for five or six minutes over the island of Hawaii.

Among the people who saw the strange craft were two Hawaiian National Guard pilots who reported spying it from their jets as they flew at a forty-thousand-foot altitude. Lieutenant George Joy noted that the unidentified object had a glowing vapor trail. A Federal Aviation Authority spokesman told newspaper reporters that he and co-workers had also spotted the thing.

Whatever the UFO was, it was clearly not a satellite. And meteors and missiles wouldn't have hovered in the sky for several minutes while hundreds watched. So the case of the UFO that visited Hawaii remains one more unexplained sighting of unknown aerial craft.

Suicide Dream

Mrs. Bertha Stone, a farmer's wife who lived in Jefferson County, Indiana, took a nap each afternoon. On June 10, 1951, she woke up from her customary snooze with a horrible dream on her mind.

She had envisioned herself at one end of a massive bridge, in a city she had never seen before. A middle-aged woman dressed in black, whom she did not recognize, came up to Mrs. Stone and told her: "I came to Abilene to jump in the river."

While Mrs. Stone watched in horror, unable to stop the suicide, the woman climbed over the bridge's railing and jumped off.

The nightmare seemed so real that Mrs. Stone decided to pursue it. Had a woman actually killed herself by leaping from a bridge in Abilene? But which Abilene?

Mrs. Stone wrote letters to the police departments of both Abilene, Kansas, and Abilene, Texas, asking if anyone had committed suicide on the day of her dream.

The Kansas police answered no to her query. But Texas officials wrote that a woman had registered under the name of Ruth Brown at the Wooten Hotel and asked how to get to the nearest river. Then she walked to the nearby bridge and leaped to her death.

The suicide victim was never identified—the name and address she gave at the hotel were fake and her clothing offered no identifying marks. Nor did Bertha Stone ever learn how or why she "saw" in a dream the tragic death as it happened a thousand miles away.

Pint-Sized Aliens

On November 28, 1954, two terrified men burst through the doors of the police station in Caracas, Venezuela. The story they related sounded so farfetched that they were immediately dismissed as drunks. But when medical tests showed they were cold sober—and suffering from shock—it was obvious that something very real and very extraordinary had happened to Gustavo Gonzales and José Ponce.

According to their sworn testimonies, the two men left Caracas in a truck around 2:00 A.M. They were headed for Petare, a town about twenty minutes down the road. Halfway there they found a glowing, curved object blocking the highway.

The craft was floating about five feet above the road and Ponce and Gonzales decided to take a closer look. As they approached the object, a small, dark, hairy, manlike creature clad only in a loincloth came toward them. Gonzales quickly grabbed him and was surprised that the "man" weighed very little, probably about thirty-five pounds. But touching the creature proved to be dangerous.

Immediately, Gonzales was thrown about fifteen feet. Ponce turned and fled toward the police station. As he glanced back, he saw two other small humanoids running toward their luminous ship holding vegetation in their hands.

The tale could not be easily forgotten by the police because it was quickly corroborated by an independent, reliable source. Two days after the men encountered the strange creatures, one of the physicians who had examined them came forward. Although he was hesitant to talk at first because he did not want to be associated with such a strange event, he finally admitted that while driving home from an emergency call he'd witnessed the entire episode. It had happened, he said, just as Gonzales and Ponce had said—UFO, hairy pint-sized alien, and all.

The Nevada UFO Crash

On April 18, 1962, reports came in that a red object had been seen in the skies over Oneida, New York, heading west. Although radar picked up the thing, it could not be identified, so when it went as far as the Midwest, the Air Defense Command scrambled jets from Phoenix to intercept the UFO.

But when the object was about seventy miles northwest of Las Vegas, it disappeared from radar screens. According to the *Las Vegas Sun*, the only newspaper that investigated the tale, the UFO may have exploded over Nevada. At about the same time the object vanished from radar screens, the paper pointed out, an explosion took place somewhere above the Mesquite Range—the blast was so powerful that the streets of Reno became as bright as day. Although many people chalked the brilliant flash up to an atomic bomb test, the Atomic Energy Commission denied that any nuclear tests were underway in the United States at that time.

A few hours later, another strange scenario that may or may not be related was reported by the United Press Service. A huge object had been spotted landing near a Eureka, Utah, electric power station. Once again, *Las Vegas Sun* reporters checked out the story, and, when they questioned a Stead Air Force Base official in Reno, they were told that the landing had occurred. The spokesman, who requested anonymity, also commented that the "impact" of the UFO's landing had knocked the power station out of order.

Curiously, few Americans ever heard about the strange objects that rocked the Southwest that spring evening—only the *Las Vegas Sun* and a couple of regional papers ever printed the news that a "flying saucer" had apparently crashed on Earth.

Biblical Archaeological Hints

Carefully studying literal translations of the Bible isn't just a pastime of the clergy. Archaeologists and geologists contend that activity has helped them find invaluable, hidden loot.

While no one had found evidence that King Solomon had mined copper, Dr. Nelson Glueck, president of Hebrew Union College, suspected that Solomon traded copper with ancient Persian kings. His belief was bolstered by this line in the Book of Deuteronomy: "out of . . . hills thou canst dig copper." But where were the copper mines located?

Glueck used planes to take color photographs of areas around a recently discovered seaport used by King Solomon. Then ground parties searched for long-abandoned water holes. Putting together his evidence, Glueck found the ancient copper mines of King Solomon in the region now known as Wadi el Arabah. He also discovered veins of copper that today, thousands of years later, are back in production.

Another scientist aided by the Bible was Dr. James Pritchard of the University of Pennsylvania Museum, who had long wondered about the pool of Gideon mentioned in the holy Book. After studying the scriptural references, he and fellow researchers located the pool, about eight miles north of Jerusalem. They discovered that when the armies of Nebuchadnezzar had invaded in 587 B.C., the conquerors stopped up the well with tons of debris and its location was soon forgotten. But Pritchard used the Bible's clues to uncover it—and today the pool of Gideon flows again, a blessing for the water-starved Holy Land.

Is this true?

The Restless Coffins in the Buxhoewden Chapel

In the Baltic Sea sits the tiny, rocky island of Oesel. The island's only town, Arensburg, contains many private chapels built by the wealthy few.

When a relative dies, one Arensburg custom is to keep the body in a weighty oak coffin in the chapel for a time. Then it is moved to an adjoining vault. But a mysterious force refused to allow the bodies lying in a chapel owned by the Buxhoewden family to rest in peace. Instead, unseen hands repeatedly tossed the heavy oak caskets around as if they were toys.

The strange happenings began on June 22, 1844, when Mrs. Dalmann visited the grave of her mother. Her horse, which was tied to a post near the Buxhoewden chapel, soon became so excited and heavily lathered that a veterinarian had to be called. Then, a few days later, other people who hitched their horses outside the Buxhoewden chapel returned from church services to find their animals in a similar state. But what could have produced such panic?

Members of the Buxhoewden family decided to inspect their chapel and vault to quash rumors that the place was somehow connected with the horses' attacks of fear. But as soon as the door was opened, it was clear something bizarre *had* gone on there—coffins had been piled in the center of the floor.

The Buxhoewdens put the unopened caskets back in place, locked the chapel door, and then poured lead into the seals to make sure no one could enter and wreak havoc with their relatives' remains again.

Not long afterward, however, eleven horses left in front of the Buxhoewden chapel for a short while became so panic-stricken that three did not survive the incident.

Once again, the chapel was opened. And once again, somehow, the coffins had been thrown in the center of the floor. Some were upside down, and one looked as though it had crashed down from above.

Again the Buxhoewden family put the coffins back where they were supposed to be, locked and sealed the door—and waited. A church court decided to investigate the matter and its representative, Baron De Guldenstubbe, visited the family vault. After the seals were broken and the door unlocked, he entered to find, as before, coffins thrown into the middle of the room.

To make sure the mysterious intruder who was moving the coffins wasn't using a secret tunnel or passageway, the investigators dug up the floor of the vault and made a trench around it. They found nothing.

Then they sprinkled ashes over the chapel's steps and the vault's floor so the intruder would have to leave footprints. Again, the door was locked and sealed and two armed guards were posted outside.

Although the guards never heard or saw any intruders and the ashes were not disturbed, when church representatives once again inspected the crypt they found the coffins moved from the opposite end of the vault where they were supposed to be. Some were standing on end.

Why the coffins were so restless in the family chapel remains unknown. Baffled and tired of the mysterious goings-on, the Buxhoewdens finally removed their ancestors remains and buried them elsewhere.

Dream of a Coming Accident

Winnie Wilkinson of Sheffield, England, could almost never nap in the middle of the day. But one afternoon in the summer of 1962 she found herself drifting off to sleep—and soon experienced a most disturbing dream.

As she later told the police, she dreamed there was a heavy knocking at her front door. When she opened it, she came face-to-face with a woman she had never seen before. The stranger excitedly told Mrs. Wilkinson that her estranged husband had been terribly injured. He had fallen off a scaffold, the dream visitor said, and his wife was to come at once.

Although she was considering divorcing Gordon, Winnie was upset at the thought he might be hurt in any way. So when she woke up she noted the time, 3:12 P.M., and hurriedly called his workplace to make sure he was all right.

Gordon Wilkinson was fine, his employers assured his wife. But the next day, at exactly 3:12 P.M., he was dead—killed when he plunged from a scaffold.

The Sleepy Murderer

While vacationing in Le Havre, French detective Robert Ledru offered to help local police solve the murder of André Monet. A small businessman with few friends but no known enemies, Monet was shot and killed on a nearby beach while apparently out for a midnight swim. There seemed to be no motive and there were only two clues. One was that the bullet had been fired from a Luger, a very common make of gun—even Ledru had one. The other was footprints in the sand, of little value since the perpetrator had taken his shoes off and walked the beach in his stockinged feet.

Examining one of the footprints closely, however, Ledru was suddenly horrified. The murderer lacked a toe on his right foot— just like Ledru himself. He made a print of his own stockinged foot next to the murderer's. He obtained the bullet removed from the victim, went home and shot his own Luger into a pillow, and compared the two bullets. He then reported to his superiors in Paris.

According to the *Encyclopedia of Aberrations, A Psychiatric Handbook*, even the police chief could not deny the evidence. Ledru, who always slept with his socks on, had awakened on the morning after the murder to find his socks inexplicably wet. It was clear that Ledru had murdered Monet while walking in his sleep.

The Calendar Twins

The term *idiot savant* describes an individual who has subnormal intelligence yet possesses an exceptional skill. According to some experts, the idiot savant, rendered important by a particular talent, will often concentrate on it, repeatedly demonstrating his ability and, therefore, improving with practice.

But according to the *American Journal of Psychiatry*, identical twins George and Charles contradicted this idea. The pair had an uncanny acuity for dates. They could recall almost any day and accurately report that date's weather. George, moreover, showed an even more remarkable talent: Although Charles was completely accurate only for twentieth-century dates, George could identify dates in previous centuries. With equal facility, the twins could also identify February 15, 2002, as a Friday or August 28, 1591, as a Wednesday, again George more accurately than Charles. And even though they didn't know the difference between the Julian and the Gregorian calendars, when they identified dates before 1582 (when the change in calendars occurred), they invariably accounted for the ten-day difference. The ability is even more impressive considering the fact that they couldn't add, subtract, multiply, or divide numbers.

Memory, learning, and recall were not abilities available to the twins. They operated, moreover, beyond the usual two hundred-to four hundred-year perpetual calendar, and in fact, could reach beyond the year 7000. While motivational factors may play a part in developing a skill, this alone can't explain the basic skill itself.

A Prince Sees the Flying Dutchman

The legend of the "Flying Dutchman," the ship captain who cursed God and as punishment was condemned to sail a phantom ship eternally over the oceans, has been immortalized in seamen's tales as well as in one of Wagner's operas.

It has often been reported sighted in storms or in fogs. Other sailing ships, drifting and unmanned, have been called "Flying Dutchmen." Encountering the *Flying Dutchman*, in the lore of the sea, has been interpreted as a warning of impending disaster.

An unusual sighting was made aboard the British warship HMS *Inconstant*, sailing the Pacific Ocean on July 11, 1861. In the *Inconstant*'s log of that date, the following entry occurs:

At 4 A.M. "The Flying Dutchman" crossed our bows. She emitted a strange phosphorescent light as of a phantom ship all aglow, in the midst of which light the masts, spars, and sails of a brig 200 yards distant stood out in strong relief as she came up on the port bow where also the officer of the watch from the bridge saw her, as did also the quarter-deck midshipman, who was sent forward at once to the forecastle, but on arriving there no vestige nor any sign whatever of any material ship was to be seen either near or right away to the horizon, the night being clear and the sea calm.

This ghost ship report is different from others because of the identity of the midshipman who wrote it. He was a British prince, doing his tour, as was the custom, in the Royal Navy. He was also later to become George V, the king emperor of the British Empire.

A Time to Keep Silent

During a war it is sometimes difficult and dangerous to admit that an event has helped immeasurably your own side.

Such a dilemma was posed by the disastrous bombing of Coventry, the British cathedral city, by German aircraft in the "blitz" against England in 1940. British Intelligence knew about the projected mass attack beforehand, having broken the German "Enigma" code at the beginning of World War II, but it could not permit even a suggestion that it could "read" secret German radio communication. Therefore, on Churchill's orders, only the usual antiaircraft and fighter plane resistance were able to rise to the defense of Coventry, instead of a mass riposte. The German attack on an unsuspecting target was successful, but the secret of Britain's possession of the key to "Enigma" was safe, to be later used with eminent success in the campaign against Rommel in North Africa and in other operations as well. At the crucial naval battle of Midway, American code translators were able to read Japanese coded communications as fast or even faster than the Japanese.

The top secret "Purple Code," a Japanese version of "Enigma," had been broken by United States cryptoanalysts before America's participation in World War II. During operations in the Pacific, an intercepted Japanese code message indicated when and where Admiral Yamamoto, commander-in-chief of the Japanese fleet, would make an inspection of the Solomon Islands' defenses. Armed with this information, United States Navy planes were able to find and shoot down Admiral Yamamoto's aircraft as well as the escort planes. Despite the propaganda value of this military coup, the operation was kept top secret to protect the United States' knowledge of the code.

Missing Links

To escape the taunts and jeers of the villagers in his Russian home, young Andrian fled into the woods. There he lived in a cave, learning to subsist on his own and eventually fathering his own children. At least two of which—a daughter who died in infancy and a son who survived and traveled with his father—resembled him.

According to a report in *Scientific American*, Andrian was an ape-man. Indeed, when exhibited at a medical seminar in Berlin in his fifties, Andrian had hair all over his body, his face, and his neck.

Andrian, moreover, was not the first human to resemble a missing link between modern man and his cousins on the ancestral family tree. Mexico's Julia Pastrana, for instance, suffered the humiliating fate of having animal-like fur and, according to *Science* magazine, died giving birth to a son who inherited the same trait.

The minds of such freaks, however, are not necessarily impaired or less than human. Discovered in Borneo, six-year-old Kra-o, for example, had thick, coarse hair that ran over her shoulders like a mane and down her back, and her resemblance to a gorilla was even more striking because of a flat nose that diagonally slanted toward her cheeks. She also had baggy cheeks in which she would store food, like apes. But, *Scientific American* said in another report, she learned English quickly and, soon after she was taken to Great Britain, was able to make herself understood.

According to experts, hair such as Kra-o's seems to develop from prenatal *lanugo* common to many mammals, but not modern humans. Among animals, the soft, downy hair gradually develops into fur or feathers. It appears that some genes of our prehistoric ancestors remain in the makeup of human DNA. At rare times, they can still assert themselves.

The Real Sleeping Beauty

On May 21, 1883, Marguerite Boyenval went into a cataleptic sleep induced by fear when the police arrived at her home. Her twenty-two-year-old body was as rigid as a corpse, the arms literally remained outstretched, in the position in which they were originally placed.

Though Boyenval was for the most part unaware of events around her, there were times when she vaguely heard what was said. After about five months, for instance, she suddenly opened her eyes briefly during a physical examination and spoke. "You are pinching me," she exclaimed.

Although she was artificially fed, her health began declining. Developing consumption, her body wasted away and Boyenval finally died in 1903—after a twenty-year-long sleep.

Sunspots and Business

Economist William Stanley Jevons believed that commercial crises were somehow related to the activity of astronomical orbs. To test that notion, his British colleague, economist John Maynard Keynes, decided to trace the history of commercial crises back almost to the beginning of the eighteenth century. Determining that business cycles seemed to occur at intervals of 10 to 11 years, Keynes was able to match economic crises to the cycle of solar spots, which become increasingly intense every 10.45 years.

Keynes, postulating an explanation for the mysterious connection, said, "Meteorological phenomena play a part in harvest fluctuations and harvest fluctuations play a part in the trade cycle. Jevons's ideas are not to be lightly dismissed."

Despite the coincidence of cyclical commercial crises and solar periods, however, the link was never proved.

Huge Slab of Ancient Glass

It wasn't until the mid-twentieth century that engineers and scientists successfully manufactured the largest glass object ever created—the two-hundred-inch reflecting mirror in the Hale Telescope at Mount Palomar. However, someone in Beth She'arim, an ancient center of Jewish learning in southwestern Galilee, managed to create a solid sheet of glass about half as heavy (8.8 tons) *thousands* of years ago.

The slab was discovered in 1956 when an ancient cistern next to some catacombs was being cleared out so that it could be turned into a museum. A bulldozer struck something huge, buried in the ground. It turned out to be a 3.40-meter-long, 1.95-meter-wide slab of solid glass. Since it was too large and heavy to be moved, it was left in the middle of what is now the museum.

The glass is opaque, because of eons of weathering, and filled with tiny crystals. When clean and wet, it appears purple with intermingled streaks of green and purple in one corner.

Researchers concluded that there was no possibility the slab could have been the result of a natural geological occurrence, nor could it be waste from the smelting of ore. Instead, it was documented as man-made—although how and why the giant piece of glass was created remains a mystery.

The Mystery Spheres of Costa Rica

Banana company workers hacked through the dense vegetation of a tropical forest in Costa Rica about fifty years ago, hoping to uncover land suitable for growing bananas. They not only found the rich soil they were looking for, but they also discovered something totally unexpected—a huge round stone about six feet in diameter.

As the workmen searched under nearby vines and brush, they found many more round stones. Some were only a few inches in diameter and weighed just a couple of pounds. But others were eight feet around and weighed more than sixteen tons. They were all so smooth and appeared so perfectly round that it took careful measuring to prove that they were not absolutely perfect spheres.

When the workmen reported their discovery they learned that few people in the area had ever seen the objects. No one—including scientists from all over the world who came to study the mysterious spheres—knew who made them, or why.

The balls were found to be made primarily of granite, although a few were made of limestone. Most were in groups of at least three, but as many as forty-five were found together. Some were inexplicably arranged in triangles and others in circles. Still others were placed in long straight rows pointing north and south, leading to speculation that some long-forgotten ancient people used them to keep track of the position of celestial bodies—in others words, a prehistoric planetarium.

Feline X-Ray Detectors

Biologists at the Veterans Administration Hospital in Long Beach, California, wondered whether cats could sense the presence of X rays. To find out, the researchers exposed the furry felines to five-second intervals of X-radiation. Using a five-millimeter-wide beam directed at specific areas, they found the greatest effect occurred when the radiation was aimed at the olfactory bulb behind the nasal and oral passages. Since directing the ray at the nose itself had little effect, they discarded the notion that the cats actually smelled the ozone created by X rays.

According to the report in *New Scientist*, however, the scientists stopped short of declaring the olfactory bulb responsible for cats' ability to sense the rays. When the olfactory bulb was removed, it turned out, the cats still retained some sensitivity to X rays, particularly when the amount of X rays increased.

There may, the scientists concluded, be more than one sensory receptor capable of detecting X rays. In fact, that possibility is supported by research showing that X-ray sensitivity is probably spread throughout the cat's body.

Mass Strandings of Marine Mammals

On the evening of August 19, 1971, three short-finned pilot whales were found stranded in less than three feet of water along the beach at Sarasota, Florida. Less than a mile away, another six whales were also caught in shallow water near the shoreline. All nine were able to rejoin their herd about 150 yards offshore only after local residents helped push the big creatures into deeper water. Then the herd slowly moved southward along the coast, traveling about 11 miles before more whales became stranded on the shore, again requiring human assistance to move back out to sea. At one point, however, the herd spread out—with some of the whales becoming stranded again—as it followed an aquarium exhibitor towing a young whale to shore. The rescue was repeated, but five days later, the whales were again stranded 160 miles away.

A number of theories, including those involving mass suicide and harassment by sharks, have attempted to explain such behavior among marine mammals. Many studying the phenomenon have pursued the idea that parasites in the sinuses and the middle ear affect echolocation, causing the animals to become disoriented and to float ashore.

Another theory comes from cetacean expert F. G. Wood, who says that marine animals may sometimes revert to the primitive behavior of their terrestrial ancestors, following the instinct to return to land when injured, sick, or attacked. Like other hypotheses, however, Wood's theory lacks hard supporting data.

Those who argue against his theory point out, moreover, that though such a trait may once have been beneficial, it is now self-destructive and should have been eliminated during the evolutionary process.

The cause of whale beachings remains unknown.

Musical Mice

Philip Ryall was often disturbed during the night by what he thought were birds chirping in the chimney. One night, however, he discovered a mouse creeping out of a crevice. It sat up on its hind feet looking around the room, all the while singing in a low warble.

The visits soon became a daily routine—until Ryall caught the fully grown female wood mouse, eventually passing her on to Samuel Lockwood, who reported on the phenomenal mouse in *Popular Science Monthly*. Lockwood kept the mouse, named Hespy, in a cage for everyone's entertainment.

In a similar case reported in *Zoologist* magazine, biologist John Farr suspected that the sound was created by grinding the teeth. But on closer observation, the throat of the mouse appeared to heave, giving the impression of a guttural sound.

If the sound emerged from the throat, however, the mice wouldn't be able to sing while eating as they often do. Nor is the singing a reaction to pleasure, since the mice also sing when chased from their nests.

In an effort to learn the secret of the musical mice, some people have tried to breed singing mice from a variety of mouse species. But this effort has not met with success. That is, no matter how the breeding was done, not all of the offspring would sing. One Maryland man bred hundreds of such mice before he found even a single offspring that could sing.

The Canals of Mars

There is an understandable tendency present among Earth-dwellers to deny the theory that we are alone in the universe or without sentient neighbors in our own planetary system.

When the famous astronomer Giovanni Schiaparelli submitted a theory about the canals of Mars, he was generally believed, because of his international reputation and because the assumption was so logical.

Schiaparelli claimed to have discovered in 1877 a system of lines seemingly connected by terminal points over the bleak Martian terrain. He named these lines "canals" (*canalli*), a name adopted by other theorists who considered them proof that a former Martian civilization had dug them to conserve the dwindling water supply on Mars. Still other astronomers who saw the sometimes straight or sweeping lines thought that they might be "game trails" trodden into patterns by herds of Martian animals over the years or, more probably, by dried up rivers that once flowed into now empty seas.

This last assumption is now more generally held, as there are strong indications that there once were rivers on Mars, and as has been observed, surface ice still exists at its poles.

Dwellers on the Moon

A purely imaginative description of life on the moon was offered as if it were factual to the newspaper-reading public by the *New York Sun* in 1835 through a series entitled "Great Astronomical Discoveries Lately Made by Sir John Herschel at the Cape of Good Hope."

The very name of Herschel, a well-known astronomer, was

enough to inspire the public's confidence, and, without a denial from Herschel, who did not know about the series until after four articles had appeared, the popular articles increased the circulation of the *Sun* by more than 650 percent.

Within a short time a pamphlet edition of the series brought in thousands of additional dollars. For some reason, *The New York Times* editorialized that the series displayed "the most extensive and accurate knowledge of astronomy." The articles were based on statements attributed to Sir John Herschel (but actually prepared by a Richard Locke of the *Sun*) that a new seven-ton telescope, installed at the Cape of Good Hope, South Africa, possessed a 42000x magnification. Focused on the moon, it allegedly made the moon's surface appear to be within five miles of the earth.

The article stated that Sir John had been able to clearly distinguish different kinds of moon animals. Some looked like American buffalos, others more closely resembled bears; there were single-horned blue goats and great cranes and other birds that flew over mountains made of amethyst. There were beaches on great lakes, one 266 miles long. Finally, there were humanoid winged creatures with faces like orangutans that flew but could also walk; these creatures appeared to be about four feet tall (the height frequently reported in modern-day encounters with extraterrestrials).

If the telescope made the moon appear as if it were only five miles away, readers wondered how Sir John was able to see such detail. But it was specified in a follow-up report that the astronomer was able to describe small animals and even the species of trees by adjusting his lens, thus bringing the surface of the moon to within eighty yards of the viewer.

Probably because of the lack of instant news communication in the 1830s, the hoax was not discovered until Locke told the truth to another journalist, who then reported it in the *Journal of Commerce*. When Sir John learned about the matter, he good-naturedly observed that he thought it was a good joke. Nevertheless, many thousands of people believed in the reports of men and animals on the moon and were disappointed when it was revealed to be a hoax.

As the Italian proberb goes, *Se non è vero, è ben trovato*. "If it isn't true, it's still well thought out."

Beyond Coincidence

Sooner or later, coincidences are bound to occur. But they can sometimes mount up to such a degree that there seems to be more than simple coincidence involved—as two car owners at a Sheboygan, Illinois, mall found out firsthand.

Thomas Baker had finished his shopping at the Northgate Shopping Center, and he was ready to go home. He walked up to what he thought was his 1978 maroon American Motors Concord and unlocked the door. But something was wrong. The seat seemed out of whack. He couldn't fit his six-foot-six-inch frame comfortably under the wheel. Glancing around the car, he noticed a caddy holding coffee cups and other unfamiliar items. Baker decided to call the police.

While he was discussing the situation with the officers, an identical Concord drove up. The elderly couple inside explained they were loading groceries into the car when they had found it contained unfamiliar personal objects. A check of the license plate showed that even though the car they were driving looked like theirs, it was someone else's.

According to American Motors Corporation (AMC) spokesman Ben Dunn, the odds of unlocking two AMC cars with the same key are 1,000–1. "But when you consider the matching color and model and the fact that the cars were parked in the same place at the same time," he says, "the odds become more like *ten thousand* to one."

The odds of this particular incident's happening shrank even more when the drivers found out they shared more than the same taste in cars. Thomas Baker and Mr. and Mrs. Richard Baker also had the same last name.

Psychiatrist James Hall of the University of Texas Health Science Center at Dallas says the car mix-up is "a good example of what Carl Jung called *synchronicity*," a term he coined to explain meaningful coincidences for which ordinary chance is not a significant explanation.

Hall adds that these kinds of multiple coincidences may reflect the underlying order of the universe. "There are deeper meanings to these kinds of coincidences," he says, "and they are research-able."

Spirited Novel Ending

Charles Dickens died in 1870, leaving his last book, *The Mystery of Edwin Drood*, unfinished. Did he find a way to complete the novel from beyond the grave? A young Vermont mechanic and psychic named T. P. James insisted that the ghostly spirit of Dickens visited him in 1873 and told him how to complete the novel.

Parapsychologist Jerry Solfvin and fellow researcher Jo Coffey, both of John F. Kennedy University in Orinda, California, are using a computer to analyze the known writing style of Dickens as well as the alleged "spirited" version of his work. The data will then be compared to determine whether the same author wrote all the material.

Solfvin emphasizes the outcome won't absolutely *prove* whether or not the spirit of Dickens actually finished *The Mystery of Edwin Drood*. "That's not our ultimate goal," he says. "What we will demonstrate is that a computer technique can help evaluate psychic information channeled from one person to the next."

The Savant of Lafayette

A native of nineteenth-century Lafayette County, Missouri, Reuben Field was a strong, heavyset man with the intellect of a child. He had never gone to school because he was considered an idiot and could neither read nor write. Nevertheless, he was able to compute and solve the most complicated mathematical problems, although he couldn't decipher written figures.

Told the circumference of the earth, in even figures, was twenty-five thousand miles, for example, and asked how many flax seeds, at 12 to an inch, would be required to circle the planet, Field almost instantly answered 19,008,000,000. If given the date of an event, moreover, he would be able to determine the exact day of the week. According to N. T. Allison in the *Scientific American*, he could also tell the time of day at any given moment without looking at a clock. Once, Allison asked him for the time and Field replied, "Sixteen minutes after three." Engaging him in further conversation, for seventeen minutes, to distract the illiterate man, Allison then asked the time again. Field replied, accurately, "Twenty-seven minutes to four."

Hair-Raising Power

At a meeting of the American Psychological Association in 1940, researcher Donald Lindsley showed the film of a man who had been voluntarily raising the hair on his arms since he was ten years old. He didn't need to scare himself, or even imagine something terrifying. He just raised his hair the same way he worked his muscles, he claimed, but a great deal more was happening than he thought. During the hair-raising experience, Lindsley pointed out, the man's pupils dilated; his heart and respiratory rates increased; even his brain waves changed. Indeed, he gave every physiological indication that he was, in fact, frightened, even though he claimed to feel absolutely no fear.

Strange Beasts of Africa

The natives call it *khodumodumo,* or "gaping-mouthed-bush-monster." In stealthy silence through the dark night, the marauder invades farms, climbing over six-foot-high fences into the pens and seizing sheep, goats, or calves. According to witnesses, the beast's "round, saucerlike footprints, with two-inch toenail marks," are unlike those of any animal known to man.

Some have identified the *khodumodumo* as a mutant hyena. Others disagree, saying the hyena always drags its quarry and is not known to leap tall fences with a calf in its jaw. The hyena, moreover, is not a *quiet* thief—it howls before a kill and shrieks afterwards. For the same reason, many say, the *khodumodumo* is probably not a lion or leopard either.

What's more, the *khodumodumo* is not alone. In the dark continent, tales of mystery beasts abound. Any hunter who has tracked African game, for instance, has heard of the strange, howling, man-eating *ndalawo* of Uganda; the *mbilintu,* a cross between a hippo and an elephant, of the Congo; and the silent, purring *mngwa,* which stalks coconut groves along much of the African coast.

Like the legendary Loch Ness, Africa has its share of water monsters as well. The *lau* and *lukwata,* for instance, are said to be immense serpents that lurk beneath the African lakes and marshes. Reportedly hundreds of feet in length, with the girth of a donkey, they make loud, rumbling noises in the night and attack marine animals and water-traveling humans. Although he never actually saw one, scientist E. G. Wayland, director of Uganda's Geological Survey, was shown an alleged *lukwata* bone and also heard it roaring through the night.

Africans also describe the *agogwe,* a small, furry, ape-man no more than four feet tall. Legend has it that if you leave a bowl of food and a gourd of *ntulu* beer outdoors for the critters, they will take the food and, in return, hoe and weed your yard.

While some of the legendary African beasts may be just myths, *some* may exist. After all, there was a time when scientists doubted the existence of the very real platypus and giant panda as well.

Australia's Enormous Egg

During the 1930s, an Australian farmer found a football-sized egg that has baffled scientists ever since. Researchers confirm that the object is an egg—in fact, a bird's egg. But they say it's thirteen times bigger than an egg laid by the giant emu, the largest egg the scientists of the Australian continent have ever found.

Though the egg remains a mystery to this day, theories abound. The egg could be from a species known as the *Aepyornis*, a bird long extinct in its natural habitat of Madagascar, some four thousand miles west of Australia. The egg could have drifted across the Indian Ocean and floated up to Australia's shore, experts suggest, as does other material caught in the juncture of the Indian and Southern oceans in the area of the find. Or the egg could have been carried by humans and abandoned on the Australian shore.

Then again, some scientists say, the egg might belong to an extinct *Australian* bird, whose fossil footprints and what is possibly its skull were found relatively nearby.

The Mass Death of the Tilefish

It was a cold and stormy Tuesday afternoon, and a strong northwest wind whipped the waves into a frenzy. All around the Norwegian fishing vessel *Sidon*, the shipmaster said, hundreds of dead or dying fish, some three to four feet long, floated on the water's surface. Traveling at a speed of six to eight knots, the *Sidon* ploughed through fifty miles of sea with the fish still slapping against its sides. Soon afterwards, during March and April 1882, the crews of at least twelve other ships related similar encounters.

Hearing the *Sidon* story, United States fish commissioner Spencer Baird began an investigation whose preliminary findings indicated the fish were cod. Still, Baird thought they were more likely tilefish, a Gulf Stream species discovered a few years earlier in 1879. When he actually saw one of the dead fish, he realized he was correct.

According to an article in *Nature Magazine*, Baird and his investigators estimated that about 1.5 million dead fish, with a conservative combined weight of more than 14 million pounds, drifted in an area 170 miles long and 25 miles wide. All manner of explanations were given for the massive kill, from volcanic eruptions and poisonous gases to heat and starvation. The most prominent theory was that the fish, confronted by a current of unusually cold water, became paralyzed and helpless, and eventually died. Be that as it may, the specimens showed no signs of illness or disease.

The species disappeared from human sight for a total of ten years and baffled marine biologists were never able to confirm any reason for the mortality of the fish.

The Mystery of the Inca's Treasure

When Pizarro and his small force penetrated and then conquered the empire of the Incas, an enormous territory covering Peru, Colombia, Ecuador, Bolivia, and parts of Chile and Argentina, he obtained for himself and Spain an enormous treasure in gold.

Much of this treasure came to his hands in a single unit. He had massacred the Indian warriors who tried to protect the Incan king, Atahuallpa, and he had taken the Inca captive. Atahuallpa, in order to secure his release, promised to fill a large room in the palace completely with gold, up to a line indicated on the wall by a standing man's upstretched hand.

Pizarro accepted with alacrity, but, after receiving a large part of the promised treasure, he decided that the Inca should be executed anyway, giving him the choice of being burned or strangled, the preferable strangulation being contingent on the Inca's being baptized. The Inca was then strangled as a Christian.

After the death of the king, the gold of the empire (statues, idols, jars, bars, plates, ceremonial weapons, and chains) continued to be brought in from all parts of the empire. Then suddenly the treasure stopped coming. Pizarro was particularly sorry not to receive the promised forged chain of gold that was said to be so heavy that sixty Indians were needed to carry it. No one ever learned what became of this treasure, often referred to as *el peje grande*—"the big fish."

A curious legend has persisted in Peru: the belief that a lineal descendant of Atahaullpa still has control of an enormous fortune, which he keeps secret, as he does his own identity. The Andean Indians tell of a distinguished and light-skinned Indian, dressed in formal attire like a white man but speaking the ancient Quechua language, who sometimes comes to mountain villages in times of trouble. This may be when certain families or the whole village is desperate for supplies, food, or money. This princely figure arrives in a large, chauffeured black car of a kind seldom seen in the mountain areas. He supplies gold to a village, sometimes for food, or for teachers, or for medicine, and then leaves. His identity is unknown and no one ever seems to remember the license number of his luxurious car, or even if it had license plates.

The Indians, however, are certain of one thing—someone is protecting them in time of need. Perhaps the mysterious benefactor is a descendant of the Great Inca, the "Son of the Sun," who still cares for his people.

The Rain Tree

Ancient journals of travelers in the Western Hemisphere recount stories of a tree that attracted clouds, invariably converting them into rain.

These stories were considered nothing more than tall tales until such a tree, its branches producing a shower of water, was discovered in Brazil during the early nineteenth century. About fifty years later, another was documented in Peru. The leaves of the Peruvian rain tree, *Scientific American* reported, seemed to condense moisture in the atmosphere and, in turn, release the water in the form of showers.

The legend of the rain tree seems to date back to the Fortunate Isles where the only "rain" was the moisture precipitated by trees. Early explorers brought home stories of similar trees in such locales as the East Indies, Guinea, and Brazil.

Today, scientists have posed a possible explanation. Many plants, in a process known as "guttation," they contend, draw moisture up from their roots, usually passing the excess into the atmosphere in the form of gas. If the air is already saturated with moisture and the water reaching the roots is excessive, then the leaves will exude the liquid, sometimes in large quantities. The process occurs mostly at night, when the relative humidity is greatest. In the tropics where atmospheric moisture is high, trees can probably exhibit guttation to such an extent that the name "rain tree" befits them, but the process cannot occur in a dry climate and rain trees cannot, therefore, act as a panacea for drought.

Creatures in the Yard

Marius Dewilde's home was situated among the woods and fields less than a mile from the French village of Quarouble near the Belgian border. Despite the fact that the National Coal Mines' railroad tracks ran along one side of Dewilde's property, the nights were tranquil. During such quiet times, after his wife and son were usually in bed, the French steelworker would sit in the kitchen and read the newspaper before retiring himself. The night of September 10, 1954, however, was different.

Hearing the family's dog barking and howling, Dewilde suspected a prowler. Taking his flashlight, he went to investigate. Outside he spotted something near the railroad tracks, but assumed it was a farmer's truck.

As the dog cringed up to him on its stomach, the steelworker was suddenly startled by a sound to his right. Swinging around, he caught a glimpse of an odd sight: two creatures with very broad shoulders, but no arms, and wearing what appeared to be diving suits and helmets. No more than three feet tall, the entities seemed to shuffle on short legs. They were heading for the dark shape he thought was merely a truck.

Dewilde ran to the garden gate, intending to cut the creatures off. Suddenly a blinding beam of light from the dark shape on the tracks struck and immobilized him; he wasn't even able to shout as he saw the creatures pass within a yard of him and head toward the tracks.

The light was quickly extinguished, however, and Dewilde continued his chase, but it was too late. The creatures apparently reached their destination, and the dark shape rose with a whistling noise as it discharged a cloud of steam beneath. Reaching a height of about thirty yards, the craft then took off toward the east, climbing higher and glowing red as it did so.

Shaken, Dewilde ran to report the incident to the police, who dismissed him as crazy. The commissioner, however, realized that he was neither mad nor joking and initiated a detailed inquiry. Investigators initially suggested that Dewilde may have suffered a hallucination, the result of a head injury.

That may have been discounted had they paid attention to the deeply cut marks in the iron-hard wood of the railroad cars. A railroad engineer estimated that such marks could have been created only by an object weighing at least thirty tons. It would have taken intense heat, moreover, to burn the ballast stones between the cars.

Valencia UFO

The Spanish charter airline flight had been delayed four hours before finally taking off from Salzburg, Austria, en route to Tenerife in the Canary Islands. The passengers' discontent was aggravated further when the plane made an unscheduled landing in Valencia, Spain. It may have been the least of their concerns had they known what precipitated the detour on that Sunday evening in November 1979.

It began after the plane had passed over Ibiza. Shortly before eleven o'clock, flight captain Commandante Lerdo de Tejada saw two bright red lights to the left of the aircraft. The object rapidly bore down on the plane from the left and a little behind. "It was moving upwards and downwards at will, all around us, and performing movements that would be impossible for any conventional machine," Tejada said. He added that it seemed to be as big as a jumbo-jet.

The unidentified object followed the aircraft for about eight minutes. About sixty miles from Valencia, the speed and closeness of the object forced the plane to make a sharp turn to avoid a possible collision. It disappeared after another thirty miles.

The airport's director, traffic controller, and other personnel confirmed seeing something with red lights. News reporter Juan Benitez also learned later that the Spanish air force had picked up the UFO on military radar in the same area as the airliner. Minutes after Tejada had landed at Valencia, two air force planes were dispatched and sighted the object, one pilot reporting close physical encounters with what he described as a UFO.

Cayce's Cosmic Knowledge

Edgar Cayce, America's best-known clairvoyant, once dreamed he was being chased by Indians on the Ohio River and that they were going to kill him. He had told only his immediate family of the dream. So he was rather surprised one day in 1923 when a young boy climbed into his lap and said, "We were hungry together at the river."

Cayce was an active churchgoer throughout his life and was inclined to dismiss reincarnation as unchristian—that is, until he recalled his own former lives. While in a trance state, Cayce was surprised to learn not only that he had been a British soldier in colonial America but also that he had been a high priest in ancient Egypt and an apothecary in the Trojan War.

Although he had been reluctant, at first, to explore reincarnation, Cayce became convinced that past lives were a reality after remembering his own—and having the memory confirmed by a past-life compatriot in the form of a young boy.

Can Animals Reason in Human Terms?

A number of animals, such as horses, donkeys, pigeons, dogs, camels, elephants, and oxen, have been trained to perform work for man. Other animals, bears, monkeys, ponies, goats, lions, tigers, porpoises, seals, and killer whales, have been trained to perform tricks, based on a system of rewards and punishments.

But sometimes it seems that to perform work at higher levels, animals would have to reason beyond instinct, and reason is something commonly believed to distinguish man from the animals.

Can animals reason like man? Certain cases indicate the possibility. German police dogs, for example, were used during World War II in concentration camp mines to count the groups of prisoners entering the slowly moving elevators descending and ascending automatically from the depths of the mines. The dogs were taught to shepherd and count the prisoners as they entered and exited up to the number of twelve and, if there were more or less, to alert the armed guards by barking.

An African baboon was used by an injured railroad worker in Africa in 1877. James Wide had lost his legs in a railroad accident and was given a less active job as signalman. His pet baboon named Jack did the housework that Wide could no longer perform and took care of the garden. Jack pushed Wide as he worked in a railroad car along the rails and worked the levers and signals, and opened and closed siding switches. Wide operated successfully like this for years and never caused an accident or delay.

Herodotus, the famous traveler and commentator of ancient Greece, recounts that the priests of pharaonic Egypt kept baboons in the temples, gave them brooms, and taught them to sweep the temple floors. The baboons learned quickly and kept the temples clean. If the baboons could reason, they may have been flattered by the fact that many temples featured statues of baboon-headed gods.

Meteorite Attack

Bound for Frankfurt, Germany, an Olympic Airlines commercial flight was struck by a foreign object shortly after takeoff from Athens on November 24, 1983. Flying at an altitude of thirty thousand feet over northern Italy, according to Athens newspapers, the plane was struck by "something" that hit the front right window of the cockpit and broke the glass. The crew managed to descend and continued the flight at a lower altitude to maintain internal air pressure. The sixty passengers didn't know that anything out of the ordinary had occurred until the plane reached its destination and headed directly for repairs.

The Fish That Came from Nowhere

In Greek mythology, Hercules once exterminated the *Stymphalides ornithes*, the wild, man-eating birds with iron claws which terrorized the people living in Stymphalis. Today, that locale in the mountains of Corinthia is mostly farmland, except for the nearby Stymphalia Lake, once big and rich in fish.

Fishermen made a fairly prosperous living from the lake until 1976, when drought caused the lake to dry up, its surface eventually reduced to less than half its original surface area of forty-five thousand acres. The fish soon died and completely disappeared from its shallow, muddy water.

Although the drought continued into 1978, the waters began to rise again suddenly in February of that year, and the lake soon returned to its original size. Fish, moreover, mysteriously reappeared. Within a month, the publication *Nea* reported, fishermen were taking their boats out and returning with eighty pounds of fish every day.

Mass Fish Faintings

Fishermen have long cast their nets in the waters around the Greek island of Elaffonisos, near Cape Malea. During the last two weeks of October 1986, however, they found the area ladened with deep-sea fish floating on the surface, alive but unconscious.

Something seemed to paralyze the fish's nervous systems, but curiously, the Greek publication *Ethnos* pointed out, fish that normally live near the surface were unaffected. Icthyological and toxicological studies of the fish were unable to determine the cause of the mass faintings.

It's not the first time, of course, that the phenomenon of mass fish faintings has occurred in Greek waters. From 1984 to 1986 alone, deep-sea fish were found floating in the Bay of Canea near the island of Crete and in the area of Gythium near Elaffonisos Island.

Prehistoric Cretan Flying Reptile

In 1986, according to the Greek newspaper *Ethnos*, Nikolaos Sfakianakis, Nikolaos Chalkiadakis, and Manolis Calaitzis went hunting along a small river in the Asterousia Mountains in western Crete. At about 8:30 one morning during the outing, they heard a strange noise that sounded like the flapping of a bird's wings. At first they paid no attention, but they eventually sighted a huge, dark gray bird gliding not far above.

The winged creature was odd looking, to say the least. Seemingly composed of membranes, its wings reminded the threesome of those of a bat, except they had fingerlike protrusions. Its hind legs, moreover, had large, obviously sharp claws and its beak was similar to a pelican's. The men watched the odd animal until it flew into the mountains and disappeared.

Returning home, the three men searched in several books until they found a similar depiction. The only picture they found that even closely resembled their bird was that of the pterodactyl, a flying reptile that supposedly became extinct millions of years ago.

The Unfriendly Skies of West Virginia

Delta Airlines flight 1083 departed Pittsburgh on June 15, 1987, bound for Atlanta. En route, the passenger plane was flying over West Virginia when the pilot sighted an object heading toward the craft. The four-foot-long, finned "missile," he told the *St. Louis Post-Dispatch*, was traveling with great speed and narrowly missed the plane as it passed slightly below it and to the side.

The Defense Department denied ownership of the so-called missile, and the National Weather Service claimed it was probably not one of its instruments. At the New York regional headquarters of the Federal Aviation Administration (FAA), spokesperson Kathleen Bergen proposed that it may have been a blimp-shaped helium balloon. The weather service, however, countered that the wind in the jet stream over West Virginia at the time was too weak to make a balloon move as swiftly as the pilot said the object had.

Nevertheless the FAA's official position was that the object was an escaped promotional balloon. "Balloons can travel pretty far," Bergen explained, adding, "We don't acknowledge the existence of UFOs."

Mexican Psychic

Under hypnosis in 1919 to treat her insomnia, Maria Reyes Zierold happened to tell Gustav Pagenstecher, a German physician practicing in Mexico, that his daughter was listening at the door to the office. To satisfy the woman that there was, indeed, no one there, Pagenstecher opened the door, but was surprised to find the child there just as the patient had claimed. The incident intrigued the good doctor and, with Zierold's permission, he began to investigate her possible clairvoyance.

Pagenstecher soon discovered that Zierold was able to give a vivid description of events connected to any object she held in her hands while in a hypnotized state. While holding a piece of string, for example, she envisioned a battlefield on a cold, foggy day. There were groups of men and continuous gunfire. "I see a big ball coming through the air with great speed," she suddenly exclaimed. "It's dropping in the middle of fifteen men, tearing them to pieces." The string, it turned out, had originally been attached to a German soldier's dog tag. The scene Zierold reported was, the soldier said, "the first great impression I received of the war."

Hearing of Pagenstecher's studies of Zierold, the American Society for Psychical Research's Walter Prince soon arrived to determine whether Zierold was telepathic or genuinely clairvoyant. One experiment he used involved two identical pieces of silk enclosed in identical boxes. He mixed them up so that even he didn't know which was which. Holding one box, Zierold described a Mexican church and dancing Indians; the other, she said, gave her the impression of a French ribbon factory. In fact, the first was from a church altar while the second had come directly from the manufacturer.

Bridey Murphy

A good dancer of Irish jigs, Bridget (Bridey) Murphy, the daughter of Duncan and Kathleen Murphy, Irish Protestant residents of Cork, also read Irish mythology and sang Irish songs. In 1818, Bridey married a Catholic named Brian MacCarthy and they traveled by carriage to Belfast. Bridey, however, wasn't an outstanding person in Irish history and we would probably know nothing about her had it not been for Virginia Tighe, a resident of Madison, Wisconsin, who grew up in Chicago.

During a number of hypnotic regressions from November 1952 to October 1953, Tighe revealed her previous life as Bridey Murphy in early nineteenth-century Ireland. Speaking as Bridey, Tighe had an Irish accent, often accurately using words with meanings that had changed since the nineteenth century: Referring to a child's pinafore, for example, she used the word *slip* and not the more common modern word *petticoat*.

Tighe had never visited Ireland and strongly denied allegations that she had ever associated with Irish people. Yet while still under her trance, she once danced "The Morning Jig," ending her performance with a stylized yawn. Her description of another dance was confirmed by a woman whose parents had danced it. Tighe also correctly described the procedure used during Bridey's lifetime for kissing the Blarney Stone.

According to Bridey (through Tighe), among other family details, her brother Duncan was born in 1796 and married Aimee, the daughter of the headmistress at a school Bridey attended when she was fifteen years old. After her own marriage, she and her husband traveled by carriage to Belfast through towns that she named. They worshiped at Father John Gorman's St. Theresa's Church and shopped in stores, which she named; she also correctly described the coins used during that period. And uillean pipes, she said, were played at her funeral.

Commissioned by the American magazine *Empire*, William Barker spent three weeks in Ireland investigating Bridey's story. He was able to confirm some of the facts, particularly the insignificant details; he proved some to be wrong, however, and was unable to confirm others.

Barker couldn't verify dates of births, marriages, or deaths because Cork officials didn't keep such records until 1864; and if the Murphys noted the occasions in the family Bible, as was the custom, its whereabouts was unknown. Nor was any information found concerning Father Gorman or St. Theresa's Church. But after painstaking research, Barker did discover that Carrigan and Farr, two shops mentioned by Bridey, had both existed. The uillean pipes, moreover, had been once customarily played at funerals because of their soft tones.

Argentine UFO

Two miles outside the small town of Trancas in northwestern Argentina, the Moreno family's Santa Teresa Ranch has its own electric power plant. When it broke down on the evening of October 21, 1963, the household retired early, while twenty-one-year-old Yolie de Valle Moreno stayed awake to feed her infant son.

The house was still and quiet when the maid, Dora, suddenly knocked on Yolie's door, crying that there were strange lights outside. The whole farmyard seemed to be illuminated. Both Yolie and her sister Yolanda went out to investigate. In the distance to the east, near the railroad tracks, they saw two bright, disc-shaped objects connected by a shining tube. It looked, Yolie said, "like a small train, intensely illuminated." They could also make out a number of shadows moving within the tube. They suspected, at first, that there may have been a derailment.

As they walked around to the front of the house, they saw two pale greenish lights near the gate of the farm. As Yolie directed the flashlight toward it, she realized it was a disc-shaped, domed object, about thirty feet wide. It hung in midair while emitting a slight hum. Through its six windows the women could see a band of multicolored light begin rotating as a white mist enveloped the object. Without warning, flames shot out, knocking the women to the ground.

Next, a tube of light, about ten feet wide, emerged from the top of the object and probed the features of the house. Three more objects appeared on the railroad tracks and directed ten-foot-wide beams of light toward the henhouse, the tractor shed, and a neighbor's house. Yolie ran inside where the temperature had risen from 60°F to a stifling 104°F, and the air smelled of sulfur.

After about a total of forty minutes, the object at the farm's gate retracted its light and joined the others on the tracks. Finally all six objects rose and flew off toward Sierra de Medina, a mountain range to the east.

The cloud that had enveloped the object nearest the house didn't dissipate until four hours later. A journalist who visited the family the next day said the heat and the smell of sulfur still lingered. What's more, a pile of small white balls, forming a perfect three-foot cone, lay beneath the spot where the object had hovered outside the gate; similar balls were found on the tracks. Later analysis at the University of Tucuman's Institute of Chemical Engineering determined they were composed mostly of calcium carbonate, with a small percentage of potassium carbonate.

In a later inquiry, half a dozen other members of the community told local police that they had seen the illuminated objects on the railroad tracks as well. One man said he saw six disc-shaped objects flying across the sky at 10:15 P.M., about the time the Moreno's ordeal ended.

Lake Guns

Each autumn, Albert Ingalls returns to Seneca Lake, where he spent months swimming, camping, boating, and fishing in his youth. Almost every day during the season, he hears distant, muffled explosions reverberating over the area. Indeed, even before the first settlers arrived, Native Americans in the region experienced the sounds, resembling the explosion of guns.

Booming lake guns, of course, have been reported in a number of countries, including Italy, Haiti, Belgium, and throughout Africa. In Northern Ireland, for example, cannonlike sounds are heard throughout the year at Lough Neagh, a lake covering 150 square miles which was created by volcanic eruptions. Although fishermen are often on the lake, no one has ever noticed any movement in the water and the booming seems always to be heard in the distance. Near the North Sea, the lake was frozen over during the winter of 1896. In that year, the Reverend W. S. Smith reported that he and other skaters on the lake heard the explosions and estimated they occurred about a half mile away. The ice, they noticed, was not disturbed.

No one knows the origin of the lake guns for sure, though theories have been kicked around. In one hypothesis, for instance, scientists have suggested that the gun sounds are created as natural gas escapes from sandstone stratum hundreds or even thousands of feet below the surface of the lakes. The gas shoots upward through the water, exploding at the surface. No large bubbles or volumes of gas have ever been seen in the lakes, the theory goes, because the gas breaks up into small bubbles before it reaches the surface.

One investigator, Rochester Gas and Electric Corporation geologist A. M. Beebee, has suggested that the guns heard in Seneca Lake may eventually die out. The reason: Rochester Gas and Electric's drilling in nearby gas wells will diminish gas pressure below the lake. The natural gas will then no longer escape through the lake.

Acoustic Mirages

Ann H. Bourhill of Transvaal, South Africa, was awakened by the apparent sound of cannons on June 14, 1903. The noise was followed by a long "whizzing," with a second explosion a few seconds later. Not long afterward, another acoustic episode occurred, giving the impression that a large structure may have been bombed. What's more, similar sounds were heard by others as far as ten or twelve miles away.

This incident, moreover, is not unique. Unexplained detonations have been reported for decades around the world. Though the cause remains a mystery, some modern experts now suggest that the sounds result from electrical disturbances in the atmosphere at the time.

One observer in Texas, for instance, claimed to have heard a whizzing sound before he actually saw a meteor entering the atmosphere. Studying the phenomenon, American meteor expert H. H. Nininger hypothesized that the sound resulted when the human ear converted the electrical activity surrounding the meteor to sound. Though no one has proposed the mechanism by which this might occur, researchers have suggested that acoustic mirages might result from electrical activity generated by supersonic jets and earthquakes as well.

Whispering Lake

S. A. Forbes was boating on Shoshone Lake in Yellowstone National Park when he heard a mysterious sound. Like others who have experienced the phenomenon there and at Yellowstone Lake, he thought of a vibrating harp or the sound of telegraph wires "swinging regularly and rapidly in the wind," or even voices heard faintly overhead.

The noise began softly, seemingly in the distance, he reported in the *Bulletin of the United States Fish Commission.* Then it grew increasingly louder as it approached, and it finally died out as it moved onward in the opposite distance. Occurring repeatedly, the traveling sound lasted from a few seconds to more than half a minute.

The sound at Shoshone Lake, as well as at Yellowstone Lake, where it occurs even more frequently, is usually noticed on bright, still mornings shortly after sunrise, but it has also been heard later in the day when the wind is blowing. Numerous theories have emerged to explain the phenomenon—electricity, whistling of ducks' wings, insects, waterfalls and geysers, or simply the wind.

Erratic Meteors

Spotted on August 10, 1972, over the western United States and Canada, the bluish white meteor was a blazing ball of fire. Traveling slowly across the sky, it left a trail of smoke that remained for at least an hour after the fiery sphere disappeared.

Once entering Earth's atmosphere, a meteor almost always strikes the earth. But this one, according to *Nature* magazine, "bounced off the atmosphere and flew back into space."

On other occasions, slow-moving meteors have been observed to bounce or dip during their trajectory en route to Earth's surface. On November 14, 1960, for example, an officer on the S. S. *Hector*, sailing from Adelaide, Australia, to Aden in South Yemen, observed such a meteor. Unusually brilliant and visible for just two seconds, it appeared to suddenly dip and then climb again. Yet other erratic meteors have never penetrated to the surface, instead skipping across the upper atmosphere like stones upon water.

Gas and other volatile materials in a meteor's composition are heated by atmospheric friction and expand, sometimes throwing the celestial object off course. Meteors, after all, are not perfectly formed spheres and, therefore, do not always appear to behave in rational ways.

The Fata Morgana

When the sun reaches a certain point in the sky and the sea is calm, you can look out across the straits of Messina and see images of arches, towers, and palaces with their balconies and windows. Also visible are rows of trees, as well as figures on horseback and on foot.

If a fog hangs over the water, moreover, the reflections of the objects appear in the air as well. Named after King Arthur's sister Morgan le Fay, who conjured up towns and harbors to lure seamen to their deaths, the fata morgana is a mirage of fantastic cities and countrysides and occurs in a number of places around the world, but most often in colder climates—in the Firth of Forth, Scotland, for example.

No one has ever adequately explained these spectral visions, though some pundits have claimed that if you fixate on rocks and a beach coast long enough, you may see things that are not really there.

Mirage at Sea

On April 15, 1949, the second officer of the *Stirling Castle* spotted a vessel off its port bow and five miles away in the English Channel. Through his binoculars, the crewman reported in the *Marine Observer*, he saw the boat's lights move for brief periods. The lights seemed to generate a double image, and as the higher image merged with the lower one, the crewman actually saw vertical strips of light.

Such mirages are usually responsible for the double images of low-altitude stars and planets, terrestrial ghost lights, and probably a number of UFO sightings. They aren't classic fata morganas, but the elongation of the images is part of the same optical process that distorts distant shores.

Apparitions of the Virgin Mary

It's not unusual for a lone witness to claim he or she has seen a ghostly apparition. But in Zeitoun, Egypt, *thousands* of people insist they've seen an eerie shining figure, believed by many to be the Virgin Mary, atop St. Mary's Coptic church.

The strange sightings began in April 1968 and continued until 1971. Then they started up again in the mid-1980s, this time over another Coptic church outside of Cairo, St. Demiana's. The figure, accompanied by a bright light, at first appeared only in the early morning. Later on, she was seen briefly several times each night.

Huge crowds gathered in the streets below, and several witnesses said the dome of the church inexplicably glowed during these visitations. Others reported that the smell of incense sometimes pervaded the entire area.

On one occasion the mysterious lady "stayed for twenty minutes," according to journalist Mousaad Sadik, who wrote about the apparition in the Cairo-based paper *Watani*. "Spellbound," he reported the next day, "the people started to plead and pray."

Pacific Coast Vikings

With the discovery of the ancient remains of Norse villages in Newfoundland and northern Labrador, few people now doubt that seafaring Vikings visited the New World long before Columbus. But there are also scattered clues that the seafarers didn't stay put on America's eastern shore. In fact, they appear to have made it all the way around the top of North America to the Pacific Coast.

As D. and M. R. Cooledge pointed out in their book *Last of the Seris*, during the tenth and eleventh centuries, when the great Viking explorers Eric the Red and Leif Ericson were roving the oceans, the Northern Hemisphere was the warmest it had been since the Ice Age. With ice floes melted or greatly diminished, Viking ships would have had little trouble navigating through the islands dotting the Northwest Passage above Canada.

The tribal legends of the Seris suggest that Norse explorers visited the Indians' homeland on Tiburón Island in the Gulf of California. According to a paper presented at the 1953 Toronto Meteorological Conference by Ronald L. Ives of the Cornell Aeronautical Laboratory, the Seri tribe told of the "Come-from-Afar-Men" who landed on Tiburón from a "long boat with a head like a snake . . . a long time ago when God was a little boy." The Seri tradition holds that these men had white hair and beards; their women were redheads.

According to the Indian tale, the strangers hunted whales in the gulf and cooked them on shore. They sailed away to the south but their ship was soon torn apart by the pounding breakers. The survivors of the shipwreck swam to shore where they were helped by the Mayo tribe. The strangers eventually intermarried with the Indians.

Is this historical fact or fantasy? To this day, some Mayo Indians are born with blonde hair, blue eyes, or both, which they say are passed down from the "Come-from-Afar-Men." In fact, until the 1920s, anyone who married outside of the tribe was expelled because the Mayos were adamant about retaining this ancient heritage.

Authors Brad Williams and Choral Pepper point out in *The Mysterious West* that actual Viking ships have been found in the American West. An elderly widow in Baja, California, found the hull of an ancient ship, with shields like those used by the Norse on its gunwales, on a canyon floor near the United States and Mexico border. And noted antiquarian researchers Louis and Myrtle Botts of Julian, California, found the dragon prow of what appeared to be a Viking ship in March 1933. It was sticking out of a canyon wall near Agua Caliente Springs, on the United States side of the Mexican border. Before they could excavate it, however, an earthquake triggered a rockslide that sealed off the canyon.

Ancient Roman Artifacts in Arizona

On September 13, 1924, Charles Manier found something on Silverbell Road northwest of Tucson, Arizona, that, according to the accepted record of world history, shouldn't have been there. The find included an array of ancient Roman relics made of lead. The anachronistic trove included more than thirty relics, including a sixty-two-pound cross, daggers, batons, spears, and swordlike weapons.

Archaeologists and mine engineers present during the digs noticed that the objects were found encrusted in caliche—a sheet of hard, crusty material that "grows" because of a reaction of chemicals and water in desert soils over many years. That such heavy deposits of caliche had developed around metal objects at such depths, they concluded, meant the Roman artifacts had to have been very old.

As the caliche was removed from the objects, Latin words, letters, and graphic symbols became visible on many of the items. Researchers, who used this information to date the artifacts to between A.D. 560 and 800, suggested that, just maybe, a band of Roman adventurers had once explored what is now Arizona.

The Arctic Metropolis

When archaeologists Magnus Marks and Froelich Rainey were in the Arctic for a second season of digging at Ipiutak in June 1940, they made an astonishing discovery. They had arrived just at the time when grass and moss in that location were becoming green—but not everywhere. Some areas of grass were higher and literally yellow, and the researchers noticed that the discoloration created a clear pattern of yellow squares. Further investigation showed that the yellow grass was growing over the ancient ruins of what Rainey called an "Arctic metropolis."

Long avenues of yellow squares marked over six hundred houses, extending east and west along the north shore. Later digs showed that more than two hundred additional houses were also buried far beneath the sand. The town was almost a mile long and about a quarter of a mile wide. Rainey estimated that around four thousand people lived in the town—an incredible number of inhabitants for a hunting village in the Arctic.

Rainey and Marks discovered elaborate and sophisticated carvings at the Ipiutak site which show that the people were most likely not related to primitive Eskimo cultures. Instead, Rainey theorized "the people of this Arctic metropolis brought their arts from some center of cultural advance."

Castles in the Sky

Every year from June 21 to July 10, "The Silent City of Alaska" appears on the Mount Fairweather glacier. Visible for about two hours between 7:00 and 9:00 P.M., the mirage is believed to be a mirror representation of Bristol, England, some twenty-five hundred miles away, further than any other mirage has been seen. (The greatest distance of any other projected mirage has been just six hundred miles.) Indeed, according to investigators, the vision includes a tower that seems to be an exact replica of one at St. Mary Redcliff.

The explanation for this mysterious mirage is not known for sure, but many experts suggest it may be the result of lenslike layers of air that magnify distant scenes.

Magnificent Memory

There have been many tales of individuals, from Mozart to King George III, who possessed the gift of remarkable memory in particular areas of knowledge. Some calendar experts have been able to report the day of the week for any date given in the span of a hundred years.

But Englishman Daniel McCartney had the distinction of remembering everything that had ever passed through his mind during most of his life. Once, at a public meeting to demonstrate and prove his ability, with someone prepared to verify McCartney's accuracy, a man in the audience asked McCartney to identify the day of the week for a particular date fifteen years earlier. McCartney replied, "Friday," and the questioner told him he was wrong. It had been the man's wedding day, he said, and it had been a Thursday. To settle the argument, the verifier checked an old calendar and determined that, indeed, McCartney was correct. McCartney's ability, however, went beyond just dates and weather reports—he could even remember what he had had for breakfast, lunch, and dinner for the last forty years. He retained his remarkable memory until the day he died in 1887 at the age of seventy.

The Incredible Building Rocks
of the Incas

Many of the monumental stone ruins of Peru and Bolivia pose architectural and archaeological mysteries. The enormous stones of the walls of Sacsahuaman and Ollantay in Peru and Tiahuanaco in Bolivia were built by pre-Incan cultures. Somehow these early peoples transported great building stones, many weighing 150 tons each, across mountains, rivers, and deep valleys and then set them up on other mountains. They remain in place today despite earthquakes that have leveled later cities built on their sites. The intervening earthquakes have not tumbled these rocks, which were linked together by angles, curves, and interstices indicating that the stones were cut and fitted together exactly more or less like a three-dimensional jigsaw puzzle.

There is no indication of how the builders could have succeeded in getting these enormous rocks to fit so closely together. Not even a thin blade can be pushed between them, and there is no sign of the use of mortar. It seems impossible that such stones could have been shaped with stone hammers or other primitive means and then lifted in and out of position until the builders obtained a perfect fit.

Colonel Percy Fawcett, the British writer-adventurer who explored the mountain and jungle regions of central South America for many years, has suggested that the unusual and cohesive joining together of the huge stones may have been made possible through the use of a liquid or paste employed by the ancient builders.

Drawing on his own experience, he tells of some wet leaves carried by jungle birds in their beaks to soften stone in walls of canyons over rivers, thus enabling them to peck out rookeries for themselves in the canyon walls. A further report tells of a man who, after crossing a field covered with low plants with red leaves, found that his long spurs had softened and melted at the ends. Indians later asked him whether he had walked through a field of such plants and told him that the plants were once used by the Incas to "melt" rocks.

A like experience of melting occurred, according to Fawcett, when some American engineers dug up a sealed container from an ancient tomb. It still had in it some liquid that they presumed was *chicha*, a strong Andean drink. When they offered it to one of their workmen, the man refused. When they tried to force him to drink it, there was a struggle and the jar fell and broke on a rock. As they watched, the rock under the puddle of liquid began to soften and then, as others came from the camp to look, it reverted to its original hardness.

Colonel Fawcett could not explain the mystery. Several years after the incident, in 1924, he made his personal contribution to South American mysteries by disappearing near the Xingu, one of the tributaries of the Amazon.

Musical Sands

Jebel Nagus, a high sand slope along the west coast of the Sinai peninsula, creates loud musical sounds when the sands are disturbed. According to native legend, the music comes from the *nagus*, or wooden gong, of a monastery buried in the area. The sound is difficult to describe, according to visitors who have heard it. In fact, it doesn't really resemble the sound of a gong or bell at all. Some have said it sounds like a harp or the noise produced by drawing a finger around the wet rim of a glass. Others have compared it to the air rushing into the mouth of an empty metal flask, the deeper tones of a cello, or the hum of a spinning top.

Similar singing sands have been heard around the world—at Reg-Ravan, north of Kabul, Afghanistan, and on the Arequipa plains of Peru, for example. Most, however, sound more like roars, booming noises, or simply squeaks. In the eastern part of Churchill County, Nevada, a four-square-mile hill of moving sand produces a deafening sound that reminds some residents of telephone wires vibrating in the wind.

The Surviving Sister

Retired teachers Margaret and Wilhelmina Dewar had been respectable citizens of Whitley Bay in Northumberland, England. Margaret's character was soon impugned, however, after Wilhelmina's sudden death. In the early morning hours of March 23, 1908, a shocked Margaret summoned neighbors and ushered them up to Wilhelmina's bedroom. There they discovered Wilhelmina's charred body lying in the bed. The linens were mysteriously untouched and there was no sign of a fire anywhere else in the house. This, Margaret said, was how she had found her sister.

At the inquest, the local coroner found Margaret's story difficult to believe. The police, moreover, claimed Margaret was so drunk at the time she couldn't have known what she was saying. The coroner decided to adjourn the investigation to give Margaret time to think about her story.

When the court reconvened, Margaret did, in fact, change her story: She had found Wilhelmina on fire, but alive, elsewhere in the house, she said. She then helped her sister upstairs, where she died. The court accepted this more plausible story, and no one even questioned how Wilhelmina had been incinerated in a bed that she apparently left unscathed.

The Largest Mammal Population

As other animal species have disappeared, or nearly disappeared, two animal groups have continued to grow, rivaling each other in numbers—human beings and brown rats.

Now, in the latter part of the twentieth century, the human

population of Earth has passed the rat population in number for the first time, and the rate of increase of the human population has been estimated to be doubling every thirty-five years. Up to now certain controls, such as wars, famines, plagues (usually spread by rats), and other disasters have served to keep the human population in check, but now, with new medical developments, the surge in the number of humans is greater than ever before. This remarkable increase may soon lead to a world food shortage as well as a lack of living space. This may already be observed in a number of countries throughout the world.

There exists an interesting human-rat symbiosis, especially beneficial to the rats, in that rats congregate in and under human cities and farmlands—in fact, anywhere people live and provide such sustenance as stored food supplies or garbage. Rats have been carried by human-engineered transportation, notably ships, to all parts of the Earth. Attempts to cut down the rats' rate of increase (female rats can have litters of five or six every six weeks!) by poison, chemicals, the use of ferrets, dogs, and cats have shown results in some areas, but rats, by some believed to be the most intelligent of mammals, seem to successfully resist all attempts to destroy or significantly limit their species.

As space probes sent to the planets and beyond become more commonplace and the search for new habitats for the world's surplus human population is intensified, it is hoped that experimental rats will not be included on space vehicles, lest they find a way on new planets to dispute man's dominion— as they have so long done on Earth.

Human Incinerators and M.D.s

While driving through Ayer, Massachusetts, on May 12, 1890, Doctor B. H. Hartwell was stopped and called into a nearby woods. There he and other witnesses saw a woman crouching as flames engulfed her body. Neither Dr. Hartwell nor other witnesses were able to determine the cause of the fire.

Although there have been relatively few open admissions, Dr. Hartwell has not been the only physician to encounter incidents of spontaneous human combustion. At a Massachusetts Medico-Legal Society lecture, held in the autumn of 1959, many doctors said they'd had experience with spontaneous human combustion as well. British physician D. J. Gee of the University of Leeds gave the keynote lecture. He was met with a round of applause and, much to his surprise, found that several doctors in attendance claimed similar experiences as well. The phenomenon was not as uncommon as it might appear based on written reports, the group declared. One doctor even said he came across cases of spontaneous human combustion once every four years.

Talking Chopper

"You needn't bother going. It won't do the slightest good," a voice said, interrupting West German dentist Kurt Bachseitz as he spoke on the phone with a patient.

Over the next couple months, Bachseitz repeatedly heard the voice. Often it was wisecracking and insolent. Calling itself "Chopper," the voice even developed an interest in the doctor's receptionist, Claudia. It was soon projecting from everywhere, including the sink and the toilet.

Suspecting electronic interference from a ham radio operator, the local telephone company investigated. It decided to install a new line in the doctor's office and re-lay the telephone cable throughout the building. Not only did the voice continue its pronouncements, but eventually it was heard over a Munich radio station. "You've taken away my switchboard," Chopper said. "But I can hear you just as well. So don't think I'm not listening in!"

Chopper's story hit all the newspapers and it seemed everyone had an explanation for the voice; psychics suggested it was a paranormal phenomenon. A philosopher said it might be a manifestation of the subconscious. Some doctors proposed that it was the mental projection of a cancer patient whose vocal chords had been surgically removed.

The truth, however, was revealed in March 1982. It had been a practical joke instigated by the dentist himself, who was also an accomplished ventriloquist. Thereafter, Bachseitz closed his office and was admitted to a sanitorium.

A Movable Light

A torpedo-shaped cloud of light appeared on the horizon of northern Europe on November 17, 1882. For months afterward, scientists debated its nature, finally terming it an "auroral meteor" because it swept purposefully across the sky like a large meteor.

A stranger event occurred over Cincinnati in 1849: A bright streak of light suddenly appeared and, after rising to a certain point above the horizon, seemed to explode, spreading over the entire sky. It was then followed by five consecutive bursts of light, all originating from the same point.

Unlike actual meteors composed of rock and metals, auroral meteors are probably disturbances moving through the upper atmosphere. No one knows exactly what causes them, but two possible suspects are gravity waves and gusts of solar wind.

The Man Who Took Photos with His Mind

When Ted Serios of Chicago recovered from a serious illness, he found he'd developed a most unusual talent. He could take Polaroid photographs of scenes miles away by just turning the camera toward his head and snapping a picture.

In 1963 a publisher in Evanston, Illinois, decided to test Serios's unexplained powers. He presented Serios with a Polaroid camera loaded with fresh film and watched as the psychic photographer held the camera at arm's length so that the lens faced him. Then Serios pushed down the shutter release.

The photograph was pulled from the camera and the publisher observed it being developed. The words "air division" showed up clearly on some kind of airplane hangar. Other fragments of words that appeared seemed to refer to the Canadian Mounted Police.

The snapshot was sent to the Mounties' headquarters and was soon identified as the Canadian Mounted Police hangar in Rockcliffe, Ontario. Somehow, Ted Serios had managed to take a photograph of an airport hundreds of miles from where he sat—just by pointing a camera at his mysterious brain.

The Native American Messiah

Sometime in the late 1880s, a Cheyenne set out from his tribe to grieve for the loss of a relative, as was the custom. During the process, he fell into a trance and dreamed that he wandered the country. He saw wildlife that had long disappeared from his people's hunting grounds, and he eventually came upon an encampment of dead family members enjoying an abundant life. As he gazed upon the settlement, he noticed a great, brilliant light that grew and extended from the village to the horizon. Along the path's light, a robe-clad figure, with skin lighter than that of the Cheyenne's own people, approached and proclaimed himself to be the Son of God. He had come, he said, to help the Indians. He could restore their game, eliminate hunger, and reunite the living and the dead. The wicked white race, he added, would perish if only the Indians worshiped and followed him.

When the Cheyenne returned home, he told no one of his dream. Shortly afterward, however, various people among the Cheyenne and other tribes began having similar visions and some heard songs and voices as well. They gathered to sing the songs, dancing to the rhythms. As in ancient traditional Indian cults, the people would fall into trances as they practiced their ritual. Soon, people were repeating tales of having seen the Messiah in the mountains near Mexico.

Although the belief in a messiah is a fundamental myth, no one could ever explain why the visions of the Cheyenne incorporated the image of Christ.

Phantom Rock Throwers

On one suburban street in Birmingham, England, the residents live a comfortable middle-class life in every way but one: Night after night, for years, stones have been hurled at the backs of their homes. Windows were broken, doors marred, and roofs damaged. And finally, unable to locate the culprits, the beleaguered residents of Thornton Road went to the police.

A routine investigation failed to reveal anything, and the matter was finally turned over to Chief Inspector Len Turley. To get to the bottom of the mystery, Turley and his men tried everything: They conducted all-night stakeouts, used automatic cameras, and even monitored the houses through periods of bitter cold. Studying the rocks themselves, investigators found they were of the type found in almost every garden, though devoid of any markings, prints, or even soil, as though they had been washed.

Resigned to this fate, the residents have boarded up their back windows and erected chicken wire screen to protect their homes. They go to the backyard at dusk only if necessary, and, they say, it is an ordeal.

Transcending Death

Does the spark of human consciousness survive death? Maybe so, according to Polish physicist Janusz Slawinski.

To prove this notion, Slawinski points to a well-known phenomenon in which a collection of cells in a laboratory dish emit a burst of radiation as they die. According to Slawinski's calculations, this burst is powerful enough to encode reams of complex information, including human memory and consciousness itself.

Slawinski believes we may sometimes emit what he terms the "death flash" while we are still alive, accounting for the out-of-body experience. This burst may also be the raison d'être for the near-death experience, in which consciousness literally leaves the body as it dies.

Says Slawinski, "electromagnetic radiation released by living systems provides a realistic basis for the possibility of life after death."

Therese Neumann

The stigmata—bodily marks resembling the wounds of the crucified Christ—usually manifest themselves in female subjects. One of the more renowned women to suffer the experience was Therese Neumann, a poor peasant girl born in Konnersreuth, Bavaria, in 1898.

Neumann's childhood seemed normal, even mundane. She worked as a domestic on neighboring farms, until a series of inexplicable illnesses rendered labor impossible. Then during the Lenten season of 1926, she "saw" Jesus and her current illness was cured. In its stead, however, her body was wracked with the

Passion—the five traditional wounds associated with Christ's crucifixion, as well as whip lashes across the back and thorn pricks on the head.

Neumann's wounds would open every Good Friday and during Lent for the next thirty-two years, sometimes gushing as much as a pint of blood and causing her to lose as much as eight pounds during the course of a single affliction.

Neumann spent a largely reclusive life, passing much of her time in bed shrouded in white linens. She was examined extensively by the medical profession of the day, but no hint of a hoax or trickery was ever remotely entertained.

Almost as startling as Neumann's stigmata was her ability to go without food or water for extended periods of time. She survived on wine and Communion wafers for the last three and a half decades of her life. Given her circumstances, Neumann remained reasonably healthy. She continued to have visions and ecstatic trances until her death in 1962.

First UFO Report

Washington State businessman Kenneth Arnold was about to fly from Chehalis to Yakima in his private jet when his flight was delayed. A Marine Corps transport plane was missing in the region, it seemed, and the air space was reserved for a search. At about 2:00 P.M., however, Arnold got the okay to take off, and he headed toward majestic Mount Ranier. He swung west to give the terrain a quick glance of his own but, finding nothing out of the ordinary, headed on.

He reported the sky clear and the air smooth, and noted that a DC-4 was behind him flying at about fourteen thousand feet. Then, suddenly, he saw a flash of light, as if the sun were being reflected off bright aluminum. Finally he saw nine vehicles in formation, heading from the north toward Mount Ranier. The craft were traveling so fast that Arnold guessed they were new fighter jets on a test flight. The size of each, he determined, was somewhat smaller than the DC-4 still overhead. Later calculations showed the diagonal line of objects, which swerved through the mountain peaks without breaking formation once, to be about five miles long. Arnold clocked the objects as moving at a speed of 1,656.71 miles per hour.

Occasionally, Arnold reported, one of the objects would dip or turn sideways, and he was surprised that he could find no tail. As he scrutinized the strange craft further, however, he was shocked to see a series of saucerlike objects with bubble tops.

Word of Arnold's sighting quickly reached the news media, and the term "flying saucer" was coined. Arnold was flooded with calls from interested citizens around the country. But no government official ever tried to follow up on his case.

In fact, the air force not only denied any unusual sightings that afternoon, it also declared that Arnold had seen a mirage.

Still, wondered Arnold and his supporters, what had happened to the pilot of the DC-4? And what became of the lost transport, which was never accounted for and, they suggest, may never have existed at all?

Croesus and the Oracles

More than two thousand years ago, Croesus, the king of Lydia, became increasingly concerned about the powerful Persians. Before taking any action against his enemies, however, the great leader decided to consult an oracle. But which one? To make his choice, Croesus decided to test seven candidates, six Greek and one from Egypt.

To conduct the test, Croesus dispatched seven messengers. Each visited a different oracle, instructing him or her to describe the king's activities at a specified time and day. Anyone, of course, could have correctly guessed the answer if the monarch had performed a routine task. So old Croesus came up with an elaborate ritual, something only a truly talented oracle would possibly know: He cut a lamb and a tortoise into pieces and boiled the flesh in a brass cauldron covered with a brass lid.

The messengers returned from their mission and the king read the descriptions. Only the oracle at Delphi had known what the king had been doing. In fact, the historian Herodotus tells us that the Pytheness, as the oracle was called, answered even before hearing the question. Croesus was so impressed he showered the oracle with gifts worth more than $100 million by the standards of today.

The Ipswich UFO Incident

At 10:55 on the night of August 13, 1956, a radar operator at the American-leased Royal Air Force (RAF) Bentwaters base near Ipswich, England, picked up a fast-moving target. It appeared when it was just thirty miles to the east, traveling at two thousand to four thousand miles per hour as it headed in from the sea.

A tower operator described the object as "blurred out by its high speed" as it passed directly over the base. Alerted by ground control, an American pilot saw a fuzzy light flash between his aircraft and the ground.

Bentwaters' controller notified the Americans at the RAF's Lakenheath base, where the UFO seemed headed. Shortly afterwards, Lakenheath radar recorded objects traveling at incredible speeds, stopping suddenly, and instantaneously changing course. Ground observers sighted two white lights that came together and disappeared. Officials hesitantly notified the RAF.

The RAF's chief controller dispatched a fighter plane toward the UFO. As the aircraft closed in , however, the UFO suddenly and mysteriously appeared behind the plane. Witnesses said the UFO seemed to flip over as it moved behind the RAF fighter, which then attempted to get behind the UFO.

According to Arizona University atmospheric physicist James McDonald,"The apparently rational, intelligent behavior of the UFO suggests a mechanical device of unknown origin as the most probable explanation."

The United States Air Force Condon Report on UFOs described

the sighting as one of "the most puzzling and unusual cases" ever to emerge.

UFO Photographs

Paul Trent's wife was in the yard feeding the rabbits at 7:45 P.M. on May 11, 1950, when she saw a disc-shaped object moving westward in the northeastern Oregon sky. Responding to her cries, Trent soon realized the unusual nature of the object and ran for his camera, already loaded with a partially used roll of film.

The silent, silvery UFO was slightly tilted, Trent recalls, and appeared to be gliding as it approached. Just before the craft passed overhead, the McMinnville couple felt a breeze. After taking one shot, Trent advanced the film and snapped a second photo, moving to the right to keep the object in view.

Hoping to avoid publicity, Trent had the film developed at a local shop and told few people about the unusual event. Nonetheless, a reporter from the *McMinnville Telephone Register* got wind of the sighting and decided to follow up. The story appeared in the local papers on June 8 and papers in Portland, Oregon, and in Los Angeles picked up the story on June 9 and 10. A week later, *Life* magazine ran the photos.

When the United States Air Force investigated the incident seventeen years later as part of what would become the Condon Report, investigators submitted the photographs to rigorous scientific examination. Afterwards, they had to admit that the photos were genuine.

According to the Condon Report, "This is one of the few UFO reports in which all factors, both psychological and physical, appear to be consistent." To be sure, Trent's photos are not the only UFO pictures that exist. But according to experts, they represent one of the few sets of UFO photos that seem to be legitimate and not the result of accidentally damaged film or a hoax.

UFOs in France

As bizarre as it sounds, grotesque dwarflike aliens in diving suits were reported in Quaroble, France, on September 10, 1954. A week later, a French farmer was bicycling near the town of Cenon when he suddenly started to itch all over. When he stopped alongside the road and dismounted, he became immobilized at the sight of a "machine" ahead of him. A small diving suit–clad creature approached, uttered strange sounds, and touched the farmer's shoulder. It then returned to the object and disappeared inside. The UFO glowed green as it rose into the air and sped away.

Some ten days later, four French children were playing in their father's barn. Hearing the dog bark, the eldest boy went out to investigate and confronted a rectangular creature that, he said, resembled a "sugar cube." Throwing pebbles and shooting a toy arrow at the ET, the boy was pushed to the ground by an invisible force. As he scrambled away, he saw the creature waddle off toward the meadow. Running back to the house, the children saw a glowing red object hovering over the meadow. The next day, investigators discovered a circle of burned grass.

A couple of weeks after that, yet another Frenchman reported an encounter with a four-foot-tall creature in what, again, resembled a diving suit. The creature shuffled along the road before disappearing into the adjacent trees. And the next day, three children saw another four-foot-tall being emerge from a "shiny machine." Later describing the creature as a "ghost" with a hairy face and big eyes, dressed in something akin to a priest's cassock, the children said the being spoke words they didn't understand.

The following day, three men from Bordeaux were driving near Royan on the Atlantic coast of France when they observed a craft hovering about thirty-five feet above the ground. Getting out of their car to investigate, they came upon four three-foot-tall creatures seemingly making repairs under a craft.

According to the experts, UFO reports seem to occur in waves. There was a rash of sightings throughout the Western Hemisphere as well as in Australia and Asia from 1957 to 1958; in South America from 1962 to 1963; and in the United States in 1964. Britain and Italy experienced a wave of sightings from 1977 to 1978. But out of all the UFO waves, the 1954 French wave was the most intense.

Prince Bernhard's Narrow Escape

The long road passed through a meadow and led to the crossing gate at the railroad tracks. Speeding down the road, a car suddenly blew a tire and ran into the gate. A lorry stopped behind it. To complete her dream, she saw the driver, lying dead on the ground. It was Prince Bernhard of the Netherlands.

When she awoke, the dreamer immediately wrote to W. H. C. Tenhaeff, who, describing the case later in the *Journal of the Society for Psychical Research*, identified his subject only as "Mrs. O of Amsterdam."

Mrs. O had described her psychic abilities and precognitive dreams to Tenhaeff before. This dream, however, disturbed her more than most. She mailed the letter almost immediately and it arrived at Tenhaeff's postmarked Saturday, November 27, 1937.

While listening to the radio the following Monday evening, Tenhaeff heard a news report about Prince Bernhard having been in a car accident that day. With the newspaper stories that later appeared, Tenhaeff was able to compare the actual accident with Mrs. O's dream:

Railroad employees, news reports indicated, were working at the viaduct of the Hilversum-Amsterdam Railway, digging sand and loading it onto lorries. As the prince's speeding car approached, one full lorry was being maneuvered onto the road that passed through meadows on its way from Diemen to Amsterdam. The right front of the car collided with the rear of the lorry on the left side. Several people who lived nearby rushed out of their houses with blankets and helped place the two drivers on them until the doctor arrived. Reports mentioned nothing about a flat tire or a collision with the gate visible in newspaper photos. Prince Bernhard, moreover, did not die.

The Year Summer Never Came

"I well remember the seventh of June," Chauncey Jerome of Plymouth, Connecticut, wrote of the year 1816. "I was dressed in thick woolen clothes and had an overcoat on. My hands got so cold that I was obliged to lay down my tools and put on a pair of mittens."

Throughout the entire northeastern United States, the weather that summer was more than unseasonable. From June 6 to 9, severe frosts killed crops. Snow fell on two occasions, though it was heaviest in northern New England, where some areas reported eighteen to twenty inches.

Summer seemed to return toward the end of the month, but in July another frost killed the replanted crops. And on August 20, temperatures dropped again, with frost as far south as northern Connecticut.

No one has ever explained the bizarre summer of 1816. But some modern meteorologists have suggested a possible culprit: volcanic dust from three major eruptions occurring between 1812 and 1817. The volcanic eruptions certainly dispensed great quantities of dust into the atmosphere, the researchers say. This might have blocked the sunlight and caused the extreme cold. Critics of this theory, however, note that when Krakatoa erupted in 1883, it created a spectacular sunset seen around the world—but no change in climate at all.

The Giant Bird of Egypt

In 1821, James Burton discovered three huge conical birds' nests along Egypt's Red Sea coast. Approximately two and a half to three feet wide at their apex and fifteen feet wide at their bases, the nests were each about fifteen feet tall. They were eclectically composed of materials that included sticks, weeds, fish bones, and pieces of woolen clothing. Fashioned into the structure of one nest was an old shoe and a silver watch designed by a watchmaker in the eighteenth century; another included a human thorax. Based on what he learned from neighboring Arabs, Burton determined that these were the nests of a giant bird that had only recently deserted the area.

Reporting on his discovery in the *American Journal of Science*, Burton said that area residents compared the species to the giant bird depicted in the tomb of the pharaoh Khufu, whose pyramid was built around 2100 B.C. The storklike avian of the pharaoh's day had white feathers, a straight, long beak, and long tail feathers. The male of the species had tufts at the back of the head and on the breast. The bird was apparently often caught by people living along the Nile Delta and offered as a gift to the pharaoh.

Because later Egyptian pyramids have no engraving or paintings depicting the birds, it had been assumed, up until Burton's modern discovery, that the creatures had probably become extinct.

Alligators in the Sewers

Claims of alligators in New York sewers might qualify for the most persistent of the urban myths. New Yorkers vacationing in Miami, the story goes, are said to have returned home with baby alligators as pets for their children. The more the alligators grew, however, the less desirable they seemed as playmates. Rather than have them skinned for their hides, parents flushed them down the toilet. Some apparently survived, living in New York City's sewers on a diet of rats and reaching a formidable size.

Is there any truth to this tall tale? Investigating the sewer alligator, cryptozoologist Loren Coleman went searching for the *real* story behind the sewer 'gators—and the origin of the myth. Reporting in the *Journal of American Folklore*, he said that he ended up with many "alligator in the sewer" reports between 1843 and 1973, but few appeared to be real.

One case, however, stood out from the rest. Recorded as fact in the *New York Times* on February 10, 1935, the story's headline read, "Alligator Found in Uptown Sewer."

Boys seemed to be having a great time as they shoveled the last of the winter's snow into a manhole on East 123rd Street near the Harlem River. Noticing that snow seemed to be backing up, however, sixteen-year-old Salvatore Condulucci investigated more closely and he saw something move. After a closer look, he called his friends, insisting there was an alligator below. One by one, they peered down into the manhole and confirmed the story. Yes, there was indeed an alligator, apparently trapped, slashing around in the ice and snow.

Using clothesline they quickly acquired from a nearby store, the boys fashioned a slipknot and lowered the rope into the hole. They maneuvered it until they worked it around the alligator and then, with great difficulty, slowly pulled it up to safety and the street.

Once the critter had been rescued, one of the boys moved to loosen the rope. Opening its jaws and snapping at him, the half-dead alligator certainly didn't seem to be very grateful for its rescue. The boys' curiosity and sympathy quickly turned to fear and animosity. Using their snow shovels, they finished the job begun by the cold water and the melting snow. They then dragged the animal to the store where they'd gotten the rope.

Measuring seven and a half to eight feet long and weighing about 125 pounds, the alligator, authorities theorized, had apparently fallen off a steamboat traveling from the Everglades which had passed 123rd Street. Attempting to escape the cold Harlem River, it swam toward shore and apparently found the opening to the conduit. Struggling through the torrent of melting snow, and already half dead, it finally arrived beneath the manhole.

In Search of Atlantis

According to the theory of continental drift, all of the earth's land masses were once joined together in a single piece. Gradually that piece broke up and moved apart to form the continents as we know them today.

The theory explains the fact that the shapes fit together like pieces of a jigsaw puzzle—all except for the bit between Europe and the United States. That missing piece seems to be the same size and shape as that of the Atlantic's underwater plateau. Could that submarine land mass once have been the lost continent of Atlantis, relegated by most to the status of myth?

Indeed, though many scientists consider Atlantis nothing more than legend, tales of the lost city can be found in every culture on earth. All races, for example, share the story of a great flood that destroyed an entire civilization. And even the name Atlantis appears in various forms around the world. In the Canary Islands there is the term *Atalaya*, whose original inhabitants were supposedly the only survivors of a continent whose mountain peaks became islands as the world was flooded. The Basques of Northern Spain, whose traditions go back to the Stone Age recall a great island in the ocean called *Atlaintica*. The Vikings described the wondrous western land known as *Atli*. In North Africa, there is *Attala*, described by the Berbers as a warlike kingdom once rich in gold and silver. The Aztecs' lore had its form of Atlantis—the legendary land of origin, Aztlán. And North American Indians living near Lake Michigan frequently referred to *Azatlán*, after their ancestors' island in the sea.

Whatever happened to Atlantis? Some six thousand years ago, legends say, the land was struck by some sort of sudden catastrophe. That catastrophe, today's researchers speculate, might have been the melting of glaciers, volcanic eruptions, violent earthquakes, tidal waves, or meteors colliding with Earth.

According to modern-day investigators, moreover, there is now solid physical evidence for the existence of Atlantis. Using sonar equipment and other high-tech tools, scientists have located underwater islands with fresh water springs in the middle of the ocean, and land vegetation has been retrieved by scientific probes.

ESP in Prague

A simple, genial Czechoslovakian, Pavel Stenpanek never claimed he was psychic. He merely volunteered to take part in an experiment designed by Czech scientist Milan Ryzl, who thought it might be possible, under hypnosis, to train someone in psi.

The project seemed straightforward enough to Stenpanek. And before long, he was showing proficiency in ESP. Ryzl's basic procedure involved placing a set of target cards, green on one side and white on the other, in a cardboard cover. They were first shuffled, then coded, and finally placed in covers to prevent any visual clues. At last they were presented to the subject, whose job it was to guess whether the green side or the white side was uppermost in the pack.

Stenpanek's performance went through various stages. At first it was merely slightly better than average. By 1964, however, his scores had declined so that he demonstrated ESP *less* than would be expected if he had randomly picked a color. Ryzl feared Stenpanek's ability was fading—until parapsychology researcher J. G. Pratt engineered a cure.

Instead of asking Stepanek to focus on the pack, the investigators now asked him to report the color of one card at a time. In that new experimental format, Stepanek's ability proved extraordinary. He was able to guess the color of the cards much more frequently than if he had chosen the color at random.

Mystery of the Healing Needle

After unsuccessful drug therapy for myelitis, a crippling inflammation of the spinal cord, a young girl is able to walk again. A man recovers from appendicitis without surgery. Another's dysentery is cured not by destroying the disease's bacteria, but by increasing the body's resistance. The miracle worker is not a religious healer, but rather the ancient technique of acupuncture—a medical art form that can cure a wide range of afflictions as long as no irreversible organic deterioration has occurred.

Acupuncture as a medical art evolved, one legend says, from observations of Chinese soldiers who, when wounded by arrows sometimes recovered from ailments they had endured for years. The earliest written reference to the art appears in the *Nei Ching*, or *The Yellow Emperor's Classic Book of Internal Medicine* dating back from 3,000 to 4,500 years ago.

The basis of acupuncture involves something the Chinese call *qi (chi)*, which, loosely translated, means "life force" or "vital energy." If *qi* stops flowing harmoniously through the body, the result is illness. *Qi*, the Chinese say, circulates through the body by means of a series of meridians, invisible channels flowing under the skin. There are two central meridians—the governor vessel, which runs up the spine, and the conception vessel, which runs up the front of the body. A dozen other meridian pairs on each side of the body are linked to the heart, lungs, kidneys, and other specific organs, including two not even recognized by Western medicine—the heart constrictor, which controls circulation, and the triple heater, which keeps the body warm.

On each of these meridians lie the "acupuncture points," two thousand in all. Stimulating the points with needles or massage affects the meridians and their corresponding body parts by easing the flow of *qi*.

The results of acupuncture vary: There may be instant relief or slow improvement over weeks or even months. Experiences range from a feeling of tranquility to an abundance of energy. Some patients have a feeling of being pleasantly exhilarated; others actually feel worse for a time. Some notice no effect at all.

Claims that acupuncture results are due to faith or suggestion are countered with proof that it's consistently successful and equally effective on animals. Why sticking a needle in someone is able to restore the body's energies, however, still remains totally unknown.

The Ghost of Redmond Manor

Sounding like a rat gnawing at timber, the tapping was heard close to the foot of the bed for about five minutes. At first slow, the sound gradually became faster and louder. Then the bedclothes began sliding off the bed as if someone were pulling them, or as if a strong breeze were blowing through the room.

N. J. Murphy had heard the rumors about the Court Street house owned by one Nicholas Redmond, who admitted that it was haunted; indeed, Redmond's wife and two boarders, John Randall and George Sinnott, agreed.

Not accepting anything on hearsay, however, Murphy and Owen Devereux decided to spend the night in the house, sitting in the boarders' room, where the activity usually occurred.

The tapping and the movement of the sheets began around 11:30 P.M., about ten minutes after the investigators put out the lights. They checked under the bed for strings or wires, but found nothing suspicious at all. After another ten minutes, the noise recommenced, gradually increasing as it had before, and the sheets began to slide off the bed. This time, when the tapping stopped, Randall began screaming. He was being pulled off the bed and onto the floor. Terrified, he was soaked in perspiration. Helping him from the floor, Murphy and Devereux persuaded him to get back into bed.

Around 1:45, the tapping began once more, but this time it came from the middle of the room. It continued for fifteen minutes and then stopped. Murphy and Devereux were unable to offer any explanation for the phenomenon. And to this day, the ghost of Redmond Manor is unexplained.

Fish from the Skies

A. D. Bajkov, a scientist with the United States Department of Wild Life and Fisheries, was in a Marksville, Louisiana, restaurant having breakfast on October 23, 1947, when a commotion arose outside. Not believing the waitress who told him fish were falling from the sky, he went out to investigate for himself. Sure enough, within an area of approximately one thousand by seventy-five or eighty feet, fresh, cold, but not frozen, fish littered the streets and yards—large-mouth black bass, sunfish, and minnows, but predominantly hickory shad. There were some spots averaging one fish per square foot. A Marksville Bank officer and two merchants had been struck by the falling fish as they walked to work.

Once when Bergen Evans, a noted debunker of scientific anomalies, asserted that all fish falls were merely myths, E. W. Gudger, a scientist at the American Museum of Natural History, responded with an array of evidence he'd been accumulating for years. In September 1936, for example, a fall on the Pacific island of Guam comprised the tench fish, common to the fresh water of Europe and western Asia.

Most often accompanying violent thunderstorms and heavy rains, fish rains usually involve a single species of fresh fish falling within an elliptical area a few hundred feet long. The explanations that a waterspout or whirlwind deposits them is acceptable when the fish comprise those that school in shallow waters. But the falls often include deep-water fish, some dead, dry, and even headless. No one has explained this last type of fish rain at all.

Driesch's Theory of Evolution

Expecting that half an egg would produce half an embryo, nineteenth-century biologist Hans Driesch used a hot needle to kill half of a sea urchin's fertilized egg. To his amazement, he discovered that each half developed into a complete, but smaller embryo of a whole sea urchin. Each half of the egg, it turned out, had a blueprint of the whole. Two whole eggs forced together, moreover, would fuse and develop into one embryo that was larger than normal. Driesch argued, therefore, that life itself is a dynamic force that "aims" for wholeness, independent of its chemistry.

According to the tenets of orthodox science, life on Earth happened by pure accident and can be explained by the laws of physics and biology. There is a reason for everything, most scientists will insist, and there is no such thing as free will in nature. Driesch and others, however, have dared to suggest that life may have its own program and its own laws.

Intrigued by Driesch's ideas, Harold Saxton Burr studied the electrical forces that initiated the construction of an organism's blueprint in the egg. He attached a voltmeter to trees and other organisms, keeping an ongoing record of their voltage. The trees' voltage, it seems, varied according to the seasons, sunspot activity, and the phases of the moon. In rabbits' ovaries, the voltmeter registered a sudden jump whenever follicles ruptured and released an egg. Attached to psychiatric patients, its reading coincided with the degree of mental illness. It could also record the highs and lows in physical illness, according to Burr, for instance detecting cancer at an early stage.

The experiments, Burr concluded, showed that all living things were influenced by their electric fields, their "life fields," as he dubbed them. A frog's egg, for example, had various lines of electrical force; when it developed into a tadpole, these lines became the nervous system. It was as if living matter were poured into the life field's mold.

Others in the twentieth century have contributed studies that support Burr's conclusions. In the 1930s, for example, Semyon

Kirlian seemed to have actually photographed the life field of a flower. Made by using high-voltage film plates, the photograph showed a glowing corona that surrounded the plant. A photograph of a torn leaf, moreover, appeared to show a dim outline of the leaf's missing portion.

In experiments at the University of Wisconsin in the 1970s, Daniel Perlman and Robert Stickgold grew bacteria in a solution containing an antibiotic that would normally destroy the bacteria. This particular bacteria, however, contained a gene that destroys the antibiotic, ensuring its own survival. According to accepted scientific views, this occurs by simply activating the defense system, which then shuts down when the danger has passed. Instead, the bacteria actually reacted by replicating the protective gene, as if it chose a more effective defense.

If life exists independently of matter, then life is the master of matter, and not the other way around, as most scientists now believe. And if it is the master, it can overrule the laws of nature. Having studied DNA programming, cyberneticist David Foster contends that Darwinian biology is most likely all wrong. He contends that complex genetic programming indicates the probability of higher intelligence than anything found on Earth. He believes the universe is, therefore, akin to a magical being and cannot be described in purely physical terms.

Dreaming of Comets

Charles Tweedle awoke around four o'clock one morning in 1886. Having just dreamed of a comet crossing the eastern sky and appearing before the rising sun, he immediately dressed and went outside. He gazed through a telescope on his observation platform, he wrote in a 1905 issue of *English Mechanic*, and saw thousands of stars shining brightly in the clear sky. Then he saw the comet sail into view. It was extremely bright and pearly white, its dense center swirling outward.

Observing the comet for the rest of the night, Tweedle was

thrilled. It was his first comet discovery, and, as soon as the post office opened, he sent off a telegram announcing his find. Almost immediately afterward, when the morning mail arrived, he read of the comet's discovery, individually viewed by astronomers Barnard and Hartwig. It came to be known as the comet Barnard-Hartwig.

Tweedle never discovered another comet, and he was never able to bestow his name on a heavenly body.

The White Blackbird

When an old woman of Somersetshire, England, had become particularly obnoxious toward her neighbors, they retaliated by following an old Shrove Tuesday custom called "crocking." Bombarding her door with all the pots, pans, and other crockery they'd collected and saved during the previous year, the townspeople created as much racket as possible to annoy her. The event, however, had an unintended victim.

Known around town for its sleek coat and sonorous voice, one neighbor's tame blackbird seemed panic-stricken by the discordant noise. For two days, it jumped around its cage and refused to eat. Although the bird eventually calmed down, the stress experienced during the Shrove Tuesday antics had a long-term effect. The bird began moulting, Alfred Charles Smith reported in *Zoologist*, and many of the shiny, black feathers were replaced by white ones. Fear had turned the poor bird gray.

Asthma Cured by Lightning

Martin Rockwell was looking out the window watching the sky grow dark and menacing. He stood with his weight on his left leg, his right hand resting on a wet board connected to the sink. Suddenly he felt his right arm and left leg go numb. In the very next instant, lightning struck the building within ten feet of him and knocked him unconscious. He came to a few minutes later, but it was days before he regained full use of his limbs.

There was a positive side to the lightning attack, however. Since childhood, and most often in the autumn, Rockwell had suffered from asthma and was often forced to rest in bed for weeks on end. But after the lightning incident, according to the *American Journal of Science*, he never had another attack.

Barisal Guns

All day long the noises aboard the steamer prevented G. B. Scott from hearing any other sounds. But at night, with his boat moored near the delta of India's Ganges River, he detected the dull, muffled booms of distant cannon—sometimes a single report, at others a succession of two, three, or more. These were the mysterious sounds of the Barisal guns.

The Barisal guns, heard no where outside the Ganges delta and emanating from the south or southeast, occur most frequently from February to October and always in connection with heavy rainfall. Many residents claim they can't tell the difference between the Barisal guns and the festive bombs fired during weddings and festivals. The wedding season, however, is very short. The guns, moreover, are heard even during the annual fast when there are no festivals of any kind.

Some researchers have attributed these detonations to underwater earthquakes or volcanic eruptions. But to this day, most experts agree that no satisfactory explanation has been found.

The Case of the Last-Minute Errand

On Saturday, January 3, 1891, at precisely 8:00 A.M., a man walked into a photo store and asked for overdue photographs in the name of Thompson. He was told they would not be ready until later that day. Explaining that he had traveled all night and could not return, the man abruptly left.

The store owner, a man named Dickenson, decided to mail the prints. First he looked up the negatives and realized that the man in the photos was the one who had stopped at the store. Two days later, he set out to make the prints. While working, however, he smashed the glass plate negative by mistake.

Dickenson then wrote the Thompsons to make arrangements for a new sitting. He learned from Thompson's father, however, that it was too late. Thompson had died on the same Saturday Dickenson saw him at the store. At that exact moment, 8:00 A.M., in fact, Thompson was actually unconscious and lying in his deathbed. The man's father added that his son had been delirious the day before and insistently asked for the undelivered photos.

Mind over Fungus

Parapsychologists have been fascinated by the subject of psychic healing for years. But studying the results of such practices is difficult since people tend to recover from sickness and biological damage for many reasons. This has led some parapsychologists to simply explore whether some individuals can use psychokinesis to disrupt small biological systems or cultures.

The researcher who pioneered this type of experiment was Dr. Jean Barry, a French physician who worked in collaboration with the Institute of Agronomy in Paris. Dr. Barry wanted to see if his subjects could use mind over matter to inhibit the growth of fungus cultures, since fungi can cause disease. Petri dishes were prepared by the institute the day before the experiments and were subsequently placed in an incubator, where the cultures could thrive. The following day, Dr. Barry's subjects would each be given ten dishes filled with the cultures. They would be asked to concentrate for fifteen minutes on five of the dishes, trying to mentally inhibit the growth of the cultures. The other dishes served as the controls.

By the time the experiment was completed, eleven subjects had been employed for a total of thirty-nine sessions. The result: The control cultures were significantly larger than the experimental ones, indicating that the subjects had successfully used psychic skills to inhibit fungus growth.

The Magus of Strovolos

Each year, Dr. Kyriacos C. Markides journeys to Cypress to talk with Spyros Sathi, a psychic healer and teacher known as *Daskalos,* or "The Magus of Strovolos." While visiting the psychic, Dr. Markides, a sociologist from the University of Maine, personally documented his powers of clairvoyance.

The incident took place when Markides brought a colleague to meet Daskalos. The gentleman had recently been bitten by a dog and was limping, so the healer asked to examine the leg. After the man had untied the bandage, Daskalos moved his hand over the wound to heal it—claiming that he was dissolving a blood clot he psychically saw forming.

"The blood clot is dissolved," he told his visitor, "but I have to warn you, you have an infection of the liver. You must avoid alcohol."

Dr. Markides's colleague didn't believe the diagnosis since he felt perfectly fine, so he ignored the remark. It wasn't until three months later that he wrote to Dr. Markides from Connecticut that he was suffering from a case of hepatitis, which inflames the liver. When the illness first struck, he suddenly recalled Daskalos's diagnosis and was attempting to find out if Dr. Markides recalled it, too. Luckily, Dr. Markides had taped their conversation with the healer, and the prediction was easily documented.

But just how did Daskalos know of the disease, which hadn't yet produced any symptoms? The healer claimed that he "saw" right into the professor's body. "Now when I was examining the professor's leg," he later told Dr. Markides, "and I concentrated within his body, I noticed inside the liver a little brown spot touching the bile. From experience I knew that there was trouble coming."

This possibility is consistent with our medical knowledge, since with hepatitis, symptoms can develop three months after the initial infection sets in.

Misguided Psi

Dean Kraft is one of this country's best-known psychic healers. In 1976, he and several other psychics cooperated in a lengthy research project conducted by parapsychologists at the Washington Research Center in San Francisco. The experimental team was headed by Roger MacDonald, who wanted to determine whether the healers could disrupt electrical and magnetic fields, cause perturbations within a sealed cloud chamber, rebond water molecules, and so forth.

Kraft's success at these tasks was fairly marginal. But something unexplained—and morbidly amusing—happened during the tests when he tried to "heal" a rat especially bred to be hypertensive. The rat was brought to the lab on the day of the experiment and placed in a restraint cage, where its blood pressure was recorded by a probe hooked to its tail. Kraft was admitted to the room only after the experimental preparations had been made. He took a dislike to the rodent as soon as he saw it.

"I tried to explain that my only previous experience with rats had been in the music store where I once worked," says Kraft. "There, fat long rats that lurked in the basement sometimes ventured upstairs and scared the hell out of everyone. I felt only hate and fear for rats, and was worried, for it had always seemed to me that I needed to have positive thoughts—loving thoughts—toward the subjects I tried to heal."

Kraft tried to lower the rat's blood pressure, despite his trepidations, by sending it healing energy. Everybody left the room when the test was complete. The shock came moments later, when a technician went back to check the rat's blood pressure for a final time. The rat had dropped dead!

No explanation for the death was ever found.

Invasion from Mars

In the years before television the performance of one particular science fiction radio show, broadcast at a critical moment in world history, had an almost incredible effect on the listening audience. It happened in 1938, when the listening public was already psychologically prepared for the possibility of a world war, just after the Munich debacle and the threatened invasion of neighboring countries by the governments of Germany and Italy.

The radio show was a dramatization of an imaginary invasion of Earth by forces from Mars, based on a science fiction fantasy, *The War of the Worlds* by H. G. Wells. The actor Orson Welles was the narrator. Although the program was pre-announced as a radio dramatization only, Welles's masterful and exciting report of the invasion of Earth, specifically of northern New Jersey, by gigantic extraterrestrial-controlled robot towers that spread destruction through "death rays" aimed at civilians and troops, as well as the on-the-spot interviews with "refugees" spread panic among the listeners who had tuned in after the program had started and, therefore, thought it was the latest news. As the listeners telephoned their friends and compared notes, they convinced each other that the invasion was actually taking place. The telephone lines were jammed with calls and the excitement mounted. There was no further declaration on the air that the program was fictional. The panic spread, and the roads in New Jersey, parts of New York, and Long Island became blocked with cars filled with refugees, police cars, fire trucks, and motorcycles. The number of cars and accidents soon brought traffic to a standstill, and it took hours for state and local police to disentangle the traffic and restore order.

Even then, many of the fleeing thousands still believed that the space invasion was taking place and was being kept secret to avoid nationwide panic.

Some time after the "Mars invasion" had calmed down, the program was rebroadcast in Spanish at at theater in Lima, Peru. Here public excitement reached such a point that rioting broke out during the show, causing fifteen deaths and many more injuries.

And two years later, in September of 1939, similar public panics occurred in Western Europe—but this time the invaders were not from Mars.

Noah's ark never existed.

Has Noah's Ark Been Found?

Among the earliest legends known to man is one that tells of a great flood and a great ark that survived it, carrying people and animals to renew life in a drowned world.

This legend is part of the lore of ancient nations and tribes of all continents. In the Hebrew, Christian, and Moslem traditions, the landing place of the ark was Mount Ararat, now in northeastern Turkey.

The word *Ararat* comes from *Urartu*, an ancient Assyrian word for Armenia. The Bible specifies Ararat and also "the mountains of Armenia" as the landing place of the ark. But it does not specify on which mountain it landed, although Mount Ararat has become sanctified through tradition and legend as the resting place of the Great Ship.

For many centuries travelers claim to have seen it frozen in the ice, mountaineers have taken purported pieces of it as religious keepsakes, military pilots have reported flying over it in both world wars, and an ERTS satellite report of 1974, taken at fourteen-thousand feet, shows something in a great crevasse "clearly foreign to anything else on the mountain." In the opinion of Senator Frank Morse, chairman of the Senate Aeronautical and Space Sciences Committee, it was "about the right size and shape to be the Ark."

Since Ararat through the centuries has been shaken by a number of earthquakes and volcanic explosions, the ark, although protected in "deep freeze" may have been damaged or broken apart. This could explain the finding of what seems to be the lower portion of the great ship at the seven-thousand-foot level. This part of the ark may have slid down the mountain and been buried in a mud bank about twelve miles from its original site (great drag anchors and part of its port side have been found along the path of its presumed downward slide). If this hull is part of the ark, the remaining upper portion must still be at the fourteen-thousand-foot level, under the ice.

This "hull" surfaced from a frozen mud slide in 1948 and has been examined by a number of researchers who, until the 1980s, were puzzled, considering that the artifact, although in the shape of a great ship, was made of stone. The measurements of the hull are almost exactly those given in cubits in Genesis, the first instance in the Bible of exact statistics. The artifact has slowly risen out of the frozen mud since 1948 and, as it does so, its lines appear consistently more shiplike.

Subsurface interface radar, brought to the site, shows metal and attached beams supporting the hull, bow to stern and port to port, as well as divisions of several decks into numerous sections. As for the stone ship, it now appears that a reed and wood framework was coated with cement (K-F-R)—mistakenly translated from the original Aramaic as "gopher" wood.

The hull is filled with solidified earth and mud and is now under the protection of the Turkish government for projected investigation by archaeologists. A newly made sign pointing the way to this unusual artifact states simply: *Nuh'un Gemesi*—Noah's Ark.

Whether or not this is really Noah's Ark, it is obviously the preserved remains of a great ship, larger than any other that we know to have existed in remote antiquity.

All Sphere Books are available at your bookshop or newsagent, or can be ordered from the following address: Sphere Books, Cash Sales Department, P.O. Box 11, Falmouth, Cornwall TR10 9EN.

Please send cheque or postal order (no currency), and allow 60p for postage and packing for the first book plus 25p for the second book and 15p for each additional book ordered up to a maximum charge of £1.90 in U.K.

B.F.P.O. customers please allow 60p for the first book, 25p for the second book plus 15p per copy for the next 7 books, thereafter 9p per book.

Overseas customers, including Eire, please allow £1.25 for postage and packing for the first book, 75p for the second book and 28p for each subsequent title ordered.